FOOD, SEX AND STRANGERS

Food, Sex and Strangers

UNDERSTANDING RELIGION AS EVERYDAY LIFE

Graham Harvey

ACUMEN

First published in 2013 by Acumen

Acumen Publishing Limited
4 Saddler Street
Durham
DH1 3NP

ISD, 70 Enterprise Drive
Bristol, CT 06010, USA

www.acumenpublishing.com

ISBN: 978-1-84465-692-9 (hardcover)
ISBN: 978-1-84465-693-6 (paperback)

British Library Cataloguing-in-Publication Data
A catalogue record for this book is available from the British Library.

Typeset in Minion Pro by JS Typesetting Ltd., Porthcawl, Mid Glamorgan.
Printed and bound in the UK by CPI Group (UK) Ltd, Croydon, CR0 4YY.

For Molly: with whom I have seen, tasted, heard, touched and smelled religion in many places, and with whom I have enjoyed the paradoxes and pleasures of trying to understand and live religion in the real world. "Always".

Contents

Preface

Food, Sex and Strangers is rooted in the fertile soil cultivated by others, including scholarly colleagues and interested religionists. Most particularly, the vitalizing compost dug into my early efforts to think differently about religion blended Te Pakaka Tawhai's chapter "Maori Religion" ([1988] 2002) with the articles in a special issue of the journal *Religion* devoted to "Native American Religions" (i.e. K. M. Morrison 1992a, 1992b; Fulbright 1992; Detwiler 1992; Pflug 1992; Irwin 1992). While my previous work has referred to and sometimes celebrated these publications (and I recommend them to you again), in writing this book I have seen new things in them. Reading them alongside some more recent works (e.g. Plumwood 1993, 2002; Primiano 1995, 2012; Abram 2010; Latour 2010; Ingold 2011; Dueck 2013; and especially Vásquez 2011) has enabled some additional understandings seeded by them to germinate, blossom and cross-fertilize other understandings. The strong influence on my work of Irving Hallowell and what he learnt among Anishinaabeg is regularly reinforced by finding that many of the colleagues who impress me also celebrate or engage with Hallowell's publications (especially Hallowell 1955, 1960). In addition to the content of such studies, I have been inspired by their provocation into seeking to learn among indigenous hosts: especially Anishinaabeg, Mi'kmaq, Maori, Native Hawai'ians and Yoruba. My considerable gratitude for generous hospitality (especially when my hosts have been tested by my veganism) blends with hope that I have not missed too many of the lessons I ought to have learnt.

I also hope to maintain my open expectation that there is yet more potential in these and other sources of inspiration. Later I will say more about the world that they have provoked me to see, and to try to dwell and work in. In short, this is a world in which religion is an everyday matter in which relational beings engage with others, sometimes across species boundaries. Religion is a project in which imagination and intimacy shape people's adaptive and evolving performances and lifeways, always in relationship with others.

I have not only learnt about religion(s) from the publications of esteemed colleagues. I have seen it happening. I have been in the midst of it. I am grateful to the Faculty of Arts at the Open University for funding, supporting and encouraging my developing and ongoing research. I am grateful to my colleagues in the OU's Department of Religious Studies and others in the faculty for similarly encouraging my efforts, including making it possible for me to incorporate some of my research into our joint efforts towards providing the best teaching and learning resources imaginable and available. I am immensely grateful to the British Academy for funding my research visits to Nigeria (December 2010), and Aotearoa and Hawai'i (March 2011), for the specific purpose of seeing religion(s) occurring there. I am grateful to those who hosted, guided and educated me during those trips: especially Tayo, Jegede, David, Che and Missy, Tony and Dotty, the Tawhai whanau, the Proctor family, and colleagues at Massey University and Te Whare Wananga o Awanuiarangi. My previous research among Anishinaabeg, Mi'kmaq and other indigenous people in North America, and among Pagans internationally, also feeds into this book in various ways. I am therefore grateful to Misel, Larry and Claire, Shine and Robert, Selena and Dennis, Tim and the other SODs, the two Philips and their Orders (OBOD and BDO), the University of the Hedge, a group of delightfully not-so-mad-after-all shamans, and Kate and Corwen and others who honour the Golden King and others who we eat. Prior to my appointment at the Open University I was honoured to work with colleagues in theology and religious studies at what is now the University of Winchester. They too encouraged research and teaching efforts that have fed into this book in vital ways.

All of my esteemed postgraduate research students have contributed massively to my thinking not only about religion but also about better ways of researching, teaching and learning about religion. By paying attention to people's performing, embodying, mattering, relating, locating, dialoguing, imagining, representing and changing of religion (in, among and between different religions) they have enriched the study of religions in many ways. I am grateful to them for all of this and for giving me hope that our discipline will thrive.

Janet Joyce at Equinox and Tristan Palmer at Acumen deserve my warmest thanks, not only for so swiftly contracting and encouraging this book but also for the absolutely vital role they play in encouraging and enabling research, teaching and learning efforts in the study of religions. I have enjoyed and benefited from inspiring conversations with Doug Ezzy at various stages of writing and revising. I also thank the various anonymous readers for comments, criticisms and encouragements that have helped me clarify my argument and presentation.

Last but not least, I thank Molly. Sometimes I have left her to do research. Sometimes she has left me to do research. But we have never been strangers. Sometimes we have done religion separately, but when we have done it together it has most often been focused around meals and music in enchanting places and unbounded movements. She will see that parts of this book are entirely due to her – and, as she is my first copy-editor, all of it has benefited from her reading. While I was thinking about and writing the first drafts of this book Molly and I enjoyed the wisdom and close companionship of Solomon (the cat with whom we lived for many happy years). While completing the final version, Salome has come to live with us, and we are grateful for that.

There are, of course, weaknesses and errors in this book. They are my fault for misunderstanding, mistyping and perhaps even misrepresenting things. But academia at its best is about continuous debate, and I intend this book to be a further opening up of conversation and enquiry. I imagine, with little difficulty, improvements and enrichments of our shared efforts to understand and discuss religion, whatever that turns out to be. I welcome the increase of intimate knowledge that flows in and through those debates. This is not the last word.

1. Of god and goats

I have sometimes set my students the task of presenting ideas about where they would take visiting space aliens who ask to be shown religion. I ask them to imagine such unlikely beings saying, "We have been observing Earth and have seen sports, politics, catering, tourism and botany, but we want to observe the thing you call religion. What can you show us?" Once they get the idea, students are usually good at this. They just need to get past the idea that religion cannot be seen because it is defined as "belief in god". Since most of my British students suppose that belief is something private, interior or personal, and that god is transcendent, neither are actually observable. My students and I find that we can do better than this. We start thinking about what people do and boldly determine to focus on religion as an everyday activity. Then we get creative. We wonder if the visiting aliens might use their senses differently and need to hear or smell religion. The competitive sonic environment of Jerusalem or the olfactory overload of temples where animals are sacrificed and incenses are wafted serve as prompts to this thought-experiment.

It is not only students who have trouble thinking about what religion might be. Many academics, even those employed to research and teach about religions, seem to find it hard to get out and see, smell, hear, taste or touch religion happening. This book might help them and their students to achieve this. It is about what we might study when we stop thinking of religion as peculiar beliefs and the strange expression of those beliefs. It seems simple enough to decide to study a particular religion (Buddhism or Paganism for example), but what is it that makes these things religions? Is Buddhism everything that Buddhists do? What about when they are washing dishes or shooting guns? Are those acts ones that scholars of religion should study or should they leave them to other people? Where can we go

1

when we want to encounter religion? To what should we pay attention when we get there?

I am not the first person to ask questions about the meaning of the term "religion" and about the focus of the study of religions. However, I am not completely satisfied with the answers that *some* of my colleagues have given. I want us to try again. Too much of what passes for debate about religion and/or religions is undermined by unfortunate presuppositions. These not only lead us to devote too much attention to strange beliefs but also encourage us to misunderstand the nature of scholarship. What I propose to do in this book is tackle these entangled issues and seek a positive way forward.

STRANDS OF THE ARGUMENT

The conclusion of *Food, Sex and Strangers: Understanding Religion as Everyday Life* is already in the title. It is that religion has everything to do with the relationships that constitute, form and enliven people in everyday activities in this material world. In particular, it is human relationships with other species that are the key to understanding real world religion. It is possible that religion began as a kind of interspecies etiquette – especially when members of one species needed to eat members of another. Religion continues today when people eat or do not eat together, when they engage or do not engage in sexual activities, when they include or exclude strangers from their communities.

To reach conclusions like these we need to reject the deeply ingrained notion that religion is belief in god. This should not be the chief focus of the academic study of religion. Some people may believe in deities, non-empirical realities, miracles and other mysteries. Some may insist that faith is more important than rational proof. But these are facts about aspects of some religions rather than data for defining religion. They are not the central matter deserving our attention. To put this another way: religion is no more accurately defined as "believing in god" than it is defined as "sacrificing goats". Religious people might do either or both of these things, but it is a mistake to think that the word "religion" always and everywhere means believing in god or sacrificing goats. I pursue this line of thought especially in Chapters 1–4. Since other scholars have already said quite clearly that defining religion as "belief in god" has misdirected attention to the wrong phenomena, I set out what some of the ignored phenomena might be. I support the proposal that we ought to pay far more attention to religion as an everyday matter. If we (scholars of religion) took seriously those religious

Tillich's UC

people who say that religion includes everything they do, perhaps we should say something about washing-up as a religious act.

It is an intriguing fact that academic books often collude with religious books in largely ignoring everyday activities. A second strand of this book's argument is that a heavy weight of tradition tends to determine what we treat as significant. Religion is defined as personal beliefs in or about deities because centuries of effort and violence have enshrined such an idea. It is part of the constitution of modernity, shaped by the European Christian Reformation, but most forcefully determined by the rise of states and all the considerable changes that entailed (Cavanaugh 1995; King 2007).[1] While I will note some previous challenges to the ongoing influence of this history on academic approaches to religion, I will devote more attention to seeking different perspectives and positions from which to study religion.

What I propose here is to try to do more than point out errors, detours and barriers to understanding whatever we decide "religion" means. I want to know what a study of everyday religion would be like when it resists modernity's gravitational pull. I experiment with starting again "elsewhere". This is an idea I first tested in editing a textbook that focused attention on the everyday lived reality of religions: *Religions in Focus* (Harvey 2009a) – about which more is said in the following section. In *Food, Sex and Strangers* the "elsewhere" theme is vital and generative. It is a mechanism that aids us to leave an illusory world in which religion is belief and scholars seek to be god-like in their objectivity. Thinking "elsewhere" aids efforts to understand what everyday religion is like in the real world of movement, change, matter, weather, hedgehogs, cocoa-bushes, flints, shining guest ants and myriad other persons, each with their symbionts and constraints, and each with their ways of respecting and/or resisting others. This is a world in which religion is lived by people who eat, make love, host guests and worry about strangers. It is a world in which religion matters to people who perform it (for themselves and/or for others) as they and the world they inhabit continue to evolve and change. It is a world of relationships and performances energized by the possibilities arising from intimacy and imagination.[2]

More is at stake than noticing that religion is an everyday activity performed by relational and material persons in a relational and material world. As importantly, scholarly activities are also relational and material practices.

---

1. I am grateful to Hugh Beattie for these references.
2. I am grateful to Byron Dueck's (2013) "inventive deployment" of the terms intimacy and imagination in a different context.

The dangerous illusion of god-like objectivity is out of date, badly jarring against the evident signs of our scholarly embodiment, emplacement, relationality and necessary participation. That is to say, the "elsewhere" real world which we all truly inhabit is the world of Darwinian evolving relationality and quantum participation. Our research and teaching about religion are likely to be more effective if we practise being in that real world and doing our academic job in tune with a science that has escaped Descartes' deluded dualism and other follies. In Chapter 4 I challenge some of what I perceive to be wrong with the ways religion is often theorized, as much by allegedly critical or scientific scholars of religion as by religionists. Chapter 5 demonstrates my indebtedness to other scholars who have engaged with significant aspects of the real world beyond modernism's not-yet-post-Reformation illusions. I indicate some of the matters that should permit an appropriately twenty-first century scientific approach to our subject matter.

Building on this, Chapters 6–11 exemplify a series of "elsewheres" (outlined in more detail below) which not only offer data about religion but also provoke consideration of ways of knowing, analysing and debating religion. Celebrating the work of colleagues who have pioneered relational definitions and approaches, these chapters present positive suggestions for engaging with real-life religion. By careful attention to what people tell us, we may find new critical terms and issues deserving yet more work. That is, these chapters are about both subject matter and approaches that deserve revisiting by scholars interested in religion.

The three strands of the book (the recognition of the problem of defining religion as belief, the critique of existing approaches to studying and the experiment of going "elsewhere") come together in a concluding chapter. This proposes that the activity called religion is something people do in everyday ordinary life as well as in occasional ceremonies. Religion has everything to do with the material world in which we humans live in multi-species communities. It is about systems of etiquette in this real, relational world. Unfortunately, a fantasy world in which humans are considered unique has dominated modern imaginations. To think differently about religion we now need to start again elsewhere.

ELSEWHERE

In *Religions in Focus* (Harvey 2009a), "elsewhere" was used to direct attention towards the everyday lives of "ordinary" religious people (who are often extraordinary). Rather than being constrained by official statements by preachers or ideologues, the book focused on the ways in which religious people perform or speak about their religions. In this, it followed the encouragement of pioneers like Leonard Primiano (1995, 2012) and Meredith McGuire (2008). Sometimes, contributors to the book wrote about those marginalized from leadership roles or about minority or migrant groups. We always tried to write about the ways in which people live religion (even when they are preachers or ideologues). Going "elsewhere" to find our examples to open our chapters, we wrote about Zoroastrians in America, Christians in the English Midlands, Jews in Germany, Hindus in South Africa, and so on.

Religions in Focus does not focus on scriptures, creeds, sermons or manifestos. It refuses to define religions by what authoritative books or preachers say people should think and do. Rather, it concentrates on what people actually do. It does not give definitional priority to the past or to the founders or great leaders of religions, but enquires into what people actually do today. Often this can include acknowledging leaders, citing scriptures and/ or responding to speeches, but sermons and creeds do not define religion as it is lived. Sometimes it is a struggle not to give the impression that religion is best observed when religious people are doing elaborate ceremonies. Nonetheless, while *Religions in Focus* discusses marriages and meditation, festivals and fasts, it also presents protests, meals and patterns of home-ownership in diaspora and in religiously central places. That is, these activities are religion, not just religiously informed acts. The *Religions in Focus* project will develop to produce more books about the actual living of contemporary religion, all starting "elsewhere".

Meanwhile, the real work of *Food, Sex and Strangers* will also begin (and stay) elsewhere. It is important to consider where you study from. Perspective and position are not random, and do have powerful effects on what you see, hear, feel, taste, smell and otherwise experience. A river is different under the surface of the water from the way it is above it or beside it. A fish is different in water and in air. A human or a heron hunting a fish is different from a human or a heron calmly admiring a river or a fish from a safe (for the fish) distance. I am not only saying "be careful with your baggage, practice *epoché*, reflect on your preconceptions", although this can be good advice and is important to the practice of research (see Harvey 2011a). However, we need this advice because we have laboured for so long under the impression that we can research and write from nowhere. We have encouraged the pursuit of something we have called "objectivity" and forgotten that this idea was

5

drawn directly from attempts to imitate the omniscient god of some kinds of medieval Christian theology.

I probably should not say "this is clearly nonsense". Some of my best colleagues in the discipline have tricked themselves into thinking the pursuit of objectivity is a secular, non-religious quest. Any hint that this modern version of imitating a transcendent deity is not desirable (let alone possible) is likely to be taken as a confession that I have stepped beyond academia's disciplined boundaries. But I am exaggerating. Plenty of scholars have recognized that the placeless objectivity of the apparently absent researcher (the kind who never tells you that they were in the middle of a fiesta or a ritual) is both nonsensical and unhelpful. Many academics in recent years have demonstrated that there are many good ways of doing scholarly work differently. It is now quite common to read about scholarly presence when and where things happened, or narratives about scholarly reflection on what happened to them while doing research. These more dialogical and reflexive approaches sometimes seem more common outside of the study of religions than within it.

This said, Ingold challenges his anthropological colleagues to resist James Clifford's separation of fieldwork from writing-up, or ethnology from ethnography (see Ingold 2011: 241, discussing Clifford 1990: 52). Nonetheless, despite the increased presence of researchers among their hosts, the more negative parts of *Food, Sex and Strangers* are about the failure of supposedly more objective scholars to proffer a definition of religion that is, in reality, much different to the early modern Christian one they imagine they have challenged. "The postulation of non-empirical and counter-intuitive realities" sounds to me quite like "belief in god". So, having belaboured a subsidiary point about objectivity, I return to considering "elsewhere".

Being increasingly dissatisfied with (divine and secular) "objective" distance I have sought to find a series of places in which I can try to see how religion is or has been lived as an everyday activity. I have deliberately travelled to a number of geographical elsewheres for research purposes. In particular, in preparation for writing this book (and with the generous financial support of the British Academy), I have been to Aotearoa (New Zealand),[3] Hawai'i and Nigeria. My previous research among Jews and Pagans has also taken me "elsewhere". It is not geography that is important, and neither are exoticism or primativity invoked. The people I have been

---

3. I use the term "Aotearoa" in the chapters that follow in preference to "New Zealand".

privileged to learn from are not strangers to globalized modernity ("most-modernity" as several indigenous friends have called it). Rather, they are "elsewhere" because their discussion of religion is not alienated from the social world, everyday reality, "ordinary" people, vernacular practice, bodily performance or action (Primiano 1995, 2012; McGuire 2008; Vásquez 2011). "Elsewhere" is away from "believers" and "those who believe in them" (to paraphrase Latour 2010). I have made efforts to be away from the world religions paradigm because if we stay with it we might as well only study theology, texts, founders, beliefs and transcendence. We can do better than that. I am honoured to have learnt from and work with colleagues who demonstrate the great value of interdisciplinary, reflexive and dialogical research and teaching about lived religion. Colleagues interested in indigenous religions often exemplify the best of such emerging practices and my desire to follow them may explain why so much of this book concerns indigenous knowledges.

Since religion seems quite as ubiquitous as the performances and ideas we merrily label (and eagerly debate) as ethnicity, class, gender and sexuality, I have found myself usefully "elsewhere" even while on holiday. For example, I scrawled rather than typed an early draft of this introduction after strolling through an olive grove belonging to good friends (Michael and Richard) while Molly (my wife) and I enjoyed a restful holiday in Aups in Provence. There, the façade of the church nearest the marketplace was badly damaged by Protestant Christians during the Wars of Religion in 1574, and was more recently emblazoned with the French Republican motto: *liberté, egalite, fraternité*. Despite being on holiday, I wondered what "religion" meant to the combatants in the "Wars of Religion" and to the later, painterly Provençal Republicans. Conversations over excellent meals (always accompanied by local gold-medal-winning olive oil and good wines) often touched on matters of religion(s): from Jewish perspectives on Israel/Palestine to the possibilities afforded by the early Roman calendar for structuring a contemporary life. In response to my attempt to summarize the argument that religion is not best defined as "belief in god", I was offered yet more alternatives to consider and some radical challenges that have encouraged me to hone the argument. Elsewhere may be everywhere, but it still requires some effort to get there and even more to be there fully and return changed.

The specific "elsewheres" of this book are real world lives and activities. Chapter 6 begins with a Maori definition of religion and considers the importance of taboo and mana. Chapter 7 considers indigenous North American interspecies relationships, clans, rituals and knowledges. In Chapter 8, the diversity of Yoruba and other African-originated ways of being in relation to a world full of competing and cooperating power is considered. A large annual pilgrimage introduces Chapter 9's re-examination of *kashrut* (the system of kosher foods and behaviours) in Judaism. Chapter 10 is about the enchantment and eclecticism of contemporary Pagans. The point of all these "elsewheres" is not that they present facts that do not fit the dominant "belief in god" definition of the world religions paradigm but that they challenge a rethinking of *all* religions. This might begin to explain why Chapter 11 is called "Christians do religion like other people" even though Chapter 3 provocatively asserts that "Christianity is not a religion". The journey between Chapter 3 and Chapter 11 is important, and the varied "elsewheres" justify the seeming contrariness of the chapter titles.

LIMBERING UP FOR THE JOURNEY

Before we embark on this journey together – trying to start and remain elsewhere – I cheekily ask you to join me in some limbering up exercises. Their purpose is to prepare us to be elsewhere so that we might alter our thinking radically. Some of these exercises are about paying attention to what might count as the data of something, not necessarily religion. Some exercises are about trying out different ways of thinking or speaking/writing about matters (again, not necessarily about religion at first). Some are about movement, presence and sensation as ways of apprehending things that might be significant. That is, they are about doing research when elsewhere.

It is, after all, difficult to rethink what seems obvious and ordinary. Old habits are difficult to resist. While it can, sometimes, be easy to go elsewhere, it can be difficult to fully immerse oneself into being fully present there. We tend to take with us technologies, mind-sets and habits of thought that keep us thinking of home. For example, our cameras can reinforce our separation from where we actually are. They encourage us to anticipate being back in the places where we will view or share the photos with others. We do not get elsewhere, but we take "here" with us. We fail to inhabit elsewhere, but force its strangeness (mild or strong) into the mould we took with us. We often constrain new and potentially challenging possibilities within our existing habits of thought and practice.

It is often said that astronauts leave planet Earth, but in reality they travel in a portion of the planet (in particular, a hybrid remoulding together of its metals, petroleum-products and atmosphere). They only observe "outer space" from a more elevated and somewhat disjointed earthly position. Unfortunately their photos of the rest of the Earth mislead us into thinking we have seen our planet home more objectively than we do when we are walking around cities or forests surrounded by bacteria and bureaucrats. Astronauts do not go elsewhere, but their photos can make us think we are not here *in* Earth. This is part of the same story of the problem of studying real life and lived religion (which might turn out to be the same thing). Put another way, and paraphrasing Latour (2010) again, the implicit mantra "we know, they believe" is a technology that keeps us at home and saves us from adjusting our preconceived interpretations of what happens.

The following exercises cannot complete the job of getting elsewhere, but they might just get us started. By practising thinking differently about describing or drawing seemingly everyday things like walking and chairs, we can learn to think differently about religion, and how to study it. If nothing else these exercises will help you see the kind of weird efforts I have made to do religious studies differently.

Exercise 1: walking

Walking seems like an easy word to define. Even people who are physically incapable of walking can use the word to describe what other people do. However, if you find a public place where you can sit and watch people for a while, you will see that people actually walk differently. Or you might try watching TV to see people walking. If you pick the wrong place or the wrong TV channel you might not see many people walking at all. More of them will be in vehicles, sitting down. That in itself is interesting when you begin to wonder whether walking is a means of getting about the world or a minority pursuit indulged in by a few. Is walking a sport, a hobby, a necessity or an exception to more common acts of mobility? Keeping an eye on walkers and drivers: how are gender and age played out here? Do women and youths walk more than middle-aged men?

What other kind of act should we most commonly contrast with walking? Is walking best defined in opposition to different kinds of movement (running or driving a car) or different kinds of rest (sitting or squatting)? While you are watching people, in addition to gender and age, can you tell a person's nationality, class, occupation, present purpose or likely destination by the style of their walk? Where does marching belong in the semantic field of walking? Indeed, since different nationalities march differently and even the same army can use different marching styles, what bit of foot, leg and body movement is best identified by the word "march" rather than "walk"?

Is walking in shoes or boots different from barefoot? Look closely. If you are a habitual wearer of shoes (as most of us are) you cannot actually answer the last question by simply taking your shoes off and seeing how you walk because you are already habituated into walking styles that are shaped by shoe-wearing. But it is worth a try. Move around. Feel the ground (carpet, floor, pavement or grass). Try it with shoes on. Does the ground or your tread feel more solid or secure? Does shoe-wearing make for a more or less intimate experience of the world? Does the last question even make sense to you? How does the weather affect ways of walking – from technical aids like footwear to practical skills like pace length and eye movements scanning the ground ahead for puddles? Some of you (I know) are lovers of high-heeled shoes, others of you (also known to me) are quite keen on minimalist foot-wear. Is it possible to walk while paying attention to how your body feels and moves in different styles (or heights) of shoes? Is it easier to notice the changes of movement in other people than in yourself? When I said, "how your body feels" should I have said "how you feel"? What is the difference?

In this exercise, some of you will recognize the impression made on me by Tim Ingold's inspiring writing. Others of you may like to read Ingold and his companions on the topic of walking (e.g. Ingold 2011: 33–50; Ingold & Vergunst 2008; but see also Amato 2004). Beyond generally encouraging careful observation and reflexivity (now standard in research), the exercise is about using your senses to attend to ordinary acts, physicality, matter, surfaces and movement. Religion, whatever else it is, is something people do in the world. It too is affected by local habits, expectations about acts appropriate to age and gender, or the weather and negotiations over access to diverse spaces.

Exercise 2: drawing what is not a chair

Having strolled briefly in what turns out to be the vast topic of walking (and the enmeshed writings of Ingold about living in the world), I now propose to draw on David Turner's writing about the Aboriginal Australian Dreaming. More accurately, my inspiration is an activity designed by one of Turner's students to enable others to *see* what Turner had learnt among the Aboriginal people of Groote Eylandt and Bickerton Island. "Dreaming" can be a misleading trans-lation of complex understandings, experiences, systems and efforts. In one of his books, *Genesis Regained*, Turner presents ramifications of one key theme: renunciation (D. H. Turner 1999). By this he indicates that the everyday reality that we experience is "renounced" into the world from "the other side", shaping all life and living, and later being "renounced" back to "the other side". It does not matter, here and now, precisely what "the other side" is or what the full implications of renunciation are in Aboriginal law and lore, or in other domains such as Sunday Morning Hockey (also discussed by Turner). What I want is for us to follow an exercise that is intended to make us *see* what people say is the real reality (using this one example to limber up for other efforts). Here is Turner's paragraph that includes the instructions for us to try out:

> Judith Asher, a former student of mine, graphically demonstrated this [the movement and simultaneous mirroring of "both sides" of reality] during one of my graduate classes at the University of Toronto by clearing off the top of my table, placing one of my chairs there and then telling us to draw "not-the-chair" that is, "the space around the chair and its parts." Try it – you'll see what it means. The space around the chair is sort of the chair in mirror image: not-the-chair, but its shadow on "the other side".   (D. H. Turner 1999: 29)

Try drawing "not-the-chair" now.

Someone else (or it may have been Turner elsewhere) has suggested trying to see – not just imagine – the space that you occupy in a bath or shower. What is the space like where there is you instead of water or air? I am not sure whether drawing the "not-the-chair" or trying to see "the space that you displace" is easier (though the former may be easier in public). At any rate, in attempting this exercise (rather than just reading it as some of you have done), you have begun to prepare (again, perhaps) to make the necessary effort to see what others say the world is like.

I am not in the least suggesting, let alone arguing, here or in the rest of this book, that we must agree with everything that people tell us about the world, about their religions, or anything else. Guests can show respect to their hosts by being quite clear about differences and divergences – and hospitality need not always be strained by honest debate that seeks mutual understanding and agreed action. I am, however, certain that we must sometimes do some mind-bending exercises before we can fully appreciate what it is that some people are doing in the world (even when they try to help us by telling us as clearly as they can). Until we do that, our theorizing is really only about ourselves and what it would be like if we did what others do. There is no guarantee that our strenuous efforts will make sense of others' taken-for-granted habits – indeed, I think it is certain that some things cannot be learnt at the late stage of life that most researchers have reached when they begin to get inquisitive again.

Nonetheless, acknowledging David Abram's inspiration here (especially in his 2013 article), at a basic and vital level, this exercise has also been about immersing ourselves more fully in the world within which we are trying to study religion. By paying attention to chairs and bodies, and the texture and changes of surfaces and things, we have almost certainly visited a distinct elsewhere from the place in/from which many scholars of religion have thought to observe what they imagined to be their subject matter or the object of their attention.

Exercise 3: describing not-copies of things

If you have ever travelled internationally you will have a photograph of yourself in a passport. If you have one, find it and open the photo page. Or perhaps you have a photo in a purse of someone you love, a spouse, child or companion animal perhaps. If so, find that. Have you ever said "this is me" or "this is so-and-so"? Or do you prefer to say "This is a photo of me/my partner/my children"? Is that only pedantic or is it ideological? Looking at the photo of yourself or your loved one, try saying "this is me" or "this is X". Then try saying "this is a photo of me" or "of X". Does one of those ways of speaking seem more true or more stilted? (These are not opposites, they are just two of the possibilities.) Is there any sense in which you are happy to affirm that a photo can be, somehow, you or someone you love? Or, is that thought something you shun, preferring to insist that a photo can only, at best, represent the person it portrays? Is the person in the photo present or absent? Does it make a difference that the photo is of yourself or someone relationally close to you? Would you feel and speak differently about a photo of a stranger?

What is the difference between a person and a photograph, drawing or model of them? Or, more interestingly, what is the similarity between the person and the image? For legal purposes, at international borders, a photo (perhaps accompanied by finger prints, a retina scan and/or a signature) are accepted as proof of identity. There is a legal identity between these things and ourselves that allows officials to identify us. The recorded "representation" *is* the person. They are not only copies. Nonetheless, photos can be destroyed with less emotion than might be generated by the destruction of our actual faces (for instance). So perhaps "identity" is too strong a word. What kind of relationship exists, then, between things and people?

Some religions are notoriously divided about the matter of physical images of deities and other living beings. Differences of opinion and practice about images have not only sharpened conflicts between religions but have also generated divisions within religions (e.g. between different kinds of Christian). Just as different answers can be given to the question "is this you or is it a representation of you?", so multiple answers have been given to questions about the difference and similarity between persons and images.

Sorry, something was wrong with that last sentence. Here we are, thinking about images, and I tried to write a sentence about persons and representations that did not prejudge the interpretation. But if an image (photo, statue, drawing) of a person *is* the person, how can I write that in English? Words like "image", "representation" and even "photograph" seem to force into our conversation the cultural assumption (trained by hundreds of years of Protestant Christian influence on the English language) that the image is *not* the thing or person. While we do not always have to agree with other people's ideas about anything, we certainly will not understand them if we unthinkingly translate their words into terms that mean the opposite. If our first task is to understand others fully, then we need to learn their language and habitual, taken-for-granted acts. This is a bit like learning any language: you know you have got it when you understand jokes or begin to dream in that language. Often we also need to unlearn habits of speech as well as taking care how we speak about what others say. In the present instance, we are struggling over words like "representation" and "image".

Let's go elsewhere for a different perspective. Among the Zuni (from the southwest of what is now the United States), a *koko* (*kachina*) mask is sacred, powerful and personal. It is simply not possible to make copies or replicas of these masks. There can be no simulacra (Baudrillard 1988) of a *kachina*. This is not because of any technical difficulty in the making of masks, costumes or figurines. In theory, almost anyone could make a *koko* mask but absolutely no one can make a copy of them. If this seems enigmatic, the point is that anything that seems to be a copy of a *koko* mask is itself a *koko* mask. It is not a copy but the real thing again. As Pia Altieri (2000) demonstrates, the only way to make a *koko* mask is to rely on Zuni sacred knowledge, and that knowledge knows no "replicas" but only masks *who* (as personal beings and therefore requiring personal pronouns) act in particular ways within the world. To concentrate on the making of things, in this case at least, is to attend to the wrong facts. While masks are made, so are all other kinds of person (human as much as other-than-human). In this case, the important facts for the Zuni – and for those who wish to understand and speak about these masks – are those facts concerned with the acts and performances of masks in various contexts.

For obvious reasons I have not asked you to replicate a *koko* mask. I am only asking you to consider what mask making, mask wearing, mask performing and mask being might involve. From this, perhaps dramatic perspective, it is worth considering what other kinds of religious objects might mean and what roles they might perform in their communities. In addition to aiding our effort to go elsewhere to see what might count as "religion", and to find out what other questions might be asked about things and acts, this exercise raises the important question of how we (scholars of religion) are going to "represent", "present" or "make present to others" the kind of things and acts that we decide, elsewhere, are definitive of religion. One of the tasks ahead of us is to show others what "religion" looks like. What are the appropriate means of reproducing "religion" in books, lectures and seminars? How will we deal with the aura of authenticity (Benjamin [1936] 1968) surrounding religion as it is done by those among whom we research when we reproduce it in other contexts? We will have to work on that more later.

Exercise 4: pointing to the past

You will have to get up and move around for this exercise too. I want you to go and look into the future. You do not need any magical equipment so do not worry about time machines and crystal balls. I am thinking here of metaphors and ingrained habits of movement. It might not be easy to do this "naturally", but I want you to try to move your head and/or your arms in ways that you and those most familiar to you normally move. Some of us gesticulate more than others, but those who normally make only the most restrained body movements might like to exaggerate now. We can try it this way: get up (so that you can move more freely) and imagine you are telling someone what happened yesterday or at some point in the recent or distant past. Emphasize your point by moving your arm and your hand to point to where the past might be, metaphorically. Or try the opposite: imagine telling someone about what you hope will happen, or direct them to do something new. Again, emphasize the point by pointing or by a head movement that looks towards the future. You might find that this makes absolutely no sense until later today or later this week when you are talking about something and suddenly realize that in saying "yesterday" or "tomorrow" you pointed or you made a small movement of your head.

Let me tell you what I think many of you will do. When you talk about the past you are likely to point behind you or turn your head slightly as if nodding to something behind you. When you talk about the future you are likely to point in front of you or make a gesture of your head to some point in front of you. It will seem quite ordinary for you to do this. The metaphors by which we live are enacted as we move – our taken-for-granted and deeply learnt philosophies are acted out in and by our flesh (Lakoff & Johnson 1980, 1999). Years of cultural entrainment drive our thoughts deeply into our bones (Grimes 2000) where they cannot but become articulated in our movements. Our habitual and culturally ordinary behaviours encourage us to think in particular ways.

So what? Well, I have been told by several indigenous people from opposite sides of the Pacific Ocean (Aotearoa and Chile to be precise) that the future is behind us and the past in front of us. It makes sense when you think about it (if it does not already). We know the past, we can pause and survey it as if it were spread out in front of us like a wide-horizoned view. We cannot see the future any better than we can see behind us. Or rather, the future creeps into view as if from behind us, slowly revealing itself to our vision over our shoulders. If you drive this thought deeply into a habit of thinking you will move differently when you speak of the past and the future. You can experiment with it now. Unless this spatial metaphor of the future-behind and the past-ahead becomes habitual you will find your hands or your head continue to point in the other direction.

What is the point of this exercise? It is another effort to pay attention to the ways we (researchers) speak, think, and move that affect the ways we see and experience the world. It is about making efforts to sit lightly in our habits so that we notice when other people are speaking or acting quite differently. We (humans) might all use words like "past" or "future" but we might make quite different assumptions about them. We (scholars) might also communicate by moving and behaving and performing in ways that make it difficult to understand the habits and knowledges of others. When we go "elsewhere" we may need to unlearn as well as to learn linguistic, behavioural, emotional and mental habits in order to grasp what is going on. Religion, I am going to argue, has remained hidden from many academics because all they can see is the one thing they have looked for: an early modern European Christian inflected system of thinking, associating or affirming (all of which can be called "believing").

TWO PROBLEMS IN SEARCH OF A SOLUTION

To be quite clear about what I seek to do in this book: I am trying to sort out two entangled problems. One is the problem of defining religion and the other is the problem of how we go about defining religion. The solutions to both problems are braided together: to define religion more adequately we need to conduct our enquiries better, and in order to research about religion we need to know what we are looking for and/or at. It is not just that we need to go elsewhere (outside academic rooms) to see religion happening, it is that we need to be "elsewhere" than the now taken-for-granted physical and performative institutions of academia to escape our centuries-old conditioning. I am, in other words, somewhat provoked by Benson Saler's recommendation that we should recognize our scholarly predisposition to root our research in familiar "prototypical exemplars of religion" (largely Christianity, Islam and Judaism) but might also "experiment" with categories familiar among the people we study (Saler 1993: 214, 263–4). The danger is that we will remain trapped among the seemingly familiar "prototypical exemplars" and fail to thoroughly explore "folk categories" other than "religion" (e.g. dharma, mana, taboo, and totem) "in their own cultural contexts" before we continue distorting them as some previous scholars have undoubtedly done (Saler 2000: 328).

Reading many of the recent books that set out, like this one, to work out what religion really is often entails a considerable surprise. There you are enjoying a good read about yet another way of thinking about what religion might be and suddenly you realize that something odd is happening. Sometimes this is because the author decides to be explicit and sometimes it is because finally it dawns that they are not being explicit. That is, you realize that far from being about religion, you are reading about what someone thinks religion should be. This is more of a problem in theology than in the study of religions, but many of our textbooks continue to present our students with the notion that religions are defined by the texts that religious leaders deem to be definitive and determinative. (This is an error vigorously followed by some of the "new atheists" but that need not interest us here.) The promotion of an ideal form of a particular religion based on selecting particular texts or preachers as representative or authoritative could perhaps be severely tested by including the Spanish Inquisition or the Nazi-ideologue theologians among such architects of imagined reality. At any rate, it is disappointing to find you have been reading about experimental manifestos or imagined systems rather than religions that can actually be observed as people live them out.

It is, in short, time to stop constructing theories without attempting to gain familiarity with what people do. It is time to talk more carefully about what Leonard Primiano (1995) calls "vernacular religion". Although, when Primiano notes that there is, in reality, no other kind of religion, we ought to follow the hint and just talk about religion. "Vernacular religion" is not distinct from the acts of institutions or virtuosi ritualists or orators (priests, pastors, shamans, medicine people, diviners, slaughterers, tohungas and so on). It is religion "as it is" rather than "as it should be" – even when it involves religious people imagining and proclaiming "how it should be". Similarly, the specialized use of the word "religious" to label some virtuosi employed by the larger population (evidenced not only in Roman Catholic references to monks but also in the cognate eighth-century Japanese use of *shūkyō*; see Reader 2004a, 2004b) does not separate such people out from Primiano's "vernacular". It invites us, however, to consider that within lived religion there are perceived to be needs that can only or best be met by employing some kind of expert. In this context, then, part of the "elsewhere" of reimagining how we might improve the way we do the study of religions is a struggle to understand the kind of thing which the many acts and passions of religious people present for consideration.

WHY IS RELIGION DIFFERENT TO COOKING?

Food, Sex and Strangers originated in a suspicion that the study of religion has been conducted in a virtual reality, or perhaps an unreal fantasy world. Even when some scholars have talked about religions as if they were talking about what real people do, mostly they are imagining something entirely different. Some have not actually bothered to engage with lived religion. They write about what religious texts say. They repeat what the ideologues dearly wish religious people would do. But such confusions are easy to set aside. I am interested here in the study of religion when that is defined as actions that people actually perform in one place or another. Those locations in which religion takes place are parts of the real world. My contention is that the study of religions has been taking place in another realm altogether.

There are scholars who argue that the term "religion" cannot be used in a properly critical way. That is, they argue that the word does not label anything that can be observed as a discrete social entity, one distinct from whatever "culture" or other terms might label. Religion, we are told, is not a critical term. It is too slippery, too lacking in boundaries, too religiously entangled, to enable us to say anything useful about humanity or the world. I entirely agree that religion as it is commonly defined by academics is actually just one small element in a semantic (mine)field. As commonly understood "religion" is wrongly applied to putatively religious phenomena. Where people do not "believe in god" and do not limit that believing to their interiority (mind or soul perhaps) and their private rather than public or political lives the term "religion" *as it is often understood* is wrongly applied.

One obvious fault here is that in modernity, because of modernity, and in order to be modern, many religious people whose religious ancestors would not have "believed in private", or would not have considered this in any way satisfactory as a definition of anything interesting or important, do now identify themselves as believers. They seek the right to believe and to express their private, interior beliefs freely where such expressions do not contravene other laws to the detriment of others. Actually, some of them are not too worried about the law or the detriment of others: they just want their rights. However, the point here is that this change is part of the subject matter that we should be studying when we study religion. But it is certainly not a good idea to make this new globalized but clearly still early modern European Christian definition of religion serve for the entire subject matter of the study of religion.

Rather than jettisoning the data that seem to gather under the umbrella term "religion" (e.g. postulations about transcendence), academics need to leave the fantasy world and start again elsewhere: in the real world. Colleagues who study catering do not, I think, have to practise *epoché* or avoid actually cooking or eating. There is something curious about the modern construction of religion that makes it a fearsome beast to approach. Mistaking religion for belief-systems has, perhaps, generated a fear that our rationality might be damaged if we are infected by postulations. Happily, a determined focus on everyday religion as a performative and material practice not only enriches understanding of religious lives but also liberates us to be better researchers and teachers. In the next four chapters I justify these assertions and propose a better place in which to study.

OUTLINING THE CHAPTERS

In Chapter 2 I set out, quite randomly, and (I hope) both provocatively and entertainingly, some of the data that illustrate what "religion" can mean. My point here is that some of these data do not fare too well when religion is

defined as "belief in god". What I do in this book is to work towards a definition of "religion" that better fits what the majority of people who do religion
do when they do religion. At present, we are still too focused on founders,
texts and ideological imaginaries of how religions ought to be believed.

In contrast, in Chapter 3 I argue that Christianity is not a religion because
the alternative is that it is the only religion. I will say more than that "belief
is a Christian category" – largely because this has been said so many times
that it ought to be unnecessary to say it too many more times. Rather, I propose that our discipline remains too narrowly focused on processes that are
almost entirely the products of Reformation Christianity and the constitution of modern states. Others have said this before.

However, in Chapter 4 I note that some of these other attempts to redefine
religion do not entirely escape the powerful gravitational pull of particular Christian and modernist emphases on belief, transcendence, spirituality,
interiority and related themes. Rather, they tend to rephrase "belief in god"
in different words that hardly do justice to their authors' more radical intentions. In large part, the difficulty of resisting the standard model of the discipline (the belief-centred definition of religion) is due to the foundational
role played by Christianity (especially in its elite textual and preached forms)
in the rhetoric and rituals of modernity, its rationalism and its Reformation
and state-making inspired secularisms.

Therefore, in Chapter 5 I survey the real world in which religion and,
more importantly, the study of religion are located, performed, enacted,
embodied and materialized. If scholars of religion are not, as we have been
led to believe, mindful thinkers confronting spiritual believers, but bodily
performers of attentive relationships, we can produce better understandings
and analyses of real-world religioning.

I then offer four chapters in which I discuss matters that shape my understand of what religion is. Chapter 6 is rooted in research among Maori and
their Oceanic relatives. It begins with Te Pakaka Tawhai's statement that "the
purpose of religious activity here is to … do violence with impunity" ([1988]
2002: 244), and proposes that we still have not learnt all that we might from
the adoption of the Polynesian word "taboo" as a scholarly term. In Chapter
7 I follow the lead of Irving Hallowell, Ken Morrison and other scholars who
have learnt from the Anishinaabeg and their relatives. In particular, but not
solely, this chapter is about "animism" (pervasive multi-species interactional
relationships) and the "totemism" that is nested within it as a more intimate cross-species relating. Chapter 8 maintains a focus on aspects of "animism" by following Harry Garuba's discussion of "animist materialism" in

West Africa into a reconsideration of the ways in which humans relate with the things they make (sometimes called "fetishes") and with the beings who "possess" them. In Chapter 9 I draw conclusions from an ultra-Orthodox Jewish pilgrimage which involves considerable efforts to contact (physically and in other ways) a long deceased rabbi. Doing so entails a revisitation of some classic scholarly thinking about purity, boundaries, transgression and sanctification. It builds on the knowledge (which is quite standard among Jews and scholars of Judaism) that this is not a religion focused on the desires of or devotion to a divinity. If Judaism is not defined as "belief in god" why should any other religion be defined that way?

Following these four chapters, in which locally significant acts, terms and knowledges are considered for their contribution to redefining religion, two further chapters widen the debate further. In Chapter 10 I offer a view of what the study of a new religion, the Paganism evolving in modernity, contributes by way of challenging received ideas about modernity and religion. Ideas about syncretism, hybridity or fusion will be considered in the context of modernity's alleged disenchantment, intellectualization and rationalism. The deliberate ongoing invention of a tradition that, in part and perhaps only partially, contests modernity's project by fusing its putative opposites (e.g. rationalism and experientialism) indicates weaknesses in common theorization of religion.

In Chapter 11, informed by having travelled elsewhere, I return to have another look at Christianity. When treated as another lived reality, a context in which to pay attention to the vernacular acts and rhetorics of "ordinary" people, Christianity looks quite unlike a "belief-system". Rather than exporting Christian theology's leitmotivs (belief, transcendence, founders, texts and creeds) and thereby promulgating "world religions", I make efforts to recognize taboos, relationality, materiality and disciplined observance as evidenced in Christian lives.

Chapter 12 brings the results of these discussions together and considers the value of redefining both religion and academic approaches to religion as it is performed everyday and often diffused throughout social and personal lives.

In writing these chapters, it has come as something of a surprise to me that I have been revisiting well-known terms. I did not set out to discuss taboo, mana, totemism, fetishism, syncretism, purity, re-enchantment and suchlike terms that have been part of the technical apparatus of studies of religions and cultures since the nineteenth century, if not earlier. I will not discuss in detail all the thoughts of earlier and contemporary theorists of religion.

The hard work of dialogue with our academic ancestors in the project of understanding religion has been done admirably and comprehensively by Manuel Vásquez (2011). Those seeking to understand how we might now make use of the best of past theorization to develop improved definitions, approaches and teaching about religion(s) as the performance of embodied and emplaced people within Earth's ecology should begin and follow along with his book. In the chapters that follow I have found myself writing about those received and contested terms entirely because they function in important ways among or in relation to the people from whom I have been privileged to learn. In the process, I conclude that *some* scholars of religions and cultures have misunderstood those among whom these words (or their cognates) originated. This is hardly surprising, as Christian Reformation and early modern statist-derived beats have too often been played at excessive volume, so that the subtle melodies of "elsewhere" songs are muted. I too may have misheard matters, but what I try to do in the chapters that follow is to exercise hard so as to begin to listen more carefully.

2. Religioning elsewhere

Among the Maori community of Ngati Uepohatu, originating in and around Ruatoria (in Aotearoa), according to Te Pakaka Tawhai, "the purpose of religious activity here is to … do violence with impunity" ([1988] 2002: 244). Tawhai discusses speeches made about the deeds and attributes of deities and ancestors, but in writing about "Maori religion" he uses the word "belief" only once. Then he only says something about the equally ill-fitting word "myth" in relation to his people's "ancient explanations" of the world, which fluidly and performatively inform debates leading to decision-making about present concerns. Instead of presenting religion as an engagement with transcendence, Tawhai evokes a world in which religious activities occur when people chop down trees and dig up *kumara* (sweet potatoes). These acts of intimate violence, or violent acts of intimacy, are required if people are to build houses and cook food to shelter and feed guests. In turn, these acts continue the processes of evolution and genealogy. But this is to get ahead of the argument. Chapter 6 will focus on Maori and other Oceanic religious activities, and the technical terms learnt from them without which it is hard to imagine how anyone could speak about major social processes in other human cultures.

In this chapter I present some of the data – facts about religion(s) – that ought to be considered as we seek to define "religion" in a way that does justice to people's lives. Some of these facts are commonplace and well known. Others are commonplace and ignored in a lot of academic theorizing and even in basic descriptions of religions. Most do not fit well in the standard paradigm that declares that religion means "belief in god" or "non-rational postulations" or downright irrational mystifications. Even colleagues who reject the "belief in god" definition of religion, sometimes continue to misrepresent religious lives and activities as "expressions of religious beliefs" or the "outworking of postulated ideas". They have not really escaped the pressure to make lived reality fit the standard model. Therefore, this orientation to some of the data about lived religion (some of which will be expanded on and/or engaged with in later chapters) is intended to suggest the kind of stuff that a useful definition of "religion" ought to be able to encompass.

My argument, to be clear, is not that scholars of religion should always agree with religious people, but that too many existing theories of religion (or its putative component parts such as rituals, myths, social institutions, individual experiences, and so on) approach ideal forms of religion rather than lived realities. It is time to work towards theories that engage with and explain real world religion (and I do not mean "world religions" as that is a crucial element of the paradigm we should have dismantled). If we do not explain religion as it is lived in the real world, we can only be colluding with the ideologues and preachers who imagine that a pure form of their religion (and perhaps others) existed in the past or will be achievable in the future. The *postulation* of the perfectibility of religious performance, of religious bodies, of religious commitment and so on, are aspects of religion that deserve study among our data. They are not definitive of religion but elements of religious performance. Our business should be to attend to religion as it is observed, as it is it lived, as "religioning" (Nye 2004: 8) in the real world. Religion, for us, should mean the acts and lives of religionists (including what they declare or share about their imaginations.

RELIGIONING FROM APULEIUS TO ZUNI

Shall we start with alleged failures to do religion and then note, almost randomly, other matters that might be of interest to us? Here (as cited by Ken Dowden) is Apuleius's "withering description of the impiety of his opponent Aemilianus in a lawsuit" of 158CE:

> Up to this age he has made his prayers to no god, frequented no temple. If he is passing by some shrine (*fanum*) he thinks it wicked to raise his hand to his lips in adoration. This is a man who makes no offerings of first-fruits from his crops, his grapes or his flocks to the gods of the countryside who feed and clothe him. There is no shrine (*delubrum*) in the grounds of his villa, no place or grove consecrated. Why mention grove and shrine? People who have been there state

they have seen on his property not a single stone which has been anointed or branch which has been wreathed.

(Apuleius, *Apologia* 56, cited in Dowden 2000: 65)

Piety, according to Apuleius, means to act respectfully towards shrines, stones and trees as well as to make offerings to divinities in acknowledgement of the provision of food and clothing. Locally appropriate etiquette for demonstrating respect included, as an absolute minimum, kissing one's fingers when passing by a shrine, anointing stones and placing wreathes on tree branches. Similar acts of piety are observable in the casual or habituated acts of people of many religions as they pass by focal points of their religions. Thus, Orthodox Christians in Bucharest, Romania, are likely to cross themselves as they walk by a church on the way to the shops. Traditionalists might at least briefly bow their heads as they walk past Eshu in his house in Ibadan, Nigeria. When secularist male French tourists remove their hats while visiting even the ruined Abbey at Cluny, we might recognize the habit-shaping influence of religious history.

Sometimes people think that others need instruction or information about correct behaviour. Religion, it seems, cannot be left to individual choice, common sense or personal preference. In Jerusalem in about 1980 there was a disused (now demolished) synagogue not far from the Jaffa Gate of the Old City. Painted in Hebrew (and only in Hebrew, though most other signs nearby at the time were also in Arabic and English) were the words "מקום קדוש אסור להשתין פה", meaning "Holy Place: It is forbidden to piss here". Perhaps it might be imagined that the words "Holy Place" would have been sufficient. Nonetheless, the need for an explicit statement must indicate something. Similarly, but also quite differently, the display (in the 1990s) of a list of forbidden marriage partners (officially "A Table of Kindred and Affinity" in the Church of England's *Book of Common Prayer*) on the inside of the door of the church at Little Somborne in Hampshire, UK, suggests it was intended to instruct those who gathered inside on the rare occasions when services were conducted. Whatever else these signs meant, they seem to indicate that beliefs or spiritual attitudes are not enough, and perhaps not even central, but that bodily acts and inter-personal relations are deemed religiously important.

In the grounds of a hotel in Waikiki, Hawai'i, there is a statue of Princess Bernice Pauahi Bishop (1834–81) reading a book to a young girl who is seated on the bench beside her. The princess's provision of significant resources for the education of Native Hawai'ian children is celebrated in this work. A

FOOD, SEX AND STRANGERS

sign declares: "KAPU. Your respect for the statue of Princess Bernice Pauahi Bishop and the Native Hawai'ian garden is greatly appreciated. Please keep a distance from the planted areas, statue and the water feature. Mahalo!" "*Kapu*" is the Native Hawai'ian dialect version of the Polynesian word "*tabu*", which has entered European and other languages to aid discourse about interesting behaviours. (The meanings of the word will be discussed in more detail in Chapter 6, and will be vital to the definition of religion that I will propose.) Like other public statuary in Hawai'i, the bronze figures of the princess and the girl are garlanded with *leis* made of vibrantly colourful flowers. That is, in addition to avoidance, someone deems it appropriate to show respect by adorning these statues.

This also provides a pointer towards a more general consideration that something about religious events seems to require particular elaborations on what people consider to be appropriate clothes and/or accessories. For some people and occasions this can mean complete coverage of human bodies so as not to reveal their sensual, fleshy shapes, or even any hint of skin. For others there are occasions that require complete nakedness. At neither extreme, however, are these preferences uncontested or absolute. Emma Tarlo's *Visibly Muslim* (2010) provides a wealth of evidence of the many ways in which British and other Muslims negotiate between displays of modesty and fashion, or between piety and appropriate adornment in which veils (for instance) need not simply equate with modesty and piety but might actually be fashionable and beautiful (Yasin 2010). Meanwhile, Marko Veisson's (2011) discussion of "Widowhood Rites in North-eastern Ghana" notes changing expectations of nudity during the funerary rites which dramatically alter widows' statuses and conditions. Another site of contestation was revealed in vehement objections to the use of Buddhist iconography on women's swimwear, despite the exuberant eroticism of some Buddhist paintings and statuary (Shields 2000).

Not only bodily display or covering are at stake in religioning. Body modifications of many sorts are commonplace. Circumcision, female genital mutilation, tattooing, hair cutting or growing, anorexia, self-torture, body-piercing, martial arts and fitness regimes, all demonstrate in some way either that human bodies are deemed incomplete and in need of deliberate alteration or completion, or that bodies, especially female bodies, are somehow inimical to the proper practice or ambitions of religion. If nowhere else, such acts also negate the duality "nature/culture" by revealing that bodies are rarely treated as purely and satisfactorily "natural" and, conversely, that modifying them can be deemed "natural". Bodies are grown and constructed.

Even when (naturally) naked, a circumcised body may be understood to be (culturally) clothed (Eilberg-Schwartz 1994: 171). Similarly, some tattooed people claim that they are now, having been tattooed, "never naked". This is a complex world in which dualisms are regularly undermined by life as well as by ideology, by intimacy and imagination.

Importantly, diverse and conflicting reasons or justifications are offered for these acts. For instance, medieval Christian women who starved themselves might not have hated their bodies or wished to punish themselves for being women. Their logic might actually require the opposite: perhaps only a loved body is a worthy sacrifice. As Jon Levenson (1993) demonstrates with reference to the logic of child-sacrifice (actual or symbolic) in ancient eastern Mediterranean cultures and their successors, "victims" are only worthy because they are first and always "beloved". At any rate, Carolyn Walker Bynum argues that medieval women's self-starvation and other austerities were ways of fusing "with the suffering physicality of Christ" (1987: 243). Monastic elites had other "technologies of the self" (Foucault 1999: 162) by which they could train their embodied selves to become what they imagined to be ideals (Asad 1993: 134). These included austerities and the control of consumption, but they also involved the deliberate structuring of time and its uses, varied tasks that included contemplation and labour which entailed changed postures and expenditure of energy. Monastic and ascetic practices in many other religions could extend this small sample of thoughts about the modification of bodies and their stances and movements. But they also invite some reflection on centrality and marginality, normativity and eccentricity, elites and subalterns, and other divisions that, once again, are likely to be more complex in lived reality.

Perhaps these are extreme examples. It is noteworthy that opposition to *some* body modification is rife among religions too. Those who circumcise may object to tattooing, and vice versa. In a similar vein, the assertion that "natural" bodies (which rarely means naked or ungroomed bodies) are to be respected is commonplace. I have been told by more than one Muslim that while all Muslims are enjoined to make pilgrimage to Mecca if they can, there are more everyday signs that someone is a "good Muslim". Each of them has used the same example: they suspect that more Muslim men have properly Islamic moustaches than ever intend to become *hajjis*. They did not say this as a condemnation (of themselves or others), but rather as part of an insistence that although great deeds are important, it is in everyday matters of modesty, hygiene and cultural style that people seem true imitators of the prophet and other trend setters. Thus, a proper examination of religion ought to be attentive to bodies, postures, movements, costuming, adornment (or its lack), diet and other forms of consumption, display and restraint.

Although researchers use critical terms or theoretical categories that seem to say something about activities in many religions there are vast differences between the form, function, structure, expressed purposes and desired outcomes of acts categorized as, for example, "pilgrimages". There may also be significant differences between what the organizers or facilitators of pilgrimages think they are organizing or facilitating and what the "ordinary" participants expect or enact. Thus, apart from the important facts of "departure, journey, arrival and return" or of "circulation" among a number of important sites (Pye 2010), people who travel to Akko, Mashad, Mel Maruvatur, Oshogbo, Santiago de Compostela, Uman, Washimiya and other destinations are hard to link together. If we boldly include virtual pilgrimage venues (a plethora of which exist in the Second Life virtual reality, some replicating real world venues), the observational possibilities and interpretative challenges proliferate.

Some links and separations suggest themselves to me: some pilgrims travel to pay respects to a deity, others to become divine; some to re-enact ancient events, others to act as fictional anime or manga characters; some to venerate immortals, others to confront mortal illnesses; some to strengthen their ties to particular religions, others to strengthen bodily fitness; some to donate wealth, others to seek it; some to accede to the authority of elites, others to find an independent voice; some to be nearer to eternity, others to be firmly placed in the world. These are just some of the possibilities. Different ways of valuing gender, bodies, physical health, financial security, communal unity, social and physical mobility, and much more are involved, performed, fleshed-out. Care should be taken not to imagine concrete boundaries around the terms "pilgrimage" and/or "religion" that might exclude some of the ambitions of many people's religiously inspired travelling. Both official imagination and vernacular performance are data for debate.

William LaFleur opens his essay on "Body" by noting that "The fact that 'body' has become a critical term for religious studies, whereas 'mysticism', for instance, has largely dropped out, can itself signal significant change in how we study religion. Twenty or thirty years ago the situation would have been reversed" (LaFleur 1998: 36). The truth, however, is a little more nuanced than this. A recent edited collection (Huss 2011) about Kabbalah (which dictionaries define as "Jewish mysticism") contains only two chapter titles that use the word "mysticism". Indeed, few chapters use the word either, seeming to prefer the word "spirituality". But the activities and performances discussed as "spirituality" or "mysticism" are often thoroughly bodily. For instance, when Zvi Mark discusses "The Contemporary Renaissance of Braslav Hasidism: Ritual, *Tiqqun* and Messianism" (2011), we read about graffiti, chanting, clothing styles and lineage conflicts.

This *is* spirituality or mysticism to the people discussed; in reading about such matters we are dealing descriptively, not reductively, with spiritual mystics. We are finding out about what they (not sceptical academics) prioritize, performatively and discursively, as their spirituality. Thus, at a massively popular annual pilgrimage in Uman, Ukraine, Braslav Hasidim visit a rabbi's tomb, recite a set of ten psalms, and donate to charity. This is their participation in, effort towards and contribution to HaTiqqun HaKlali, "the Universal Rectification". At the original centre of this *tiqqun* (rectification) is the putting right of the pollution and serious sin of having a nocturnal emission. In the same manner, at the same time, a person's gaze may "turn toward the good, rather than (merely) away from evil" (*ibid*.: 111) in every area of life. It is far from insignificant that this pilgrimage occurs at Rosh haShanah, the Jewish New Year, when the world is created anew. In short, the study of mysticism, ritual, myth and calendar customs – often listed as core elements, sub-categories or even as definitive of religion – are implicated in a decidedly earthy engagement with bodily issues.

When asked what she thought of a selection of textbooks that purport to be about the Hindu tradition, Vasudha Narayanan replied "with some hesitation ... that none of them discussed some important features of the tradition" (Narayanan 2000: 761). Asked what was missing, she elaborates:

> "Food," I said and continued, "my grandmother always made the right kind of lentils for our festivals. The auspicious kind. We make certain vegetables and lentils for happy and celebratory holy days and others for the inauspicious ceremonies like ancestral rites and death rituals. And none of the books mentioned auspicious and inauspicious times. (*Ibid*.)

Still few of them do. Narayanan's article offers a wide range of other elements of Hindu tradition as "reinforced ..., subverted ..., challenged ..., enjoyed ..., [and], above all, ... transmitted" (*ibid*.: 776) by Hindu living and performing. While many discussions of specific religions do deal with "holy days" and "inauspicious ceremonies", too few of them do so in relation to cooking and grandmothers. Neither Narayanan nor I propose that there should be a precise equivalence between academic and religious discussion and definitions of

29

religion or specific religions. However, academic descriptions, at least, should be recognizable as addressing what people do and how they live. That first foundational level of our work is vital before we categorize, analyse and theorize. A failure to do so is a failure to engage with religion and a travesty of our chosen disciplinary or subject label: "study of religion(s)".

If food and drink are not yet sufficiently part of our theorizing of religion, neither is cleaning. When I used to take students to a Greek Orthodox church in southern England, the nun who usually showed us around (until the year that the priest took over, possibly suspecting we were hearing odd things) was most keen that we brushed any mud off our shoes before the visit. This, certainly, was a practical matter, and one of politeness to our hostess who, after all, had to clean the floor. However, when we got to what we might call the business end of the church (if we are minded to privilege priestly sacred space), the nun gleefully announced that "only men can go beyond this *iconostasis*, only priests ... except that they expect me to clean in there, so I'll go behind there now so I can tell you what happens at the altar". I imagine that things are different at monasteries like Mar Saba and Mount Athos where no women are allowed inside the gates. Nonetheless, alongside a hint of rebelliousness, this nun was entirely reverent towards her tradition and her sacred space. Cleaning, for her, was part of her religious duty and offering.

What are we to make of the common insistence by people in many religions – perhaps all – that *every* part of life is part of religion? If this is so, most certainly the setting of tables and the washing of dishes after meals is important. If we need to attend to the preparations people make for rituals and if many of those rituals include feasts and fasts, then definitions of religion cannot exclude preliminary and post-event cleaning. Indeed we might find that cleaning is definitively ritual or religion, not merely a precursor or posterior to ritual or religion. We might, then, take interest not only in the *samu*, "(ritual) work" of sweeping autumn leaves in Zen Buddhist temples (Reader 1995), but also of the ordinary(?) house work, home making in which religion can be rooted-in and made sense of in everyday life.

Actually, Ian Reader already takes steps in this direction by noting that:

> Housewives sweeping outside their houses are not, unlike the members of new religious groups who [are] described [in his article], taking part in explicit religious actions. They are, however, performing actions that have an identifiably ritualized (and, I would add, implicitly religious) content whose meaning and nature clearly transcends the simple act of cleaning. (*Ibid.*: 227)

Reader is fully aware that both temple sweeping and home sweeping are meaningful elements of world- and order-making:

> Of course, [cleaning] involves far more than simply removing the unclean for, as Mary Douglas [1992] has amply demonstrated, what is classified as clean or unclean is itself a matter of great cultural and ritual significance. Consequently, cleaning itself is innately connected with ideas of restoring or establishing a sense of order in the surrounding environment. In so doing it thus signifies the preoccupations and attitudes of the social milieu in which it occurs.
>
> (*Ibid.*: 227)

One example of a religious encouragement to do (ordinary) sweeping religiously is provided by a Buddhist primer's assertion that "whatever we do, we should do it carefully, with proper thought. We may be studying, or cooking, or sweeping the floor ... whatever it is, we can try to do it with a clear mind" (Sangharakshita 1998: 133). It would, I think, be good to see how other religions might parallel this thought. Sweeping and cleaning could, perhaps, contribute to definitions of religion when performed, even outside temples, by people who insist that "all of life" is "religious life", without remainder or exception.

It may seem contrary to follow this by pondering the fact that religions often entail the employment of experts. There are at least aspects of the doing of religion that are deemed to be the sole preserve of priests, shamans, tohungas, diviners, pastors, sacrificers, medicine people, theologians and other trained and/or initiated ritualists or teachers. In extreme contexts religion might be something left to experts. Indeed, "religious" and its Japanese cognate *shūkyō* have, sometimes at least, been technical terms for dedicated officials, contrasted with more "ordinary" or "everyday" persons (Reader 2004a, 2004b). Among the Amazonian Shuar everyone, including young children, is encouraged or enabled to do something we might call "shamanizing", ingesting vision-granting plants to know the future and also (importantly) the rules for proper, respectful and healthy communal living (Rubenstein 2012). However, Siberian shamans are "charged by the[ir] community" to represent them in diplomacy with other-than-human persons of various kinds (Hamayon 2013; see also Pentikäinen 2009) and similar virtuosity is expected in Mongolia (Humphrey & Onon 1996), Korea (Kim 2003) and perhaps among the Amazonian Marubo (Werlang 2001). This tension between what everyone is expected to do and what experts are employed to do can be evidenced in many places and ways.

Another version of this, or a similar tension, is identified by Grace Davie as "vicarious religion" (Davie 2002: 46): "the notion of religion performed by an active minority but on behalf of a much larger number, who (implicitly at least) not only understand, but, quite clearly, approve of what the minority is doing" (Davie 2007: 22). Although Steve Bruce and David Voas complain, "Vicarious religion clearly exists; our objection is that it seems to be the exception in the contemporary world" (Bruce & Voas 2010: 245), my suspicion is that the term could usefully be hijacked to refer to a far more general phenomenon. Davie is certainly clear (and reinforces that clarity in her 2010 response to Bruce and Voas) that she intends to cast light on a temporary European phenomenon in which people willingly maintain religious institutions despite their non-participation or non-performance of religion, and even their avowed secularity.

However, it seems entirely possible to categorize many, perhaps most religious ceremonies as vicariously enacted by a minority on behalf of a more passive majority. The performance of the liturgy behind screens by clergy alone among Orthodox Christians, the performance of the mass by priests facing away from their congregations, the entering of trance by those willing to be "horses" for possessing deities or ancestors, the entering of hermetic mysteries or enduring of privations for the great good or enlightenment of the many, and the careful approaching of angry ancestors or "animal-owners" to offer appeasement for others' wrongs, and many other examples could be adduced as evidence of a minority being employed to do religion for the majority.

Religion may be or become visible in other places and acts too. Thus, in discussing Kabbalistic rituals, Mark notes that:

> Even a person who takes a brief trip across the country [Israel] cannot avoid coming across the presence of Braslav Hasidim: graffiti with the mantra, "*na, nah, nahma, nahman meiUman*", men wearing the emblematic large crocheted white cotton yarmulkes and vans out of which emerge joyously dancing Hasidim. (Mark 2011: 101)

Mark's traveller is, perhaps, like the space-aliens I invite students to imagine, showing some example of the "religion" category. What kinds of things or acts can be shown to either such being that would advance their understanding? Graffiti, public statuary, buildings that enable community gatherings and other things might provide solid material for discussion. In some countries, road names can also provide interesting data about religion. Sometimes this can be more about the fossilized remains of long past religions, such as most (but not all) place names that refer to saints or "holy wells" in Britain. But in other cases, the structuring of towns and villages along and around their "church roads" may indicate something worth considering about "sacred geography". More dramatically, in Nigeria many shops appear to declare allegiances to one religion or another: a "Holy Family" bakery and a "God is Great" photographic shop. The common assertion that Nigeria is fifty per cent Muslim, forty per cent Christian and ten per cent traditionalist could perhaps be tested in relation to such labelling traditions. The counter suggestion that in fact Nigeria is fifty per cent Muslim, forty per cent Christian and *ninety* per cent traditionalist may also be tested by visiting the back rooms of shops to see if "traditional" amulets or material forms of the *orishas* (deities) are present alongside the affirmation of Islam or Christianity on the public face of the building.

Given all this religioning outside of religious buildings, what takes place inside religious buildings? Are all acts in religious buildings religious? I have sometimes asked students whether they could explain to those imaginary naïve aliens whether the drinking of Eucharistic wine and the drinking of tea or coffee in a church building are equally exemplary of religion. There are some obvious performative differences: only small amounts of wine are drunk while the tea or coffee are probably more stimulating; the two acts of drinking often take place in different parts of the building (or the complex of buildings); the wine is most likely served by someone in more elaborate costume than the tea or coffee; and in some churches the serving of wine is likely to be done by men, that of tea or coffee by women.

Nonetheless, even a non-reductive interpretation of these acts of consumption (i.e. one that does not see them as expressive or constructive of community [if that is not what religion really is]) might recognize, in the theological language of Christianity, that both the wine and the tea or coffee feed and unite the communal "body of Christ". Is tea or coffee truly Eucharistic too? There are, I recognize, Christian churches where wine, tea and/or coffee may be banned. In relation to such venues, my questions could be about the sharing of grape juice or water.

A similar enquiry might address the meaning and power of flower arranging and sermon preaching in church-related practices. Both could be treated as displays, celebrations, offerings of respect to significant others, efforts to unify congregations and perhaps far more. Preaching may seem more obviously to fit the purpose and design of religious buildings, but perhaps that is to collude with elite and official imaginations and desires. Perhaps as many people comment on the flower arrangements as discuss the sermon later. Perhaps the flower arranging is a more communal act than the sermon. It is not uncommon for researchers to be told that "oh, we don't really listen to the vicar preaching, that's not why we're in church", but, importantly, people would feel cheated if the vicar did not preach. That is, the preaching and the flower arranging are expected elements of the ritual life of these social groups, and if they are rituals or ritualized acts, they may be valuable invitations to yet further thinking about finding and theorizing religion.

Another favourite exercise for students involves checking for reports of anything that might count as "religion" in any selected newspaper. The results can be revealing. If they were one's only source of information, newspapers might give the impression that far from being about faith, goodness, community cohesion, anticipating eternity or celebrating compassion, religions are definitively divisive, prejudicial, hypocritical and dangerous. For instance, at the same time that Anglican/Episcopalian Christians were participating in "inter-faith" ventures built on the notion that "people of faith" could benefit wider society by working together, the most media-worthy events were divisions over homosexuality and gender. That is, since the turn of the millennium, if not for longer, this "communion" has (according to the media at least) been torn apart by support for or objections to homosexual and female clergy.

Most recently, the mere possibility of there being female bishops has angered many. Some of the Christians involved are allegedly willing to accede to the existence of gay male priests as long as they are sexually celibate. Others, however, are reported to have officially requested that Christian groups be excluded from the provisions of human rights laws. That is, quite astonishingly, they are said to have actually requested permission to be bigoted in deed as well as in thought. "Marriage", we are frequently told, is defined as something that can only be done by heterosexuals, and we are expected to conclude that the documents that enshrine this definition are, almost uniquely in human history, unchangeable (which seems unlikely).

Meanwhile, global media reports about Roman Catholicism commonly relate either to papal announcements about contraception or to sexual abuse by clergy. Once again, the distinct impression of two major branches of a religion focused on sexuality and gender is promulgated. In the context of concern about how theologians represent and reinforce an image of Christianity as centred on believing, Tom Beaudoin insists that "the theologian risks decadence without their work bearing the weight of the scandalous abuse of persons and power, and concomitant redefinitions of religious practice" (Beaudoin 2012:

242), alluding to the "physical-spiritual violence towards thousands and thousands of young souls in the past several decades" (*ibid.*: 236).

In 2011, Kenyan newspapers (among others globally) reported that the failure of the Catholic hierarchy to prosecute (or have prosecuted) abusive clergy led to calls for the Pope to be tried at the International Criminal Court (Mutiga 2011). However researchers test the veracity of media reports, the question here for scholars of religion is a less awful one than how sexual violence and bigotry might be dealt with. Our question is about how we incorporate sex, gender, abuse and bigotry in our definitions of religion.

There has been a tendency to equate religion with positive ambitions. Perhaps this has been more common among religionists than among scholars of religion, but it is not unknown among them. Typical responses to "the Troubles" in Northern Ireland, to Jewish and Muslim militancy in Israel and Palestine, to Buddhist and Hindu conflict in Sri Lanka, and to violence in many other locations, have insisted that these are not really examples of religion but of ethnicity, economics, politics, history or immorality. Conversely, in an equally deluded but contradictory direction, some violent conflicts have been put down to "fundamentalism" as if only the over-enthusiastic practice of religion could be dangerous. When the idea of states reshaped Europe in the early modern period, it was aided by a rhetorical sleight of hand that still persuades us to write about "the Wars of Religion" rather than "the Wars of State Making" (King 2007). The community building and transnationalism of Catholic and Protestant Christian religion had to be delegitimized in order for states to gain control. Somehow we remain persuaded that violence is only justified when conducted by states. Religious violence matter-of-factly demonstrates how unmodern and illegitimate religion is. The term "fundamentalism" can be hijacked to reinforce that polemic. Instead, we might treat the refusal of the subjectification, internalism and individualization of religion as an act of resistance to the ongoing violence of modernism.

This is not to say that religious violence should be deemed acceptable or a cause of celebration. It is only to reimagine the relation between religions and other social complexes (states) differently and to resist a specific plank of early modern polemic.

It is not, at any rate, difficult to find examples of the twining of religion and violence in many places and times. The Doctrine of Christian Discovery on which the colonial expansion of European power and peoples spread worldwide (promulgated in papal bulls and royal charters) certainly provides evidence of an intimate relation between religion and violence (Newcomb

2008). The mere absence of a "Christian prince" is the fundamental justification offered for subsequent acts of conquest, enslavement and genocide. No reference to peaceable texts and charitable efforts balances the preponderance of replacement and subjection to the "civilization of Christianity". Perhaps other expansionist religions with universal ambitions have produced similar charters elsewhere. Certainly, any definition of religion that ignores violence, division and self-aggrandizement is inadequate.

A somewhat differently conceived link between religion and violence underpins Maurice Bloch's theory of "rebounding conquest" (e.g. Bloch 1992), which points to a generative association between violence and ritual. In addition to the initiation rites from which his theory arose, supporting evidence could be drawn from the public and national ceremonies that memorialize those killed in state-supported military conflicts. War memorials and military parades are key features of a tradition in which the apparent finality of death and mourning are contested (not merely transcended) and made into the beginning of (new) life. They are initiatory of the imaginary that participants are supposed to more fully embrace and seek to vitalize. Those who challenge this civil religion with an alternative typically do so with ritualized acts drawn from a similar repertoire. The proponents of (non-militarized) peace and (non-state) justice can also mobilize in pilgrimages, with candles, flowers and other efforts "against death" (Davies 1997).

Another example of the continuing vitality of early modern efforts to subjugate religion is evident when religion is defined as something that should be kept out of "politics" (just as "politics" is sometimes defined as something that should be kept out of "sport"). This is commonplace and examples from many places could be offered. Indeed, a significant strand of the secularization debate concerns the degree to which religion is separated from politics. Here, however, is an example that offers a contrast. After a conversation with an indigenous council leader, a friend said "there was more politics than spirituality in that!" I disagreed. Only because of a spirituality of intimate relationships with place (as a multi-species community of embraided responsibilities) and care for communal, bodily and material well-being could that particular leader engage politically and diplomatically with the politicians of the engulfing nation state. Rather than lacking spirituality, he had successfully resisted full incorporation into the modernist state's constraints (to echo Cavanaugh 1995).

Religion is also often contrasted with economics. Seemingly endless debates about ethics or morality revolve around the question of whether a seemingly "good deed" is undermined if it brings any financial (or other "worldly") benefit to the deed's doer. Charity could be asserted to be defined as the gift of resources to the needy out of purely motivated generosity. However, Islamic and Jewish systems of charity can be free of the burden imposed by the attempt to "disappear" the donor. By tradition and teaching, Jews and Muslims are supposed to give to others – and they can be applauded for doing so. Donors are not meant to consider themselves morally better than the recipients of charity, only economically better off. Being seen to be doing charity does not undermine it as a moral act. The Kantian sense that the "right thing to do" is only right so long as it is only done because it is the right thing to do, and not because one might look good, seems like a fine sermon but an unlikely description of genuine and praiseworthy motives.

More controversially, religious leaders or groups who make money are frequently condemned as lacking in spirituality or morality. It is often implied that making money, especially in significant quantities, invalidates actions as "religion". What place might be found in definitions of religion for phenomena involving money-making? Should they be a negative, "not-religion" or "anti-religion", that helps us more clearly see what religion really is? Interesting examples for consideration include Christian capitalists, New Agers and Scientologists. Thus, Susan Thistlethwaite (2011) notes that "According to some Christian conservatives, unregulated capitalism, with all its inherent inequalities of wealth, is God's plan". She robustly criticizes this view and argues that "Not only do we need to understand that 'Christian Capitalism' isn't Christian, we need to understand how it is distorting capitalism" (*ibid.*). But since she and some of those she cites identify others as both "Christian fundamentalists" and "market fundamentalists", we have to assume that, whether or not this is Christianity, it is religion in some sense. New Age is commonly dismissed as a "pick and mix" merchandising venture in which products derived from real religions are randomly appropriated and curiously blended for marketing to gullible others.

A more nuanced critique is offered by Jeremy Carrette and Richard King in $elling Spirituality: The Silent Takeover of Religion (2005). In an era when everything else has a price and a market(place), it would be naïve to think that religion should be different. More interestingly, any fit between contemporary spirituality and contemporary economic systems might encourage us to consider earlier and other relations between religion and economy, politics, society and similar elements of complex reality.

Meanwhile, Scientology has been labelled a "business enterprise" by the German government (Kent 2009: 507), as if that equated with the movement's not being (also) a religion. In fact, almost everything about Scientology's self-presentation has been treated by one writer or another (from undergraduate students to newspaper sensationalists to otherwise insightful researchers) as if it delegitimizes any claim to the status of being (a) religion. This is somewhat as if Catholic Christianity was declared to not be religion because its churches contain statues, or Islam not a religion because its mosques do not. It does not make sense to use what people declare to be important *as* and *within* their religious practice and ideology as reasons for dismissing them. Simultaneously, any particular religion's key features or obsessions should not be benchmarks against which all other religions might be judged.

Whether or not particular religions, religious activities or religious people transgress the economic, moral or political boundaries preferred (but ineptly policed, evidently) by hostile observers, some forms of religion are inherently more fluid. That is, the fact that some people identify as Buddhists, Christians or Jews *and* as full participants in "alternative spiritualities" (or the events, therapies and communities they offer) is inescapable. Indeed, there are now Quaker Pagans, Buddhist Christians, Jewish Witches (or Jewitches), and many other examples of what Giselle Vincett calls "fusers" (2008). The very idea that religions are discrete phenomena – that there is something called Christianity that is not an African or Amazonian religion, that is there is a Japanese Buddhism that is not of interest to Shinto ritualists, and so on – is most unlikely *if* the lives of real people in the real world are the focus of study.

On the beach of Durban, South Africa, self-identified Christians perform purification ceremonies that are not immediately distinguishable from those of practitioners of local African traditional religions. Nigerian shop-keepers and politicians who identify themselves as Christians or Muslims rarely feel that this should prevent them from seeking guidance from "traditional" Ifa diviners. The cathedral in Lund, Sweden, has rediscovered the value of its place in the Santiago de Compostela pilgrimage network even if the "pilgrims" unhesitatingly self-identify as Lutheran Christians or secularists who walk not for salvation but for a range of other purposes. Examples could be multiplied. They amount to a challenge to any sense that words like "syncretism" or "hybridity" do anything other than label the normal processes by which people learn and borrow from one another.

Well, obviously the label "syncretism" often functions as a condemnation of people who are deemed to wrongly and foolishly blend, for example, Catholic Christianity, Yoruba traditionalism and Amazonian animism into something like Candomblé or Santo Daime. Eschewing such polemics as unhelpful hangovers from elite imaginings of bounded and pristine traditions, we might treat the fusers as the norm rather than the exception. We gain little from obsessively tracing the Islam and Hindu roots of Sikhism and ignoring its lived and still evolving reality.

We do, however, need to attend to the presence of polemic, differentiation, hostility and prejudice as common aspects or elements of religiosity. Religions may have fluid boundaries, but they also frequently entail boundary marking rites and rhetorics (which often resonate with the "cleaning" and body-perfecting activities noted earlier). At their extreme, these tendencies present us with the necessity of accounting for accusations of witchery, sorcery and devilry. They necessitate inclusion of the divisive, violent or otherwise negative aspects of religion as well as socially cohesive, identity forming and otherwise affirmative trends within our efforts to define our subject and our scholarly approach. This is, as I hope to demonstrate, somewhat less contentious a pursuit if we begin elsewhere than among those religious leaders and texts that attempt to persuade others of the general niceness of religion.

Elsewhere, where tricksters are rampant (Malotki & Lomatuway'ma 1984), or where the creator of this rather difficult world full of illnesses, drought and disharmony is dramatically made *not* welcome (Platvoet 2001), or where some deities desire to feast on human blood (Whitehead & Wright 2004), it might be utterly straightforward to contemplate the negative performance, functions and outcomes of religion. It seems unlikely that careful attention to explicit unpleasantness in religions will encourage the "new atheists" (actually old-fashioned Protestant atheists with a better grasp of evolution and a new audience) to understand that religious people are well aware that deities are not necessarily "nice". Religion is not always treated or resorted to by religious people as a comforting opiate that will fend off painful reality until something better comes along. Knowing religious views about more shadowy concerns (e.g. divisions and demons) better might improve our attempts to define religion honestly, with reference to the full range of available data.

When the marketing department of the Open University were collecting images for a leaflet about the religious studies department's work they offered one entitled "a man alone with god". It showed a man, with his head bowed and his hands clasped in front of him, sitting on the summit of a mountain at dawn or twilight. This was supposed to illustrate something definitively religious – something that might perhaps be called spiritual, mystical or numinous experience. My immediate response was to ask if the man was sitting on his god. My colleagues and I rejected the image because, although we might say something about religious experience in the teaching and learning materials we prepare, we do not privilege such experiences as defining our subject.

In contrast, William James provocatively requested that "religion [should be taken] rather arbitrarily ... to mean ... the feelings, acts, and experiences of individual men in their solitude, so far as they apprehend themselves to stand in relation to whatever they may consider the divine" (James [1902] 1997: 42). Rudolf Otto is even more extreme, reducing James's "experiences" to one definitively religious experience, being apprehended and overwhelmed by the numinous (Otto 1958). However, commentators like Melissa Raphael (1994), Brian Bocking (2006) and Manuel Vásquez (2011) convincingly demonstrate not only that Otto's "experience" is that taught and encouraged by his religious context, but also that the study of experience is embedded in modern (post-Enlightenment) notions of individual selfhood.

Further thought might suggest that the "man alone with his god" (whether this is James, Otto, or the anonymous mountain sitter) does not necessitate a probe into individual psyches but, rather, already invites consideration of material, embodied, emplaced and relational activities. The fact that there are mystical schools and systems reinforces the recognition that religious experiences too can be shared and caught. Then, the construction of elaborate buildings, calendars, liturgies, musics, narratives, meals and emotionally powerful events demonstrate that people put considerable effort into making it possible to have religious experiences over and over again. The study of religious rites (Whitehouse 2004) and emotions (Davies 2011) further reinforces and enriches this line of enquiry.

Location and practice are increasingly popular terms both in academic studies of contemporary religion (especially regarding "alternative religions") and among people who seem to prefer to identify as "spiritual" rather than "religious". While this duality deserves careful attention (alongside historical and cross-cultural comparison), it is the forceful intervention of place and performance into critical studies that is currently enriching our subject. Emplacement and religious activities should not be surprising: histories and ethnographies of particular religions have consistently noted locations and what takes place there. The construction and utilization of shrines, temples, meeting houses, venues for sacrifice, liturgy and teaching proliferate. Orientations to sunrises and other cosmic relationships abound. Nonetheless, a pervasive academic somatophobia (Spelman 1988: 126–32) and a fear of matter (Pels 2008: 266)[1] have delayed or derailed a

---

1. I am grateful to Amy Whitehead for alerting me to these terms and works.

thoroughgoing materialist approach to religion. Perhaps that is changing now. If feminist studies of religion led the way back to consideration of bodies (and related themes of gender, sexuality, performance, everyday life, power and more), now materialist studies (such as that of Vásquez 2011) are bringing the study of religion into dialogue with work in anthropology (e.g. Ingold 2011) and a wide interdisciplinary debate (e.g. Latour & Weibel 2005).

I contend that scholars of indigenous religions deserve greater attention in this arena both for what they have already contributed and for their potential to lead the way to a far better understanding of religion in the real world. Anticipating the powerful argument of Latour (2010) about fetishes and "factishes", John Fulbright's (1992) article (and the other articles in that special issue of *Religion*) already demonstrated the rich potential for rethinking many of our discipline's critical terms and debates. If other scholars of religion paid more attention to the actions and relations of prayer-sticks among Hopi and Zuni peoples, we would gain a richer sense of the importance of relationality and materiality in defining and debating religion.

GETTING LESS RANDOM

The intention of this chapter has been to present some of the many phenomena, possibilities and polemics that can be (and sometimes have been) considered by those interested in understanding the lived realities of religion(s). The following chapter considers one of the two barriers to treating the doing of religion as the chief matter that requires the attention of scholars of religion. This is the idea that religion is properly defined as "believing". Subsequent chapters will tackle the second, larger barrier: this is the theologically inspired notion that experts can and should be objective.

3. Christianity is not a religion

Some Christians and scholars who study religion claim that Christianity is defined by and as "belief in god". No other religion is properly defined in terms of beliefs or believing. This means that either Christianity is the only religion, or it is not a religion at all. This is hardly a new thought but I put it more starkly here than I have seen it put before. It is a commonplace of the study of religion that belief and believing are not at the heart of religion (though they *may* be at the heart of Christianity). If so, belief and believing should not be permitted to direct our attention when we research and teach about religions. This chapter sets the scene for thinking again about what "religion" might mean by reflecting on this recognition that believing is a definitive act for Christians but has been wrongly applied to defining religion itself.

It may be important to note, in passing, that by saying that Christianity is not a religion I do not mean that Christianity is not a human creation. I do not mean that it is something different from some sort of social or cultural phenomenon. I most certainly do not mean that Christianity is (uniquely or otherwise) a divinely revealed truth. Some Christians make this pious assertion of the exceptionalism of Christianity, insisting that "religion" is "man-made" (where they do not think it is a satanic counterfeit) and quite different from (their kind of) Christianity. When Karl Barth (1956) asserts this, his insiderly and polemical understanding of Christianity provides further examples of rhetoric for scholarly consideration. He is preaching and simultaneously demonstrating how different theology can be to the study of religion. But we know that. Anyway, we should set aside Barth's parochialism and seek a better understanding of religion and of ways of doing research and teaching.

The question for this chapter is, what was it about Christianity that made Christian ideologues, and those influenced by them, define religion as "belief in god"? In order to understand the difficulties faced by scholars interested in religion, we first need to understand that belief and believing are uniquely Christian acts and therefore unhelpful in defining anything other than Christianity. Since this is a deliberately polemical statement, I willingly add the coda that belief and believing are also evident in colonial- and globalized-modern phenomena constructed to be like Christian believing.

PECULIAR BELIEVING

Wilfred Cantwell Smith insisted that:

> The peculiarity of the place given to belief in Christian history is a monumental matter, whose importance and relative uniqueness must be appreciated. So characteristic has it been that unsuspecting Westerners have ... been liable to ask about a religious group other then their own as well, 'What do they believe?' as though this were the primary question, and certainly were a legitimate one.
>
> (W. C. Smith [1962] 1978: 180)

Similarly, Ken Dowden notes that "students of ancient religion are well aware that paganism did not promote 'faith'", that the collocation "believe in" is "a peculiar piece of jargon which we derive from New Testament Greek" (πιστις εις) and that "Paganism was not creedal but a matter of observing systems of ritual" (Dowden 2000: 2). The evolution of Christianity out of the proliferating ferment of Mediterranean intercultural encounters in antiquity is firmly anchored to the deliberate emphasizing of belief in Christ. Ever since then, the spread of Christianity globally was the promulgation of believing. Not only did Christians promote believing in their deity, they often conducted a mission that sought some hint of believing among not-yet-Christians. Either in practice or in the rewriting of history after Christian conversion, Christian mission activity usually involved creating the illusion of prior (false or inadequate) belief which could be claimed as a foundation for teaching the truth.

Little has changed. Indeed, so dominant is the association of belief with religion that it is now the common experience of students and scholars of religion to be asked by taxi drivers or new acquaintances, "so what do *you* believe?". Perhaps we only have ourselves to blame for not contesting the

44

association of religion with belief – and the association of studying with affirmation – more vigorously. Thus, Tom Beaudoin asks:

> Is it ethical to analyze whether people are Christian in the ways that we have? … I mean, is it ethical to give people the impression that this is what counts as Christianity? That this is what it is to be religious? In a media culture, by asking people about their religious beliefs and religious practices, scholars propagate not only data about religion, but a way of handling religion, a way of thinking about it, that is picked up by other scholars, students, journalists, government offi-cials, the educated public. (Beaudoin 2012: 239)

In Chapter 4 I intend to show that academics interested in religion have not, despite protestations to the contrary, always securely removed "belief" or "faith" from its imperious position in definitions of religion. For now, I need to say more about Christianity as believing.

Malcolm Ruel cites Wilfred Cantwell Smith's statement (cited above) about the peculiarity of the place of belief in Christian history as a good summary of his own argument about "Christians as believers" (Ruel 1997). In this, one of his "reflexive essays on a Bantu Religion", he concludes with four "shadow fallacies" demonstrating the folly of attributing belief to non-Christians. The first fallacy is that "belief is central to all religions in the same way as it is to Christianity". Illustrating this, Ruel says:

> Much of [Martin] Southwold's critical commentary [on "religious belief"] is highly relevant to any discussion of religion but why focus the discussion on the nature of belief? And does not the framing of the question thus itself determine the kind of answer that will be obtained? Namely, that "basic religious tenets are (1) empirically indeterminate (2) axiomatic (3) symbolic, and (4) collective" (1979: 633). Christian Belief is historically and conceptually more precise in its references than this, but take belief (the shadow idea) to apply to other religions (as one might take the Judaic *torah* or a shadow extension of it) and one may well find the correspondence to be inde-terminate and indirect (symbolic). (*Ibid.*: 56)

Ruel here combines two critiques: that belief is not central to all religions and that Christian belief is not just "belief" but "belief in". Whether belief means acceptance of ideas, assent to doctrines or commitment to a person, it not only has content but its content is vital within Christianity. (In Chapter 9 I will accept his implicit invitation to think what would happen if we took "the Judaic *torah* or a shadow extension of it" to be definitive of religion – but to do so I will have to insist that it is studying, not text, that is central.)

Ruel goes on to identify a second fallacy, that "the belief of a person or a people forms the ground of his or their behaviour and can be cited therefore as a sufficient explanation for it". He cites his own teaching experience as an example:

> Along no doubt with many others, I regularly set my first-year students in social anthropology an essay on Zande witchcraft usually in the first few weeks of the course. One topic I commonly use runs: since Zande oracles must often give false answers, why then do Azande continue to believe in witchcraft? and, all being well, the essay that is returned duly rehearses Evans-Pritchard's [1937] situational analysis of Zande reasoning. But, not infrequently, all is not well and my (I think now misguided) weak use of "believe" is turned into a strong use: the evidence in the book for individual Zande scepticism is ignored, as is much else, to present Azande with such unalterable firmness of conviction as would make a Calvinist jealous.
> (Ruel 1997: 56–7)

He further notes that this fallacy leads to the "relativization" of putative Zande "beliefs" as "something to do with *them* (rather than the world they experience)". These "beliefs" cannot then be compared with what we or others also "experience of the world", because if "We all have our beliefs: all peoples have their beliefs". That is, within relativism we all exist in neat and discrete belief- or worldview-boxes which hardly touch the real world (if such a place exists) and therefore cannot or should not be tested against each other. Ruel's argument here resonates with a tradition of critiquing relativism, the separation of religion and science, and the modern and scholarly invention of "believers", which can be exemplified in the works of Michel de Certeau (1985) and Bruno Latour (2002, 2005) (discussed further in the following two chapters).

The third fallacy challenged by Ruel is that "belief is fundamentally an interior state, a psychological condition". Again he roots this fallacy in the application of some version of Christian believing to all other Christian and other cultural domains. While, for instance, Luther and all reciters of Christian creeds may, at least sometimes, have had inner psychological experiences of believing, or held private thoughts about reality, they also stated, recited and acted on official Christian teachings. Furthermore, when anthropologists attribute belief to, for instance, the Azande, "To assume that *our* presentation of their belief carries the same force as though *they* said 'We believe …' is to misunderstand the semantic conjugation of the verb and to transpose Christian assumptions unwarrantably" (Ruel 1997: 57).

Finally, Ruel examines a fourth fallacy about belief, namely "that the determination of belief is more important that the determination of the status of what it is that is the object of the belief" (*ibid.*: 59). He explains:

> In Christianity to be a believer is to acknowledge an allegiance and to declare an identity: the person does not always have to be clear about the full content of his belief. The same circumstance transposed to non-Christian religions makes much less sense. To say that a people "believe" in this, that or other abstraction (witchcraft, God, spirits of the ancestors, humanism) tends to bracket off ideas that they hold about the world from the world itself, treating their "beliefs" as peculiar to them, a badge of their distinctiveness, and all knowledge of the world as our privileged monopoly. (*Ibid.*)

Other people are marked out as believers while scholars claim a firm grasp on knowing and knowledge.

What all of these fallacies amount to is that "belief" is something that some Christians do some of the time, or something that some Christians have insisted is a necessary thing to do. But even when studying Christianity we need to recognize that it is not only "believing" that is important to Christians, the object/subject of belief is crucial. Those Christians who assert the importance of belief are vehement that it is important to believe correctly (i.e. in the correct facts, realities and persons). Precisely because Christian believing is specific (because the word "believe" is properly followed by "in" and other words), it cannot be sufficient to extend "belief" to make it definitive of religion.

PERFORMING AND REFORMING BELIEVING

The long tradition of belief in Christianity is admirably surveyed and discussed in many scholarly publications, including those cited above. Some highlights from that history may clarify what Christians have meant by "belief" and "faith". Donald Lopez writes:

> Religious belief is, furthermore, often resistant to contrary evidence and oblivious to negative consequences. Tertullian's paradox is *Credo quia absurdum*, "I believe because it is absurd." Aquinas argued that belief (or faith) is superior to reason because it is an assent to a transcendent truth, and that by definition, to believe (*credere*) is to believe in what is true; if its object is not true, it cannot be faith (*fides*).
>
> (Lopez 1998: 23)

If Aquinas's faith is inextricably woven together with transcendentalism, it is matched by Augustine's encouragement of interiority: "Do not wish to go out; go back into yourself. Truth dwells in the inner man" (Vásquez 2011: 88). The interplay of interiority and transcendentalism evidence the twin(ned) referents of "spirit" in Christianity: belief links "the true inner person" with "the divine reality".

Bodies, though the locus of incarnation and redemption within Christian ideology, require discipline and (sometimes) subjection to allow the (inner) spirit to connect faithfully to the transcendent divinity. Tertullian and Origen illustrate the way in which "early Christian communities made the body of the crucified saviour the model for authentic faith: in order to have life in abundance, the believer must ultimately lose him/herself, literally die to the world" (*ibid.*: 28). Martyrdom and monasticism are two of the ways in which bodies could be disciplined to the benefit of the inspired believer or believing spirit. While this could tempt some Christians into dualism, the dominant (elite) tradition or imaginary continuously affirmed the value of believers' suffering bodies. The venerated relics of Catholic martyrs and the restrained lifestyle of pietistic Protestant sectarians are on a continuum of embodied and enacted believing.

Martyrdom helpfully (for us) brings believing into contact with both unbelieving and wrong-believing. The martyrdom of Christian believers by non-believers is represented in Lopez's article by a short paragraph on the crucifixion of "The Twenty-six Martyrs" in Nagasaki, Japan, in 1596 (Lopez 1998: 27). Lopez notes that although "belief, portrayed as an inner state, was again employed" as the Christian explanation for these deaths, this was "a surrogate for more visible concerns". In particular, Lopez suggests that martyrdom for their faith provided other Christians with a more palatable explanation that that these people were killed because they became entangled in a deadly disagreement about the ownership a foundered ship's cargo.

Even in celebrating the exemplary faith and alleged witness of the victims, Matthew Bunson (undated) notes the tangled causes involved. He also contrasts the faith of the missionaries and rapidly growing number of Christians with the "traditionally accepted divine origins" of the emperor. The "belief" of one ruler that allowing the building of "such a church might help to establish a trade relationship with Europe" is contrasted with a persecution initiated, it is claimed, because of "the rapid growth of the new faith". In that persecution Christians were "compelled ... to abjure their faith". Furthermore, "the shoguns believed the new religion might curb the influence of the sometimes-troublesome Buddhist monks in the islands". Bunson notes a difference between Jesuit missionaries and other "assorted Catholic missionaries who lacked the subtlety of the Jesuits arrived in Japan and failed to respect Pope Gregory's decree" (*ibid.*). Presumably Bunson means Franciscans here, but cannot say so without impugning at least six of the martyrs. In short, either different kinds of "belief" or different political and material interests resulted in violence. The entanglement of "faith" (Christian believing) with other kinds of believing, thinking, plotting, expectation and desire takes precedence in Bunson's article (and others like it) even over contrasts between Christianity and Buddhism and emperor-veneration. While it seems possible that the martyrs understood their deaths to be a testimony of their faith (summed up as "man can find no way to salvation other than the Christian way") they must (also) have suspected that a conflict of interests over cargo and leadership got them into trouble.

Chapter 7 will provide another opportunity to consider the mismatch between Christian discourses of belief and the understandings of those they attempted to convert. I will, for example, summarize Ken Morrison's (2002) arguments about what the Jesuits and eastern Algonkian people understood to be at stake in their encounter in north-eastern North America. A similar mismatch between the worlds, knowledges and expectations of Christians and indigenous peoples is evidenced in Claude Lévi-Strauss's encapsulation of differing attempts to judge the nature and culture of others:

> In the Greater Antilles, some years after the discovery of America, whilst the Spanish were dispatching inquisitional commissions to investigate whether the natives had a soul or not, these very natives were busy drowning the white people they had captured in order to find out, after lengthy observation, whether or not the corpses were subject to putrefaction.   (Lévi-Strauss [1952] 1973: 384; see also
> Lévi-Strauss [1955] 1961: 80)

Lengthy deliberations about the humanity and humaneness of both invaders and indigenes involved Catholic Christians in debate about "Indian" souls and rationality, while Puerto Rican "Indians" undertook protracted observation of Spanish bodies. Belief in the Christian faith was one of the key issues for the Europeans, but was completely unmatched by interest in beliefs for the indigenous enquirers into the naturalness of invaders.[1]

Returning to martyrdom, for a while, along with confrontations of "believers" with "unbelievers" (or perhaps more properly "not-believers"), Lopez draws attention to the contrast between true and false belief. His example of "heresy" (and it is interesting that "belief" requires such an antonym in Christian discourse) again involves martyrdom. Peter Martyr's axing to death by Cathar "heretics" in 1252 generated Catholic hagiographical texts and paintings such as the one described by Lopez (1998: 21) in introducing his article. In this, the dying Peter has written *Credo*, "I believe", in his own blood on the ground. Lopez notes (*ibid.*: 24) that some accounts have Peter writing *Credo in deum*, "I believe in god" or (perhaps more provocatively in the presence of dualistic Cathars) *Credo in unum deum*, "I believe in one god". Again, however, Lopez points out that there were possible causes of violence other than a difference over beliefs. While Peter may well have understood the ultimate cause of his death to be his desire to testify to his faith (in the sense of both his inner beliefs and his vigorous promulgation of Catholic Christianity), his persecutors may have had quite different motivations. The confiscation of Cathar property may have led to the hiring of assassins to remove the threat Peter posed to wealthy families. Lopez concludes that "Peter was not murdered for his beliefs but for his deeds" (*ibid.*: 26). Nonetheless, the official justification for Peter's activities was "the contents of men's and women's minds", their beliefs rather than their properties. It was as people condemned for believing wrongly they were judged to be deserving of the confiscation of wealth, land and life.

If belief was a matter of life and death in such encounters between Catholics and non-believers or wrong-believers, it became even more prominent in Protestantism. Indeed, the preaching of the need for belief, and the preaching of what to believe, replaces all other possible activities in the defining repertoire of Christianity (at least as it is officially taught and represented). Thus, the first purpose-built Lutheran church was designed as a place for

---

1. Caroline Walker Bynum's *Christian Materiality* (2011) offers a challenge to Lévi-Strauss's contrast by emphasizing the sustained paradox of materials and bodies in late medieval Christianity. Further discussion of this will be offered in Chapter 11.

speaking, hearing and responding to "god's word" so that belief could be encouraged, established and enacted. Luther's sermon at the inauguration of that church, in Torgau in 1544, proclaims "That we come together in the congregation is due neither to my words nor my acts but occurs through all your wills and because of the whole church" (Koerner 2005: 415). All that mattered (and all that materialized the true, ultimately invisible Church) was that the congregation could believe and could demonstrate their will to believe. Physically, the church building was oriented, for pragmatic reasons, to the northwest rather to the previously traditional (sacred) east. Its real architectural focus is the elevated pulpit attached to the north wall. Koerner demonstrates, point by point, that from this pulpit, in his "first and only church dedication", Luther explicitly and systematically contested what had until then been normal practice in church-dedication rites. He established Lutheran Protestant Christianity in practice here as much as he and other Protestants established it rhetorically in declarations, articles or confessions. Basically, he preached a sermon that he could have preached on any other occasion in any other venue. He made the congregation of believers and potential believers, as hearers of read and expounded scripture, the ultimate focus. Liturgical rites conducted by priests separated ideologically and spatially from congregants were rejected. The building became only an easily identifiable place for gatherings.

The elevation of belief as the definitive marker of Christianity could be further traced in the Zwinglian, Calvinist and other Reform movements. For instance, in Zwingli's insistence that the Eucharistic statement, "This is my body", "was to be understood, not in a real, literal and corporeal, but only in a symbolical, historical or social sense" a "wedge was decisively driven between symbol and reality" (J. Z. Smith 1987: 99, citing Uberoi 1978). Here, at the foundation of the modernist dualism dividing matter/body and spirit/mind, Christians are separated from ritual and reconstituted as only believers, as believers or not Christians at all. They are offered symbols or signs of a radical transcendence that seems to solidly reinforce Michel de Certeau's claim that, by offering belief, believers defer benefit to a future epoch of divine presence (de Certeau 1985: 193–5, cited by Lopez 1998: 28). So much hung on the small word "is", reversing its apparently obvious indication of equivalence (bread is body, wine is blood, spirit is embodied, religion is deeds) to enshrine and encode the centrality of belief, interiority and transcendence.

Ferment continued (and still continues) about "belief" among Christians and those Enlightenment thinkers who, despite their putative post-Christianity, reveal the imprint of Christian emphasis on belief (spirit and transcendence) in derivative emphases on non-physical minds, intentionality in ethics, intellectualism and other interiorities. It is, hopefully, sufficiently clear that Christianity has belief at its core. This is belief with a specific focus, so that Christians can define non-Christians as non-believers, and other kinds of Christians as wrong-believers or heretics. Perhaps what is not yet sufficiently emphasized is that this obsession with belief is not central in other religions.

BELIEF IN WORLD RELIGIONS

Around 1880 Buddhism became a "world faith" and at least some Buddhists became believers, or some people came to believe in the Buddha and Buddhism. This happened when the co-founders of Theosophy (Colonel Henry Olcott and Madame Helena Blavatsky) visited Sri Lanka and became impressed by some kind of Buddhism. When Olcott produced *The Buddhist Catechism* ([1881] 1947), a kind of Buddhism became, like Christianity, focused on belief. As Lopez summarizes, Olcott's activities were:

> the inevitable consequences of an ideology of belief, that is, an assumption derived from the history of Christianity that religion is above all an interior state of assent to certain truths. In Victorian Europe and America, the Buddha was seen as the greatest philosopher of India's Aryan past, and his teachings were regarded as a complete philosophical and psychological system based on reason and restraint; opposed to ritual, superstition, and sacerdotalism; and demonstrating how the individual could live a moral life without the trappings of institutional religion. This Buddhism could be found in texts, rather than in the lives of modern Buddhists of Ceylon.
>
> (Lopez 1998: 31)

This Buddhism was what Olcott tried to teach the Sinhalese, and it is recognizable as a Protestant Christian Buddhism. Its language, feel, promulgation and dissemination are all about belief. Adherents were to assent to teachings about revealed truths. Perhaps it is enough to note, as Ruel does, that "Gombrich, writing about Buddhism, struggles awkwardly for two pages to find an equivalent to the verb 'to believe' or 'to believe in' before moving directly to the term ('best not translated at all') *dharma*" (Ruel 1997: 50–51, citing Gombrich 1971: 60).

We might quest after traditional parallels to the term "belief" elsewhere. We may even find some words that seem like them. But we will not find them performing the generative function of "belief" or "faith" in Christian texts, sermons and discourse. Jews can recite statements that sound (in translation) like Christian creeds. The twelfth-century "Thirteen Articles of the Faith" produced by Maimonides are still published in the prayer books of various Jewish movements. In Singer's *Authorised Daily Prayer Book of the United Hebrew Congregations of the British Commonwealth of Nations* these begin "I believe with perfect faith [אני מאמין באמונה שלמה] that the Creator, blessed be his name, is the Author and Guide of everything that has been created, and that he alone has made, does make, and will make all things" (Singer 1962: 93).

Nonetheless, despite the presence and antiquity of this formulation, Jews do not make a big issue out of "believing with perfect faith". They tend to disagree more about observance or practice than about beliefs. The varieties of Judaism are generally not the result of differences of belief but of observance. Similarly in Islam, while a Muslim may be called a "believer", (مؤمن) this has more to do with what Ruel calls the "quality of a relationship, that of keeping faith, having trust" than with the "content of belief". As he says, what Islamic teaching elaborates, and what Muslims differ about, has to do with "the duties of relationship: the practice of ritual, the following of Islamic custom, the observance of Islamic law" (Ruel 1997: 50). Indeed, Muslim "believers" are more than ordinary Muslims; they are an ideal, role models of complete submission and disciplined devotion. In Islam and Judaism we need to look elsewhere for terms that play the kind of role that "belief" does in Christianity. These would be powerful terms that point to creative and divisive matters without which Muslims and Jews would not recognize their religions and their religious disputes. Later chapters endeavour to do that: to go elsewhere to find what religious people are if they are not believers.

I hope to have reinforced the understanding that religions are not about belief and are not like Christianity, especially in its capitulation to modernist state power (Cavanaugh 1995). I note, however, that some scholars of religion continue to compare religions as systems of belief. The term "world religions" (which appears in the title of far too many books and degree courses) embraces a Olcott-like notion of (proper) religions as being like Christian believing. The term leads to an approach to religions in which some of our colleagues introduce religions by first referring to founders and/or deities, then surveying key texts and statements of allegedly fundamental beliefs, especially those to do with transcending the world, e.g. with words like "salvation" or "enlightenment", and then noting some exemplary figures.

Contemporary religious life might be mentioned, usually with frustrating brevity, and often rather negatively in comparison to the attention paid to great teachers and authoritative texts. In short, there are still rather too many scholars who believe in and promote "world religions". Some also seem to believe in belief.

BELIEVING IN BELIEF

Although this is really part of the subject matter of the following chapter, I want to note here too a few examples of scholarly belief in belief. I do not mean that some scholars of religion are members of religions. That may be true and it seems to upset some of those who claim "objectivity". My point here is that despite publications that clearly set out good reasons for being critical of the unwarranted application of the term "belief" in studying religion(s) (e.g. Asad 1993: 43–8; Ruel 1997; Lopez 1998; Nye 2004: 105–28) the term is still rampant. Princeton University's Shelby Cullom Davis Center for Historical Studies has recently announced a new topic for focus: "Belief and Unbelief". The announcement asks:

> How has the line been drawn between religion and other forms of deeply held conviction: secularism, secular religions, political theologies, and the like? At issue are not just questions of demarcation and definition but processes: secularization, proselytizing, conversion. How does belief manifest itself in lived experience, in ritual, observance, and daily-life practices? (Dav 2011)

It concludes that "As always, we hope to address these questions from a wide variety of periods and places, from prehistory to the present and from all parts of the world". All this is to say, the traditional themes constellated around "belief" are alive and well. Religion is about "conviction" and can therefore be contrasted with other intellectual systems. By implication at least "religion" is "manifest" in activities but is truly about "belief".

Similarly, a call for papers for a 2009 Columbia University conference entitled "Belief Matters: Reconceptualizing Belief and Its Use" announced that:

> In recent decades, sociologically- and anthropologically-minded scholars of religion have attempted to shift scholarly attention away from belief and doctrine to rituals, practices, identities, and institutions. This turn away from belief-as-doctrine has helped scholars see

religion as a dynamic phenomenon that exists beyond the confines of peoples' [*sic*] heads. At the same time, however, has this shift kept scholars from examining other ways in which belief and believing remain central to how people conceptualize what religion is and how it operates in the world? By reexamining what it means to "believe," this conference explores if and how belief matters.

(Burchett & Vaca 2009)

The description of the themes about which papers could be offered strongly suggests that the organizers reject the rejection of belief and wish to revivify the ailing topic.

The woeful effect of emphasizing belief, of insisting that religions be defined in Christian terms, is felt every time a legislature or court seeks to determine and judge someone's freedom of religion as freedom to believe. It is felt when Pagans have to frame their religion as a system of beliefs in order to gain charity status in the UK. It is felt every time US judges make decisions about equality, free exercise, establishment and separation with reference to "systems of religious belief" (e.g. Sullivan 2008). The "new atheist" opponents of "religion" seem fixated on the folly of what putative believers believe. Religion is enshrined as belief legally, educationally and polemically.

As a final example of the continuing influence of "belief" in definitions of religions, the publisher's catalogue blurb for Enzo Pace's *Religion as Communication: God's Talk* (2011) claims that the book provides "an insight on a new approach to religious studies, drawing from systems theory to consider religion as a means of communication, and offering a critical alternative to the secularization theory to explain why religion persists in modernity" (Ashgate 2011). And yet, for all the promise of approaching religions as communication, it is asserted that "The crucial passage from living word to holy scripture is a fundamental device in the construction of a system of religious belief" (*ibid.*). Religion is, once more, belief. What is communicated about is belief rather than any of the myriad other activities that interest and motivate religious people.

LOOKING FOR A RELIGION CALLED CHRISTIANITY

Academic belief in belief and believers has misdirected attention away from what is definitive and/or generative in religions. The export from Europe of the modern constitution of states, citizens, individuals and societies further elevated particular Christian ideas into necessary elements of modernity.

55

Christian theological imaginaries (belief, spirit and transcendence) have then created more Christian-like phenomena – such as "what Buddhists believe", "wrong-believers" and "belief-and-practice". Scholars have studied these quasi-Christianities as if they were something else, proper Buddhism, folk religion or, in the use of the refrain "belief and practice", religion itself. So now there are hybrids (as powerful as those discussed by Latour 1993) that are religious belief-systems like Christianity. This does not mean that we should bow to the pressure of the dominant current and define religion as belief, "belief in" or "beliefs and practices". It only means that our research should engage with belief where we find it, and nowhere else. Christianity may, then, be a religion that involves belief, and some kinds of Buddhism may not be religions that involve believing. The bigger question, however, is whether there is religion as well as belief-system or Christian-like-ism in these new hybrids. Indeed, is there a religion called Christianity? This is really the topic of Chapter 11, and I propose here only to note some of the data that seem not to fit well within the still dominant definition of Christianity as believing.

When, in the 2011 UK census, 59.3 per cent of the population of England and Wales declared themselves to be Christians (Office of National Statistics 2012), how might we understand what Christianity is? Some colleagues have proposed that there are increasing numbers of people (worldwide) who "believe without belonging" (Davie 1990), others who "belong without believing" (Halman & Draulans 2004) and many who are "spiritual but not religious" (Fuller 2004). Does any of that amount to Christianity or religion? If it does, how "religious" are Christian oppositions to women bishops, homosexuality and magic? What about proclaiming or testifying to "faith" verbally or by holding venomous snakes, drinking tea in church, full immersion in the sea by members of the Nazarite Baptist Church, and the seemingly global fashion among Christians for intoning prayers in strangely accented and rhythmic patterns? Do these phenomena amount to a religion called Christianity?

LOSING FAITH IN RELIGION

If Christianity really is all about belief and believing it may be a "faith" or a belief-system but it is not a religion. Even though some religions have adopted the terms belief and faith, Christianity is unique in promulgating the centrality of believing. Perhaps religions that reinvent or re-present themselves as faiths and belief-systems, remove themselves from their heritage, their tradition and their religion-ness. Either that, or in reality Christianity is the only religion and scholars studying other phenomena need a different title, discipline and approach.

Some have concluded (if not in these words) that scholars of religion have, in reality, only been studying Christianity. Other phenomena have attracted attention only after they have been forced into a Christianity-shaped mould. Or, rather, and more damningly and dangerously for our discipline, the process of "studying religions" has largely been a process of creating Christian-like phenomena to be a focus of attention. Some have argued that this so undermines the study of religion that the whole project should be abandoned. Others have at least implied that scholars of religion should confess that they have been theologians all along.

A more radical solution might be to start again elsewhere, to seek an understanding of religions that does not assume Christianity is a primary model. Here I have boldly taken one step further and raised the possibility that Christianity is not a religion at all. If so, it cannot be taken to be a model for anything other than itself. It is also more than likely that Christianity-as-believing may have only ever been an imaginary, a powerful model of what some people wish to do, namely "believe" properly. I am not that interested in trying to find a name for what Christianity-as-believing is if it is not a religion. Perhaps "belief-system" is enough. Since "belief-system" plays no role in the remainder of my argument, then its use as a label for whatever Christianity is (if it is not a religion) is not in conflict with my proposals about more helpful and accurate definitions of religion. Perhaps there is a Christianity that is not Christianity-as-believing, not a belief-system, and perhaps this other Christianity might be a religion. That is a possibility that deserves further attention. That attention will be given in Chapter 11 after we have been elsewhere to seek alternative – and hopefully better – understandings that might contribute to redefining religion.

First, there are some other matters that need addressing. The work of recognizing where we are (where we have been until now, where we need to leave to start again elsewhere) has only tackled part of the equation. If Christianity is a belief-system, we need to pay more attention to the fact that Christians are not just "believers" but people who "believe in". So, following on from the fact that religion is wrongly defined as "belief", the putative (quasi-Christian) objects of believing, e.g. "the sacred" and "god", have also misled scholars into focusing on Christian-like themes among other-than-Christian religions. This is part of the matter to be tackled in the next chapter. After that we will go elsewhere and see what religion looks like there.

4. Talking like a pirate

In 2005 a new religion was invented: Pastafarianism. The fact that it is a spoof religion, a polemical make-believe in a creator called the Flying Spaghetti Monster, casts light on common perceptions that religions necessarily possess certain components. Without agreeing this early in our venture that religions should be defined by some canon of "necessary and sufficient" elements or by a set of family resemblances (Wittgenstein [1953] 2001),[1] this chapter makes use of the writings and acts of those "touched by the noodly appendages" of the Flying Spaghetti Monster to further develop an argument about the need to start "elsewhere" in order to rethink and better define religion. Pastafarianism is not an "elsewhere". It is too closely moulded by the phenomenon it opposes, namely Protestant Christian Creationist efforts to get "intelligent design" taught in schools as science rather than religion. Precisely because Pastafarianism insistently contests "irrational beliefs" or non-falsifiable metaphysics, it mirrors the pervasive contemporary obsession with belief. But more is involved here than strengthening the argument of the previous chapter.

This chapter also hoists a pirate flag to announce not only that the flagship of "belief" needs challenging, but that there are other treasure ships in the normative fleet that need to be pursued aggressively. The cargo conveyed by many textbooks and even research monographs is, ultimately, minted from Christian theological materials. Beliefs about "the sacred" and a peculiar inflection of the word "god" have gained currency where they should have been rejected as the coinage of a particular, singular worldview. Thus, the task here is not to take over that cargo and distribute it differently. It is to sink the globalized universalization of a specifically Christian alloy of "belief",

---

1. I am grateful to Tasia Scrutton for questioning me on this point.

"god" and "world religions" ideas so that the academic study of religions can more easily pursue the real treasure: a better understanding of lived religions (in the past or the present).

So, piracy is afoot, challenging the dominance of discources of belief, guaranteeing no easy journey for traders in founders and scriptures, and hybridizing a new creole language in which to converse about religions. My target is not the allegedly religious study of religions. Rather, to signal my intent with clarity, I seek to show (a) that some scholars of religion have been misled by Christian theologians into privileging a particular definition of deity, and (b) that some of us have adopted the pose of that deity (transcendent, impassive and omniscient)[2] and called it "objectivity". To do so, it examines some putatively non-religious phenomena (Pastafarianism and rationalism) and some "alternative" phenomena (Jedi, Sith and Star Trek-inspired movements) to establish that it is now taken-for-granted that believing and transcendence define religion. A discussion of the uses and associations of words like "sacred" develop the argument that one Christian trajectory has come to dominate in global modernity's constructions of the world. This dominance has not been accidental or natural but an aggressive colonization of ideas as well as of persons, nations and ecosystems that has impoverished and endangered the world. While this book cannot tackle all the ramifications of such facts, it does challenge the unhealthy influence of ideas about divine omniscience on academic pretensions towards strong forms of objectivity.

In the end, this is transitional. Its purpose is to reinforce the point that religion and scholarship have been wrongly defined. But more is at stake that merely noticing that "the secular" is only the theological flipside of "the sacred". Etymologies rarely do more than reinforce genetic fallacies. If successful, this chapter's effort ought to demonstrate the pressing need for us to go elsewhere to find better academic ways of approaching religion. Following chapters will extend our vocabulary with richer critical terms and theoretical approaches. Instead of seeking the shadows of some kind of Christianity in (other) religions, they will enable us to focus on the everyday phenomena of lived religion. It is likely that when we look again at what Christians do (which we will do in Chapter 11), Christianity too will almost certainly turn out to be quite a lot like how people do religion elsewhere.

---

2. I recognize that such ideas are in tension with other Christian beliefs about incarnation and participation. However, imperialist approaches have had a more dominant influence than cooperative ones.

PASTAFARIAN PIRATES

Pastafarianism began with an open letter from Bobby Henderson (2005) to the Kansas State Board of Education. It attempted to derail Creationist efforts to get "intelligent design" taught in schools as science. The majority of the letter pretends to offer a "concerned citizen's" religious belief that the universe was "intelligently designed" by the Flying Spaghetti Monster, that any contrary evidence is either mistaken or deliberately placed by the Creator to mislead, and that Pastafarianism requires the wearing of full pirate regalia. Henderson explains the pirate regalia both as the will of his deity and also as an effort to reduce the effects of global warming on the grounds that in the last two hundred years there has been "a statistically significant inverse relationship" between the average global temperature and the number of pirates. The letter clearly parodies the kind of arguments made by Creationists attempting to present "religious beliefs" as "scientific theories". Henderson's real point is made in his final sentence:

> I think we can all look forward to the time when these three theories
> are given equal time in our science classrooms across the country,
> and eventually the world: One third time for Intelligent Design, one
> third time for Flying Spaghetti Monsterism (Pastafarianism), and one
> third time for logical conjecture based on overwhelming observable
> evidence.   (Henderson 2005)

The logic of the satire is that in fact science lessons should be concerned with scientific theories, logic, observation and evidence.

Henderson and the rapidly growing number of Pastafarians have produced an entertaining, informative and activist website (www.venganza.org). Throughout the site, and well exemplified by a discussion about producing a Pastafarian billboard, it is insisted that the Church has a "positive message" and is not best represented by "satire and nonsense", although there is plenty of that. Complaints (often published on the site's "hate mail" page) that some point, polemic or parody is "not funny" are often met by the rejoinder that it is not meant to be funny, but it is meant to encourage the separation of rationality and irrationalism. While challenging irrational belief (which might be tautological in Pastafarian discourse), the website suggests that many members are experimenting with the creation of a religion. They playfully elaborate beliefs and justifications, rituals and texts that parallel or parody those of other religions; for example, a section of the Church's "holy book", *The Loose Canon*, is entitled "The Torahtellini" (FSM Consortium 2010). The project, therefore, reveals common assumptions about how religion might be defined: religions are popularly supposed to have transcendent but self-revealing deities, texts, cosmologies, rituals, hierarchies, and probably a degree of hypocrisy.

INVISIBLE PINK UNICORN, JEDI AND SITH

The Church of the Flying Spaghetti Monster (FSM) is not alone. Other advocates of rationalism and/or opponents of religious irrationalism have made use of the idea of an Invisible Pink Unicorn, "an invisible dragon breathing heatless fire" (in Carl Sagan's garage) and Bertrand Russell's "cosmic teapot". They raise a range of similar questions about rationality, evidence, logic, proof and provability. They contest "faith" as if religion should be defined as its synonym. Most of them insist that belief in the existence of a god is irrational and therefore unscientific. Pastafarians are different. Although they challenge the rationality of some religious ideas and arguments, notably Creationism's "intelligent design", they do not deny that religious people can be rational. Indeed, the Church's website often notes that many Christians treat the Bible as an inspiring book but not one to take "literally" (or as "inspired" in the fundamentalist sense). Most Christians are no more Creationists than they are observant of (biblical laws about) Shabbat or Kashrut.

Whether the Church of the Flying Spaghetti Monster is a religion, whether there is a difference between "spoof religion" and "religion", or whether some Pastafarians are atheists or believers, are not really the main issues here. Rather, I am interested in the choices made by Pastafarians about what counts as "religion". Because of the core desire or need to challenge Creationist Christian projects, much of the Church's activities emphasize beliefs or ideas that further illustrate the privilege Protestantism (inflected by modernism) has in contemporary ideas as to what constitutes "religion". Even if their own alleged beliefs are regularly contrasted with rationality and scientific method (summarized as observation, reason, experimentation and evidence), it is still "believing" that is deemed definitive. Rituals are frequently noted as being optional, although dressing as a pirate and talking like a pirate, especially on weekly or annual occasions, seem popular (and a significant means of evangelism). Behaving respectfully towards others, including taking care to argue responsibly, is high among the moral themes inculcated among Pastafarians. This too might resonate with the Protestant and Enlightenment background of the religion.

Pastafarianism is also not alone as a newly invented religion. There are other groups that purport to blend science and religion, or at least technology and ritual. A worldwide effort to have "Jedi" and/or "Sith" recognized in those national censuses which include questions about religious affiliation, identity or practice has generated considerable internet traffic. There are also groups that playfully experiment with blends of religion and popular subcultural or literary genres. There are Anglican churches that conduct "Goth Masses" (in which "Goth" is not to be confused with Gothic architecture) and Druids who perform Star Trek rituals. Together this ferment of possibilities invites further consideration that, by and large, illustrates the dominance of thoroughly modern, Protestant and Enlightenment approaches to defining religion. That is, they tend to conduct rituals in the service of individualized self-development (the improvement of "faith" or "inner knowledge"), build networks of largely solitary beings who treat institutions as optional services, and carefully inculcate rational interpretations that support personal spiritual growth.

All this makes Pastafarianism and other spoof and playful religions ideal entry points to a larger exploration of the better charted waters of debates about religion, sacrality, secularity and theoilogy (words about many deities).

WHAT IS NOT SACRED?

As already noted, occasionally people accuse the Church of the Flying Spaghetti Monster of making fun of serious matters or sincerely held beliefs. These criticisms might be summed up in the common exclamation, "is nothing sacred?!" Elsewhere, freedom of speech is sometimes asserted or, conversely, challenged when comedians and cartoonists make fun of religious people, activities or ideas. Perhaps the freedom to say negative, insensitive things about religion is definitive of the rights, freedoms and secularization that emerged out of the modernist state-making wars (often misrepresented as Protestant versus Catholic "Wars of Religion") and the European Enlightenment that eventually followed. More is at stake, however, than an equally modern concern that people should, in fact, be respectful and sensitive towards others. The putative contrast between "the sacred" and "the secular" or "profane" (which includes but is not limited to the things that can or cannot be spoken publicly) has been an important aspect of some modern definitions of religion.

In the technical language of classical Roman sacred architecture, there are "profane" areas, literally, outside temples. This has been extended as a metaphor that creates areas (physical, discursive or imagined) that are "not sacred". These are separate from religious areas (whatever they may be), and/or are subject to different authorities and organizations. While these distinctions emerged slowly, and in the context of varied political experiments, they feed into contemporary understandings that religious matters should be separate from political and other matters. "Profane" also spawned ideas about "profanity": not merely as a spatial contrast between inside and outside (albeit that this contrast bore implications for appropriate behaviour), but also as a synonym of "inherently wrong". A profanity is now an (almost) inexcusable rudeness, a defilement. Things have become rather fixed and concretized. Any decent Pagan Roman could move from inside sacred temples to their profane outsides without compromising anything. Today, as illustrated by reactions to the Flying Spaghetti Monster, sacrality and profanity are treated as if they ought to be separated by a wide gulf.

Similarly, another Latin word has been given larger tasks than those that it was originally employed to conduct. "Secular" once meant something like "of this time", "contemporary" or "of this generation". But the Christian theological notion of a deity outside of time and somehow separate from the physical cosmos encouraged an expansion of "secular" to embrace contrasts between "now" and "eternity", "the immanent world" and "transcendent reality", or "everyday necessities" and the "eternal liturgy". It made space for "secular" rulers as well as "religious" leaders and authorities.

Later in this book (especially Chapters 6 and 9) I will seek to recover a more dynamic understanding of sacred–profane and religious–secular transitions. Perhaps a sense of that is gained by noting the more verbal and active senses of the terms. While things can be profaned (made ordinary if not negative in some way), they can also be made sacred, especially by acts of sacrifice. The richness of these flows seems lost in the more mundane contemporary dichotomy of "the sacred" and "the secular". What was once profane, outside of the temple, was still connected to the sacred inside of the temple. Sacrificial animals were selected from among animals destined for "ordinary" meals. Ritual leaders could be expected to behave appropriately (i.e. with restraint) for some period in preparation for entering temples. But the modern "secular" realm is separated off from religion. Or, rather, efforts are made to separate religion and politics, church and state, sacred and secular domains or pursuits. One religion's internal struggles have created a world that is now too often treated as natural, necessary or normative.

As Tim Fitzgerald argues:

> a necessary part of the ideological process of creating the modern category religion has been the simultaneous attempt to conceptualize the non-religious. This has been facilitated by the transformation of the old mediaeval religious/secular dichotomy within Christendom into some presumed universal distinction within all societies. ... The creation of the secular – non-religious, the scientific, the natural, the world as it is simply given to rational observation – can be seen in this light as the mystifying project of western imperialism, for it disguises the western exploitation of the world and the unequal relations which in fact exist between nations. One task here then is to analyse the role played by the modern category religion in this process.
>
> (Fitzgerald 2000: 14–15)

Fitzgerald's challenge to that mystifying project of exploitative imperialism and only partially masked processes is, in important ways, developed not only by an analysis of "western" texts and practices but also by discussion of Buddhism, Hinduism and religion in Japan. In short, Fitzgerald goes "elsewhere" to test, elaborate and enrich his argument – though I note that his argument and data are contested by Ian Reader (2004a, 2004b), among others. I am trying to do something both similar and different in this book. I am intrigued by the possibilities provided by learning from elsewheres, hopeful that it can be made even more evident that modernism is a project not a given, but not entirely convinced that "religion" has no translation equivalents in other-than-European languages. I am, rather, excited by the idea that religion (everywhere and everywhen) is, in real reality, better defined by terms, interests and matters learnt elsewhere than by the European rooted traditions of dualism and hyperseparation.

For now I propose to accept that modernity has been shown to be something other than a natural sea within which we all swim. Rather it is an imperial warship that (peculiarly for this metaphor) has been hiding its real nature and context with costly illusions. Chief among these are the artifice of separation between mind and matter, culture and nature, and humans and the rest of the cosmos. But a pirate fleet is gathering. Among its weaponry is the illusion-busting announcement that we are confronting an "-ism" not an "-ity": the effortful project of making modernism happen rather than the mere presentation of a given modernity. If Latour is correct that "we have never been modern" (1993) it is not only because modernism has always been an impossible project (creating its own unmodern hybrids, among other difficulties), but also because we and the world have always been resistant. But let's come back to that and the "factish gods" (Latour 2010) of modernism later. There is more to be said about "the sacred" to enhance our ability to see the deceitful chimera of modernism's damaging separations.

SACRED NOUN AND ADJECTIVE

In *The Loose Canon* (FSM Consortium 2010), the Church of the Flying Spaghetti Monster's "collection of really important words" (or incipient scripture), the term "sacred" occurs fourteen times. It always and only occurs as an adjective. It qualifies certain places, trees, pasta-related consumables (including beer), pirates and one "law" concerned with public etiquette. Admirably, "sacred" never occurs in the barbarous nominal phrase "the sacred", the misuse of which is traced by Jonathan Z. Smith (1978), Bill Pickering (1994), Terry Thomas (1994), Melissa Raphael (1994), Veikko Anttonen (1996, 2000, 2005) and Kim Knott (2009). This nineteenth-century neologism was made unhelpfully oppositional to "profane" in Émile Durkheim's sociology (e.g. Durkheim 1915: 37), but reached its apogee in the theologies of Rudolf Otto (1958) and Mircea Eliade (1959). It has never escaped its theological parochialism: while it pretends to aid objective, cross-cultural and/or critical discussions of religions, it generally reinforces the tendency to universalize elements of Christianity.

"The sacred" sometimes collaborates with "experience" to attempt to seduce us into believing in and/or researching about one universal experience of a unified religious realm (like Otto's numinous). Sometimes use of "the sacred" scuppers any attempt at understanding others by spreading contagion with the insistence that any experience of transcendent divinity is ineffable. In short, "the sacred" does not open up possibilities for cross-cultural or inter-religious conversation, and nor does it serve as a truly critical term in debating such encounters. Rather, it is a mask thinly disguising the face of a modern Protestant kind of deity and, with "experience", is a call to believe. The mask is too flimsy and should be jettisoned.

If "sacred" should not be a noun in religious studies, its traditional use as an adjective remains potent. While we need not accept that there are sacred people, places, times and things, we will fail to understand some of the dynamics that could be definitive of religion if we do not appreciate that others do accept such matters. To that end, once again, I pick up this thread later (especially Chapters 6 and 9) where, for instance, I attempt to strengthen the dynamic sense of things, people, places, times and so on shifting as they relate differently to other facets of life. I do this in relation to *tapu/tabu* and *qadosh* – only partially cognate Maori, Polynesian and Hebrew terms. At least, I propose to argue that the dynamics of these terms (in context) would greatly enrich our understanding and use of "sacred".

Here, however, recognizing that "the Sacred" and "religious experience" are flimsy masks for Christian theological notions is intended to cast light on two other matters. First, there is the unfortunate effort to find a deity like the one of elite Christian theology in places where no such being exists. Second, there is the effort by scholars to be like that deity.

SEEKING DIVINITY AND TAKING LAND

The Flying Spaghetti Monster is, first and foremost, a creator. Indeed, the monster is *the* creator – the intelligent designer, albeit a rather eccentric and entertaining boffin. He (being almost certainly male) may be a drunk, can be lazy, and is more likely to ignore his followers than to punish his detractors. Nonetheless, in many respects he is like the god of some Protestant Christian theologies. In particular, he is a deity who invites efforts to believe faithfully in irrational, non-scientific metaphysics. However, he is neither omniscient nor impassive. Also, because he is, in the end, a spoof, he actually invites contest, debate and challenge. Pastafarians are unlikely to be seduced into sectarianism or fundamentalism. Indeed, they regularly contrast themselves with humourless fundamentalist atheists.

The point here is that deities are not all the same. In ignorance of this, the aggressive expansion of European imperialism was founded on two notions: that (a) there is one true and authoritative deity, and (b) those who do not believe in this deity ought at least to believe in a deity like the one of Christianity. A brief consideration must suffice to illustrate the far from ironic and far from just results of the devastating application of this theo-politics.

When the subjects of Alfonso V of Portugal and, soon afterwards, those of Ferdinand and Isabella of Aragon and Castile arrived in new (to them) places they looked for signs of the presence of Christianity. They needed to know whether there was a Christian ruler in charge of the people they encountered.

67

They also needed to know whether the inhabitants were either Christian or at least human enough to be capable of being converted to Christianity. The first of these (a Christian ruler) was of primary importance. If there was no Christian ruler then the subjects of European Christian rulers were commanded "to 'capture, vanquish, and subdue the saracens, pagans, and other enemies of Christ,' to 'put them into perpetual slavery,' and 'to take all their possessions and property'" (Newcomb 1992, citing Davenport 1917: 20–26).

The command came from Pope Nicholas V in the bull *Romanus Pontifex* (1452) and was reinforced by Alexander VI in the bull *Inter Cetera* (1493). It resonates throughout European ruler's decrees and justifications for invasion, enslavement and impoverishment (i.e. colonialism) from then on. It underlies the many assertions of the United States to own the multiple territories of indigenous nations over which it spread(s) itself. It harmonizes (albeit in a barbarous song) with the concept of *terra nullius* that verbalized the fantasy, contrary to all evidence, that what is now Australia was an unused, unclaimed or unruly land prior to the arrival of Europeans. Other ramifications of European land-ownership and life-ownership ideas could extend these few examples globally.

A particular constellation of ideas about legal authority and land-ownership are, in these and similar contexts, fundamentally linked with notions of deity. The attempt to find evidence of ability to believe in the existence and graciousness of the invaders' authorizing deity played a significant role in defining the humanity and/or rights of indigenous peoples and individuals. The failure of Samuel Marsden (1765–1838) to find a means of converting-and-civilizing Aboriginal Australians contrasted, in his mind at least, with his success among Maori. He says of Aborigines that "The natives have no Reflection – they have no attachments, and they have no wants", but describes Maori as "a very superior people in point of mental capacity, requiring but the introduction of Commerce and the Arts, [which] having a natural tendency to inculcate industrious and moral habits, open a way for the introduction of the Gospel" (Marsden, quoted in Yarwood 1967).

What Christian missionaries, worldwide, particularly needed was what Christian colonialists benefited from the absence of (i.e. notions of land-ownership and divinity that Europeans could recognize). They mistakenly judged Aborigines to have nothing with which Christians could dialogue. Equally, but differently, however, they misjudged Maori as having both "primitive" and "rudimentary" notions of land-ownership and deity. As in many other places, Europeans were looking for individuals with title to property, authority to negotiate, and the capacity for interior "belief" in a transcendent deity. Actually, whether they found such people or not, the end result was largely the same: people were removed from their lands, had their choices ignored, and their traditions belittled (or converted into curiosities). The religion part of the Euro-expansion project is, ironically perhaps, well expressed in William James's putative definition of religion: "Religion, therefore, as I now ask you arbitrarily to take it, shall mean for us the feelings, acts, and experiences of individual men in their solitude, so far as they apprehend themselves to stand in relation to whatever they may consider the divine" (James [1902] 1997: 42). Civilizing involved destroying emplaced communities, reforming people as increasingly hyperseparated individuals, and rendering religion down into occasional overwhelming experiences of subjection that might, paradoxically, console alienated individuals.

Even among Maori, what Marsden and others found was more communal and less supernaturalist (to note one prevalent bit of dualism) than the theology of elite Christian theology. Being omniscient, omnipresent but largely transcendent, probably impassive, certainly singular and definitively "creator of all", makes this deity different from almost all other deities and decidedly separate from other beings. Although there are other elite monotheistic theologies that present a similar complex of ways in which the one god is definitively "different", in lived reality the practised relationships of most Christians with their inspiring others is not so transcendent. They ask for help with bodily and material concerns, and they seek emotional support from immediately present and often materialized (incarnate or enstatued) sacred persons. But missionaries typically expect more of people (Christians or potential Christians) than this. They seek an idea that they can use to preach the desirability of "feelings, acts, and experiences of individual men" who can, on that basis, fully encounter and properly relate to the divine.

GOD IN THE ACADEMY

An almost global quest to find "high gods" who can be compared (less than favourably) to the Christian deity is not only evident among Christian missionaries. It also affects the assumptions some scholars make about what sort of being is referred to by the word "god". Apart from the imperial deity of expansionist Europe, deities are rarely omniscient, omnipresent, omnicompetent and so on. Some may participate in creative acts, but they are more likely to shape and look after aspects of the cosmos than the whole of it. They may be resorted to for advice, but there is no logical reason why any powerful being must be continuously pleasant to all other beings. There are, according to many religious traditions, good reasons to take care in all relationships, especially with persons who are capable of self-centred acts. In some places, possibly, prior to the arrival of Christianity or Islam, people noted the existence of beings beyond the multiple personal and involved deities, ancestors and the diverse community of earthly life. Perhaps a single being initiated the whole cosmic process or show. But they are rarely of any great interest – just as they seem only rarely interested in the world. Even "Mother Earth" and "Father Sky", where people mention them at all, rarely have elaborate rituals devoted to them. As among Maori, it is their children who are addressed and engaged with, reciprocally. This seems a more common pattern than that in which "god" refers to a singular, unique kind of being.

I will expand this enquiry about the nature of deities in Chapter 8 in an engagement with Yoruba orishas that may further aid a consideration of how religion might be defined in relation to proximate and engaged deities rather than a transcendent one. Similarly, I will argue in Chapter 9 that Judaism demonstrates that "god" need not refer to the kind of being postulated in the preached or creedal theologies of Christianity.

None of this is to agree at all that deities are projections of human concerns or anthropomorphisms. Rather, it is to take seriously a pervasive indigenous insistence that the world is a community of persons, most of whom are not human, but all of whom (when healthy at least) are capable of relationship, communication and intentional acts. Humans are not definitive of personhood (or the abilities that seem definitive of personhood) but are one kind of being among many that share broad similarities. Deities are like humans only in as much as they are also like other living, relational beings. Of course, some humans do portray and (perhaps) experience their deities in human-like shape. But that is another matter. The point here is that it is easier to think and talk cross-culturally about divinities if one is not burdened by notions imported from only one religion. In particular, the legacy of Christian theological thinking about one deity should not be treated as definitive elsewhere. Perhaps, indeed, deities from elsewhere might aid an improved understanding of everyday Christian life. An ecology of divine beings seems more achievable if these are treated as participants in a larger, multi-species community. But this is true in regard to an ecology of humanity too, as the next section and the next chapter will explore.

One really obvious effect of the importation of Christian notions of deity into academic theorizing about religion is that a set of dualisms have too often become a focus of attention. Some academics rather too casually use dichotomies like natural/supernatural, immanent/transcendent, worldly/ divine, and so on as if they were natural and universal. Like "secular" in relation to "sacred" or "religious", each member of these pairs implicates the other. So, calling Paganism a "nature religion" can contrast it with putatively "supernatural(ist)" or transcendentally focused religions. Less helpfully still, it may imply that there is a "supernatural" realm to contrast with "nature". Provoked by similar dichotomies, Ken Morrison deemed it necessary to critique Åke Hultkrantz's presentation of "The Concept of the Supernatural in Primal Religions" (Hultkrantz 1983) at some length (K. M. Morrison 2002: 37–58). Morrison's work (here and elsewhere) demonstrated the great value of attending to local relational understandings of divinity and personhood and considering how it might enrich our critical efforts more generally. Both Paganism and the indigenous religions discussed by Morrison are not pervasively generated or defined by dualisms. Indeed, those dualisms are endlessly problematic even where they arose, as the effort to enact or enliven them in reality conflicts with our inescapable embodiment, emplacement and relationality. Care should be taken with the assumption that religion is definitively otherworldly even when it does involve dealing with deities.

Perhaps even more detrimental to the effort to understand particular religions in their own terms, is the contagious assumption that "god", and therefore "religion", has to do with ultimate concerns or highest values. In part, this tendency may arise from an effort to be inclusive or pluralist. Thus, non-theistic Buddhists, polytheistic Hindus and atheistic Humanists might all have a place in dialogues about "ultimate concerns". In part, too, it may arise from a desire to find a place for "religion" beyond the matters now colonized by the sciences. If the creation of modern states forcibly pushed religiosity into increasingly private and individualized spaces (Cavanaugh 1995), it also required god to be concerned with only non-mundane matters: life after death, ultimate values, and the meaning of everything. Some deities and some religions are certainly concerned, sometimes at least, with such issues. But religions should not be ghettoized and/or codified statically. We should follow Asad's (1993) critique of Clifford Geertz (1973: 90) in devoting attention to negotiated practices of embodiment, materiality, power and discipline rather than defining religion as symbolic or representational of ultimate concerns.

It seems evident that whenever religious preachers elevate deities or religious goals beyond the concerns and reach of ordinary life, "lesser" deities or goals intervene. But we need not worry about the place of saints, icons, statues and other revered persons (and thing-persons) in relation to "high gods". Rather, we should forcefully resist the notion that religion and "god" are best defined in relation to ultimate, transcendent or supernatural entities or facts. As Bruno Latour provocatively argues:

> Religion does not even try ... to reach anything beyond, but to represent the presence of that which is called, in a certain technical and ritual idiom, the "Word incarnate," which is to say again that it is here – alive – and not dead over there, far away ... Religion, in this tradition, does everything to constantly redirect attention, by systematically breaking the will to go away, ignore, be indifferent, blasé or bored. Conversely, science has nothing to do with the visible, the direct, the immediate, the tangible, or the lived world of common sense: of sturdy "matters of fact". (Latour 2010: 110)

As Latour's sentence about science indicates, this is a powerful polemic that deserves further consideration. For now, I cite it so as to agree with him that modernists have mis-identified both religion and science, making the former (under the conditions of modernity) "abandon its goal of representing anew what it is all about, making all of us gaze, absent-mindedly toward the invisible world of beyond that it has no equipment, nor competence, nor authority, nor ability to reach, and even less to grasp" (*ibid*.: 112).

In short, religion has much to do with material, physical, embodied, emplaced, performed life. I propose, then, that words like deity, divinity, god and goddess refer to quite different kinds of person to the kind of being identified as "god" among elite Christian theologians. It is time to return our gaze to the ways in which people perform religion when not torn asunder by unlikely elite dualities. But to do this we must also tackle the problem that some of us (academics) have been trying to imitate that omniscient and transcendent deity.

SECULARIZED SURVEILLANCE

Scholarly objectivity can be a trace of divine transcendence. There are all sorts of ways in which we come to know things and many ways of seeking certainty. Ethnographic disciplines have evolved their practice from observational to participant-observational and other even more engaged forms of research. Nonetheless, the ideology asserted by many academics resolutely insists on the desirability and possibility of objectivity in its strongest senses. That is, just as the transcendent deity is supposed to have better than a bird's-eye view of the entirety of things, so the trained and disciplined scholar is supposed to be able to represent reality completely to others. But there is no remote position from which reality can be seen entirely and adequately. There is always another side or an inside that is not visible, touchable or observable. Bracketing out matters is only helpful if the researcher acknowledges that they only desire a partial view, and undermines claims to have engaged with all relevant issues.

Happily, of course, most of us (scholars) are well aware of the folly of claiming transcendent-god-like powers. We seek understanding through particular kinds of relationship with those among whom we research. We work hard so as to find ways to speak what others would insist is (religiously) ineffable or (sceptically) solipsistic. But where we read or hear contrasts between objectivity and subjectivity, outsiders and insiders, observation and participation, rationality and faith, and a range of similar dualities, we are witnessing the "fugitive pose" (to pick up a resonant term from Gerald Vizenor 1998) of the deity our colleagues believe themselves to have rejected. God is not in the gaps but in the surveillance. His traces are discoverable in transcendence, impassive observation and certain knowledge.

Vásquez offers some other ways of considering the modern self (especially as performed by academics), its inheritance from Protestant Christianity and its surveillance techniques. Two of these are resonant here. First, Vásquez builds on Ivan Strenski (2006) to contend that:

> the rise of the phenomenology of religion as a core method in the academic study of religion was the result of the convergence of German Idealism, Protestant Pietism, and the Husserlian (Cartesian and Kantian) temptation of transcendence and his adherence to the Augustinian motto "Do not go out; go back into yourself. Truth dwells in the inner man." Phenomenology of religion operates with the notion that the self has a "glassy essence" (Rorty 1979), that the religious subject is potentially self-transparent, having privileged access to its thoughts, feelings, and emotions, which once retrieved can serve as the foundations for a theory of religion. Protestant Pietism and the early Husserl shared a mistrust of the "external" world and situated praxis, the former because it wanted to avoid appealing to mediation in the relation between the believer and God (arguing against the efficacy of works in Catholicism) and the latter because it saw the contingencies of the external world as an obstacle to the recovery of the transcendental ego.   (Vásquez 2011: 88)

Anti-Catholicism, particular as anti-ritualism, undermines any effort to engage with the doing of religion at the same moment as it (mis)directs attention to ultimacy or transcendence. Scholarship may have been secularized but it is not (yet) entirely secular – both because it continues to perform religious methods and because it focuses on a transcendent rather than this-worldly contemporary reality.

Similarly, Vásquez builds on Michel Foucault in showing that:

> The Cartesian self is the central epistemological figure of the modern epoch. … Foucault argues that the modern epoch is characterized by the dual constitution of the self as both subject and object. This split is made possible by the generalized use of self-reflection, the same kind of optics that accompanied the othering of the mad persons. … What defines modernity is "an analytic of finitude," where the human self has taken the place of God, as both the sovereign spectator of the world and the object of his/her own gaze.
>
> (*Ibid.*: 134, citing Foucault 1973)

There are resonances here with Linda Holler's (2002) recognition of the elective schizophrenia of Descartes and other philosophers. Vásquez and Holler both propose a material, embodied, performative and localized practice of scholarship and of self-construction (one in relation to religion, the other to moral reflection and agency) and contest business as usual among moderns.

There have been other challenges to the religiousness of the varied kinds of phenomenology (e.g. Flood 1999), but with Vásquez, at last, we find a far more wide-ranging critique. Modern rationalist science too requires a Protestant style subject to become a (Protestant) god-like self: an omniscient and omnipresent but impassive observer. The quest for a meaning outside of "immediate reality", in some kind of transcendence signalled by material forms and relations, hints (where it does not shout) at the traces of those same-old fugitive poses. Thus, Vásquez (building on Asad 1993) can critique Clifford Geertz (1973) and others who propose a conception of religion that:

> has its roots in the notions that "social reality is fundamentally symbolic" and that our apprehension of the world is not immediate and complete, but always uncertain and partial, always "mediated by the whole of explanatory procedures which preceded it and accompany it".   (Vásquez 2011: 215, citing Ricoeur 1979: 99)

BEYOND CRITIQUE

The misjudged and mistaken Protestant-style defining of religion as "belief in god", "belief in spirits" or "postulated metaphysics" is not the most damaging infection of academia by the abiding interests of a single religion. The widespread effort by some academics (sometimes asserting their ownership of the label "scientist") to be transcendent, omniscient and impassive has more severely damaged our scholarship.

That it is not enough to criticize some ways of studying religion as being religious is demonstrated by the evidence that modern ways of doing scholarship are themselves religious. The "secular" has not separated from "religion" – indeed, it is questionable whether we would need a word like "secular" if it was not somehow defined as a term within a religious vocabulary. When scholars of religion continue seeking a character from the Christian theological pantheon among communities and practices when such a being is an alien (including, that is, among many Christians) they continue the Christian mission by other means. The definition of religion by reference to transcendence and ultimate values maintains the boundaries of a partisan pursuit. But so does the assertion of the ability of scholarly training to shape the modern self into the divine–king's all-seeing replacement.

Different notions of deity might help. Tricksters and other deities who are passionate about the world might, for instance, invite us to rethink what we might look for when we set out to find religion in the world. The Flying Spaghetti Monster might remind us that some deities are not expected to be omni-competent or entirely rational. I am not certain that any particular "elsewhere" other than the still dominant, overly normative "here" of Protestant-derived rationalist modernity will provide a better understanding of religion. It is possible that I will only insert another localized view into the profligate diversity of things that scholars of religion study and their ways of studying. However, by starting elsewhere, by thinking about performance and materiality, the everyday and the ordinarily dynamic, I suspect we will work towards far richer engagements with and understandings of the world. Small and large acts of piracy, sinking the dominant Cartesianism and transcendentalism (of deities and scholars) can, I think, only aid our ability to manoeuvre among the lived realities that we encounter. In the next chapter I want to try to evoke a sense of the real world in which religions and scholarship take place.

5. Real world

I have learnt two things from listening in on the conversation of birds. First, although the larger-than-human world is full of conversation, most of it is not about humans. Second, although most of the conversation of the larger-than-human world is not about us, it does not ignore us. We are not central, but neither are we absent. Although other species do not share our anthropocentric obsession, we are not separate from them, or they from us. Birds and our other relations do not ignore us; we aren't alien to them, we live in the same place-communities, we co-evolved in the same world. Our acts are of some importance to them, but what we do and what is done to us are not the only significant happenings in the universe. Just as birds are not here for our benefit and use, nor are they particularly motivated by our every act and obsession. But sometimes they are.

We are part of the community of life, the society of Earth dwellers. We live alongside others of many species, all our lives are braided together, all our acts co-create the emergence of all that is, moment by moment. There is no environment separate from the lives we and all other species live. There is only ecology: the at-home acts of multiple related species. We are made, mattered, embodied, carnated perhaps, in the same way as other Earth evolved creatures. We are not and cannot be individuals (despite the best efforts of Brian, Monty Python's not-the-messiah). We are necessarily communal beings. Furthermore, our "here", our ecology-home-Earth, is not made around us while we do what we do, but "it" is made by and of the combined actions of all of us dwelling here together. There is no separation between our verbal dwelling and our nominal dwelling (our being/acting at home). Our emplacement and our embodiment are co-extensive.

It does not really matter how you take my claim to have understood the language of birds. It works as well as a poetic and mildly ironic evocation of a thoroughly scientific understanding of the inter-relatedness of all existences as it does as an animist-mystic testimony. Listening to birds is most certainly not intended as revelatory, nor as a necessary stage in the defining of "religion". This chapter is not about a religious interpretation of reality or religion. It does not fuse the many different things that religions involve or imply into yet another description of reality (however adequately I could do that). It is not my intention to judge the veracity or value of religions by their agreement with any particular view of reality. Religions do not have to fit any cosmology other than their own. It is up to religious people to work out how to deal with disjunctions between traditional or taught worldviews and anyone else's views (whether they be religious, scientific or both). More to the point, it is up to religious people to deal with how they might live, act, behave or perform religiously in the real world.

My goal is to continue the work of the previous chapter in sketching out how academics might do a better job of researching and teaching in the real world. That is, I want to know how we might do more than criticize and deconstruct. I do not want to spend much more time and energy arguing that the world is not well described by Cartesian or post-Cartesian modernism, postmodernism or most-modernism. Scholars as varied and excellent as Val Plumwood (1993, 2000, 2002, 2009), Bruno Latour (1993, 2002, 2010), Antonio Damasio (1994), David Abram (1997, 2010), Charlene Spretnak (1999, 2011), Tim Ingold (2000, 2011), Linda Holler (2002), Mary Midgley (2004), Karen Barad (2007), Manuel Vásquez (2011), and many others, have demonstrated this more eloquently and more completely than I could hope to do. So too have many of the indigenous, environmentalist, global justice and feminist activists who speak and act better worlds.

We need to know more than that the old maps were wrong. If "we have never been modern" (Latour 1993), we must ask what we have been. Depressingly, Latour correctly argues that we who live under the conditions of modernity, inside the project of modernism, have been expending a lot of effort to be(come) modern – and we have been willing or unwilling contributors to modernizing. Similarly, Michael Steinberg (2005: 143) may well be correct that "we are becoming the species best fitted to the capitalist world". Happily, however, he continues, "enough remains of our old life that we find the process painful". All is not lost. But I want more! I want to know what we might become if we stop trying to be moderns in the mould of separatist-fantasists like Descartes.

Taking note that Steinberg warns against simplistic solutions (looking back, looking inward, looking sexy and looking mystified), and not wishing to participate in endless deconstruction, neither do I want to resort to construction. As I am sure others have said, that is a tired and tiresome metaphor. We readily and correctly assume that our houses, pubs, universities, law courts, sports stadiums, restaurants, gardens, farms, and transport and communication networks are constructed. It is not worth commenting on. Just so, it is time to think about the ways we live and act within our world. It is time to see how others live and act within this world. It is time to find an academic practice for the world that is not as we have imagined. Or, rather, we need to ask how we might do academic work in the world that we are once more beginning to understand, now that the edifice of Descartes' error has collapsed. For example, how can we do research as symbiotic beings rather than as individuals? How can we be cognizant of religion's performance in a multi-species world in which humans are neither separate nor exceptional but emplaced and integrated?

I propose to summarize and riff off some works that show us how to perform academia in the real, "deep" world – a phrasing that might show that I have learnt something from Ronald Grimes (2002). Since we cannot have ever truly ceased living in the real world, despite the abundance and seduction of our illusions, our curious worldviews, I have tried to pay attention to diverse signs that show us where we really are. No, that is the wrong metaphor: these are not signs pointing somewhere, they are cairns that invite us to stop, become present, and add our piece. But, still, the real world is as yet elsewhere than modernist individualism, consumerism and separatism of the late-anthropocene era[1] and its dominant way of performing academia.

The real world might also be elsewhere than any particular religion's proclamation about reality, but that is not particularly interesting. Indeed, it is entirely unremarkable as we seek a better way to *study* religions. Once we are firmly back here, elsewhere, where we have always really been, in the real world with all our relations and all our bodies, then we can move on as researchers. We can study religious worlds as they are imaginatively and intimately lived out in the real world – whether or not they "fit" that world. In part, I am provoked by the thought that defining religion as a "cultural phenomenon" (with Clifford Geertz 1973) or as a "natural phenomenon"

---

1. "This era in which the impact of humanity on earth systems has gained the force of a geological era"; see the Ecological Humanities website, www.ecologicalhumanities.org/about.html.

(with Daniel Dennett 2006) requires us to define what "culture" and "nature" mean. Are we, in fact, using words in ways that preclude us understanding the world? Understanding that the world is not dualistic as the use of terms like "culture" and "nature" commonly imply, I propose to summarize some alternative views. At times I will juxtapose ideas and approaches that seem, to me, to resonate interestingly (although perhaps not always in ways antici- pated by their originators).

BEING PREY (NOT SEPARATE)

Val Plumwood's analysis of our modern(ist) situation is astute, powerful and ultimately empowering. She writes:

> Human-centredness is a complex syndrome which includes the hyperseparation of humans as a special species and the reduction of non-humans to their usefulness to humans, or instrumentalism. Many have claimed that this is the only prudent, rational or possible course.
>
> I argue contrary to this that human-centredness is not in the inter- ests of either humans or non-humans, that it is even dangerous and irrational. (Plumwood 2009)

This assessment of reality is rooted in an earlier essay, "Being Prey", in which Plumwood (2000) wrote that "we remake the world in that way as our own, investing it with meaning, reconceiving it as sane, survivable, amenable to hope and resolution". Plumwood's realization that this kind of world-remaking is a dangerous fantasy occurred when she was attacked by a crocodile. When she wrote about death in relation to the prevailing anthropocentric delu- sion she was not writing about her own near-fatal experience but about the ongoing human assault on the world. Her various publications amount to a sustained examination of the forcible hyperseparation of humans from what is too often labelled "the environment", "nature" or just "the world" which, coterminously is reduced to resource and possession. This is expressed, performed or habituated in what Plumwood labels as "dematerialization": the practised ignoring of the physicality of human relations with the world (Plumwood 2008, drawing on Ehrenreich 2003).

Far from being separate or distinct from other species, we are prey. We are also predators, but while we need to think about this (especially in relation to over-consumption and myriad injustices), it is "being prey" that should most completely disrupt the fantasy of human dislocation, hyperseparation and exceptionalism. We are full participants in processes by which all bodies are continuously growing and decaying, all matter and nutrients continuously circulating, and all beings continuously conversing. There is no place in which we can fulfil fantasies of separating ourselves out from or above others.

The implications of our embeddedness in complex and sometimes difficult relationships are worked out by Plumwood in a rich fusion of feminist and ecological analysis. Throughout her publications, she consistently demands that we attend to our complex delusions (hyperseparation, objectification, anthropocentricism, consumerism) and to our complex emplacement within relational networks in which we ought to act responsibly and carefully (not least as prey and predators). As she says, "This is not a dilettante project". Rather, a consideration of gender, bodies, matter, place, labour, hierarchy and much more contributes to a project of finding "ourselves in dialogue with and limited by other species' needs, other kinds of minds" (Plumwood 2009).

UNROUND WORLD AND THE YUK FACTOR

According to Mary Midgley, we are beings who, rightly, experience the "yuk factor" – a "sense of disgust and outrage" when encountering acts we find objectionable, and we live in a world that "fails to be round" (Midgley 2004: 105, 129).[2] The alleged imperfect rationality of humans is matched by the alleged imperfection of the world. In saying such things, Midgley provokes us to consider that what some of our intellectual ancestors considered imperfections are actually positive facts. Our emotions are as important as our rational thoughts, and our kinship with others in a messily evolving world invites us to act honourably towards all bodies.

Midgley debunks the "symbolism of height" (*ibid.*: 145) to demonstrate that we can know ourselves, our world and our cosmos better if we stop imagining a set of perforations along which we might divide bodies from minds, matter from consciousness, humans from other animals. Neither can we continue to cut maleness from femaleness (whether in relation to bodies,

---

2. This "disgust" of Midgley's is of a different order than that rightly criticized by Martha Nussbaum (2004, 2010).

minds, emotions, knowledges, labour or much else) and then privilege male-ness above femaleness. In the new world of Darwinian-inspired evolution-ary theory into which we have not yet fully brought academia, we should reimagine our relations horizontally not vertically. Even Darwin's "tree of life" metaphor for evolutionary relationships could misdirect us to think of higher and lower species. Instead, nothing has ceased evolving, nothing is living at a more primitive stage of evolution, there are no "living fossils". There are only the continuously co-evolving beings of a continuously chang-ing world, some better adapted to their current place than others.

The fantasy that humans (or white, male, self-reflecting humans) are the point at which the universe becomes conscious of itself is a hangover from the fantasy that the cosmos was designed for us. We are not a necessary stage of evolution, let alone its pinnacle or ultimate goal. Rather, we are mem-bers in the ongoing experiment of reality. Like other animals, our senses co-evolve with the air, light, water and soil that form and inform us. Contrary to Descartes' doubt, we know as emplaced-body-minds and not as hyper-separated minds.

Midgley's "yuk factor" emotional knowledge, which propels us to want to improve the world, making it more just and more habitable, is no less vital than the bodily knowing by which light, sound, smell, taste and touch enter into us. These, too, are no less important than our knowing-with-others as we respond to communication from outside the skin-bags of our bodies. In fact they are all entangled and only separable heuristically – as, indeed, is it only temporarily useful in a limited way to think of ourselves as inside a "skin-bag". In reality, the heuristic value of such separations is diminished by their fantastic entanglement with the deadly atomism and reductions that deny our always participative relationships within the living/lived world/community.

BODYMIND PLACE

Adrian Harris's Bodymind Place blog (Harris 2013), building on his unpub-lished PhD thesis (2008), expertly navigates the stream of current debate about our place and our nature, providing an unrivalled source for energizing ideas and discussion. Thus, he proposes that although we have what Gendlin (1981) calls a "bodily sensed knowledge" or a "felt sense" which enables us to act meaningfully without necessarily thinking consciously, deliberating rationally or reflecting systematically, we are not defined by minds entirely fixed within our "skin-bag bodies" (citing Clark 1997). In fact, the "outside" world "is part of our being" (citing Lakoff & Johnson 1999), "organism and environment enfold into each other" (Varela *et al.* 1991) and, more strongly yet, "organism (mindbody) and environment (place) are 'one indivisible total-ity'" (citing Ingold 2000). Thus, we are "corporeally embedded" in a "living landscape" (Abram 1997).

Blending and distilling these varied proposals, Harris's contribution to reformulating how we understand and speak about ourselves and our world is itself of exceptional importance. The kaleidoscope of ideas that he presents resolve into a holistic image of a dynamic materializing of human selves within the varied relationships that we might express as "placed-bodies". We are not and cannot be dislocated minds. Neither can we be dislocated persons. Alienation results from a wrong-headed effort to ignore our bodies and our world, just as the alienation of labour results from a wrong-headed effort to ignore other's bodies and worlds (to paraphrase Marx and Ehrenreich). Thus, we and the world would be better off if we put our efforts into different activities. Time spent in the larger-than-human world, especially in less-human-dominated places (which, with care and poetry, we might call "wilderness" – see Harvey 2012b) greatly aids our return to a visceral sense/ knowledge of our place in the world.

PETER RABBIT AND ELBOW CROOKS

Ironically, perhaps, it is sometimes alleged that attempts to situate humans in relation to other animals, or to engage with the consciousness or personhood of other-than-human animals, are either anthropocentrism or anthropomorphism (the unwarranted projection of human-likeness). On the contrary, the recognition of human kinship with other animals and with all other life on Earth requires that we dethrone "the man" and expect to celebrate a host of similarities and likenesses between all beings. It is in this vein that Irving Hallowell (1955, 1960) considers the implications of (Native American) Anishinaabe ontology and epistemology. "Person" can, he demonstrates, be used as an umbrella term over all the taxonomy of species names so that he can write about "human and other-than-human persons". This too has been criticized as a re-enthronement of humanity and, therefore, of anthropocentricism and anthropomorphism (Bird-David 1999), but this misreads Hallowell and those he learnt from. Hallowell's point can as easily be made by writing about "bear and other-than-bear persons" or "rock and other-than-rock persons". (Indeed, this should be localized to refer to hedgehogs, wombats, sparrows, mosquitoes or some other species in your local community.) The word "person" is prioritized, the species are all nestled under that umbrella. Or, put another way, "person" recognizes similarities among species, while specific species names recognize differences. Indeed, difference within similarity (and vice versa) can be a cause of celebration rooted in the dynamic relational interplay of imagination and intimacy.

When Beatrix Potter wrote and painted Peter Rabbit and all the other characters of her "little books" she was doing something far more interesting than attributing human likeness to animals. Even though she painted Peter Rabbit wearing a blue jacket, she "criticised Kenneth Grahame (author of *The Wind in the Willows*) for describing 'Toad' as 'combing his hair ... A mistake to fly in the face of nature – A frog may wear galoshes; but I don't hold with toads having beards or wigs!'" (letter to Mrs M. E. Wight, 26 June 1942, cited in Victoria and Albert Museum 2012a).

Potter's own meticulous observations of animals, insects, plants, countryside, furniture and costumes justify her assertion that "all writers for children ought to have a sufficient recognition of what things look like" (*ibid.*) and, by implication, how they behave. Thus, in her stories, animals are not mere ciphers for humans, however entertaining and educative that might be, but her "cats long to eat mice, rats terrorize kittens, rabbits can end up in [pies]" (Victoria and Albert Museum 2012b; final word missing in original). She also wrote about the familial relationships of animals. But there is more to Potter than her "little books" for children.

Beatrix Potter wrote those global bestsellers after her careful observations about lichens (revealing these to be symbiotic communities) were rejected by the Linnean Society. Not only would this all-male group not allow Potter to present her own work, neither did they take the theory of symbiosis seriously. Even male botanists like Simon Schwendener and Anton de Bary were treated derisively when they presented similar arguments and evidence. However, Potter and others did demonstrate that lichens are symbionts: a mutually beneficial fusion of fungi and algae. Their analysis has become orthodoxy and an inspiration to others seeking to understand the relational nature of the "natural" world.

While Potter's life story is important and fascinating (as myriad websites, articles and a biography by Linda Lear show; Lear 2007), it is this close observation of symbiosis that contributes most to an effort to rethink the world. What is a human being but another symbiotic community? I confess, this might not be the right terminology. But the following paragraph from the *New York Times* suggests to me that as well as the better science that has been conducted since Potter's rejected efforts, we need better words than anthropocentric English currently offers us. Nicholas Wade (reporting on an article in *Genome Research*) writes:

> Since humans depend on their microbiome [the entourage of all microbes that live in people] for various essential services, including digestion, a person should really be considered a superorganism, microbiologists assert, consisting of his or her own cells and those of all the commensal [creatures that eat at the same table with people to everyone's mutual benefit] bacteria. The bacterial cells also outnumber human cells by 10 to 1, meaning that if cells could vote, people would be a minority in their own body. (Wade 2008)

Neil deGrasse Tyson qt

Not only are our guts necessarily full of "good bacteria", without which we would not be able to digest nutrients, even the crook of our elbows is:

> a piece of highly coveted real estate, a special ecosystem, a bountiful home to no fewer than six tribes of bacteria. Even after you have washed the skin clean, there are still one million bacteria in every square centimeter ... they are giving something of value in return. They are helping to moisturize the skin by processing the raw fats it produces. (*Ibid.*)

It seems unlikely that "six tribes of bacteria" breed promiscuously in our elbow crooks solely and generously in order to "moisturize the skin" of humans. Nonetheless, whatever they are up to for their own benefit, benefits us. Without them, what would we be? Would we still be humans, but humans with bad skin? I think that the only conclusion we can draw is that "humans" are symbiotic communities. Most of the cells of our bodies are not precisely, uniquely or solely human. The bacteria are genetically richer than the non-bacteria bits of the community we call a "human". We are not "superorganisms" in the sense of "an elite" (just because bacteria "help" us), but "we" are a human–bacteria symbiotic community. Even before human skin touches animal fur or tree bark (or meat or wood) we are already thoroughly and inescapably relational, non-individual, participative, engaged members of localized, materialized, living communities. Evolution, it turns out, is propelled less by competition among individuals than by mutualism and cooperation among symbionts and other relational beings (Wakeford 2001; Bartley 2002).

85

Those who level accusations of anthropomorphism against others commonly ignore this relationality while simultaneously conducting research in a fantasy realm riven by hyperseparations.

This all too brief reflection on humans as symbionts is not intended to stand alone. The "more" that needs saying about what makes us ourselves should not reintroduce individualism or some essential core of, for example, self-consciousness, human intellect, or a guiding and unifying "soul". Our relationality constitutes us in every (only heuristically considered) part and is approached from different perspectives throughout this chapter. One vital implication of this pervasive relationality for the study of religion is the necessity of approaching our subject matter (religion, religions and not-religions) as performative and material engagements of embodied, emplaced and relational beings.

MARS, AMERICA AND OTHER BODIES

A perennial platform of American presidential elections since the Second World War has been the promise to put men (preceded by dogs or monkeys, and followed by flags and women) into space, on the moon or on Mars. Regardless of our inability to relate well with life on Earth, or even with other humans, some of us seem obsessed with the question of whether there is life in places that are so remote that even a positive answer will have no practical value. (I resist the temptation to ponder reports that Vatican Observatory scientists hope to evangelize alien beings.) We are not so different from previous generations who wondered about the aliveness and/or humanness of beings encountered in remote lands.

In Chapter 3 I noted Lévi-Strauss's encapsulation of the different means employed by European and indigenous Puerto Rican enquirers into the humanity of others. Lévi-Strauss contrasted Spanish Christian investigations into whether indigenous people had souls with indigenous tests as to whether Europeans were bodies. Research among Amazonian peoples has led Eduardo Viveiros de Castro to build on that emblematic discussion of cultural or natural difference. He proposes that:

> Amazonian cosmologies concerning the way in which humans, animals and spirits see both themselves and one another ... suggest the possibility of a redefinition of the classical categories of "nature",

"culture" and "supernature" based on the concept of perspective or point of view. The study argues in particular that the antinomy between two characterizations of indigenous thought, on the one hand "ethnocentrism", which would deny the attributes of humanity to humans from other groups, and on the other hand "animism", which would extend such qualities to beings of other species can be resolved if one considers the difference between the spiritual and corporal aspects of beings.   (Viveiros de Castro 1998: abstract)

That is, from one perspective, similarities or differences between species are observed in terms of cultural characteristics, behaviours and ideas, and from another perspective they are observed in terms of natural, corporeal or physical matters. In Levi-Strauss's terms: can natives believe? Do Spaniards rot? Most radically, Viveiros de Castro argues that while modernist European-originated discourse inculcates a difference between "nature", a single thing, and "cultures", always plural, as take-for-granted and self-evident, Amazonian discourse does the opposite. It makes it possible, indeed necessary, to assume that all living beings share a single "culture" (dwelling in houses, eating cooked food, organizing families and clans) while having different "natures", bodies that have different perspectives. Each being sees itself doing culture but, except in extreme conditions (e.g. shamanizing) does not see other species doing culture. Thus it becomes necessary to test the kind of body, not the kind of mind or soul, that one meets.

While Europeans can easily speak of "multiculturalism", Amazonian peoples could easily recognize the value of Viveiros de Castro's coinage: "multinaturalism". Things have become more complicated recently because evidence of animal cultures is mounting. Not only have some birds and some mammals been observed using hooks, pounding stones and spears, but members of the same species are recorded as using these and other tools differently from their relations. That is, they meet what are sometimes claimed to be minimum requirements for having or doing culture. Similarly, it seems straightforward to argue that animals and plants communicate in various ways, especially if scare quotes are inserted (animals "communicate") in order to distance the arguer from saying too much. Braver souls like Marc Bekoff, however, provide copious evidence, based on careful and long-term observation, that animals do not only communicate within the range typically expected of them (i.e. about territory, breeding, fear and aggression). Consider the following:

Cows, for example, are very intelligent. They worry over what they don't understand and have been shown to experience "eureka" moments when they solve a puzzle, such as when they figure out how to open a particularly difficult gate. Cows communicate by staring, and it's likely that we don't fully understand their very subtle forms of communication. They also form close and enduring relationships with family members and friends and don't like to have their families and social networks disrupted. (Bekoff 2011)

Here and elsewhere in his *Psychology Today* "Animal Emotions" blog (and in his publications; e.g. Bekoff 2004, 2008a, 2008b, 2010; Bekoff & Pierce 2009), Bekoff demonstrates that cows and other animals plan, anticipate, hope, enjoy, love, fear, mourn, commit, play and do many other things that require communication skills. Notions of self-identity and relationship are also implicated. To want to open a gate means that cows have an idea of a better future. Their expression of sorrow when their calves are taken away indicates that cows and humans are not so different from one another.

Human relations with other animals, and perhaps plants too, are central to Debbie Rose's (1998) discussion of "totemism" (see also Rose 1992, 2004). She argues that Aboriginal Australian understandings of kinship and mutual responsibility and inclusivity cross species boundaries. All local co-dwellers are expected to look after the well-being of the community which is formed by their being and their relating. Each species may play a different role in relation to others, but together as one community, care is taken to curtail over-consumption and other threats to wider society. Research about indigenous environmental knowledges or, more broadly, traditional environmental knowledges, often concerns the bodies of these co-dwelling plants and animals. To be treated as scholarly, it seems, people have to say less about minds, emotions, desires, and ways of communicating. Nature not culture is privileged. But now that so many studies are collapsing the boundaries between nature and culture, making the reference of those terms far less certain, we might have to think again about the world.

In doing so, we return to the situation in which indigenous peoples and European immigrants pondered each other's nature and culture. Ken Morrison (2002) identified the key question for Algonkian peoples of northeast North America, confronted by Jesuits, fur-traders and settler/invaders: what kind of persons are Europeans? Are they cultured enough to seek the good of others or are they cannibalistic individuals bent on over-consuming all they encounter? In an intersubjective cosmos (K. M. Morrison 2000), and with little interest in the hierarchical separations of nature, culture and supernature (K. M. Morrison 1992a, 1992b), the important questions had to be about kinship, neighbourliness, mutuality, guesthood, participation, sharing, gifting, and other markers and modes of local(izing) relationship.

INTRA-ACTING ANTS AND SPIDERS

"The universe is agential intra-activity in its becoming", according to Karen Barad (2007: 141). In *Meeting the Universe Halfway* she argues that the "con-joined considerations" of many scholars "make possible an understanding of the entangled co-emergence of 'social' and 'natural' (and other important co-constituted) factors that are needed in efforts that strive for the responsible practice of science" (Barad 2011: 4).

What this understanding amounts to is a vision of myriad actions of many players (constituted by their performative intra-activity) mattering the entire universe in a way that further challenges our (scholarly and general) separation of nature from culture or sociality. From the quantum level to that of the physicist socialized into a way of doing science with particular apparatuses, the universe is relational, each agential actor meeting others in both material and discursive ways. This rich incitement to do scholarship and other modes of participation in life differently has further implications for our approaches to religion.

Encouraged by Barad's influence on Vásquez (2011), in setting out some perspectives on the real world in which both scholarship and religioning take place, I propose to accept that we live among others who are more like us than they are different. It is not only curious ethnographies that suggest this. Hard scientific observation and theoretical physics demonstrate that matter acts consciously, deliberately with, always with, other matter. It is a mistake to think of animals, plants and bacteria as merely instinctive or mechanically responsive objects. Such beings make choices and intra-act together, benefit-ing local multi-species communities even if they do not always benefit every individual. In such a participative cosmos (in which humans have co-evolved among related intra-active kin) how could we mistake religion for the interior thoughts of solitary individuals?

In following Barad, I note that Tim Ingold warns against too strong a use of the term "agency". As he says:

we give the name "agency" to [an] ingredient ... [which] is the supposed cause that sets otherwise inert matter in motion. But if we follow active materials, rather than reducing them to dead matter, then we do not need to invoke an extraneous "agency" to liven them up again. (Ingold 2011: 16–17)

Happily, use of the term "agent" is possible without the attribution of a magical ingredient called "agency" to beings who act. Barad's "agential realism" does not need it. Nor, I suspect, does Latour's (2005) "ANT" (actor network theory), even though Ingold proffers a "SPIDER" (skilled practice involves developmentally embodied responsiveness) in playful counterpose to what he sees as the over-serious use of the network idea (2011: 89–94). While Latour's ANT can appear to require interacting individuals, connected together in networks, Ingold emphasizes the interactions out of which actions and relations emerge. What is important is not whether one or other model is correct but what we wish to pay attention to at any particular moment. The point of both models is to demonstrate the pervasive working together of many beings (constituted by their intra-actions and performances) to form (without pre-ordaining or designing any agreed outcome) what emerges, moment by moment, as the real world.

LIQUID REALITY

Ingold is right though: there are flows of material, meshings of activities, but there are no permanent, secularly bounded individuals. Zygmunt Bauman's phrase "liquid modernity" (2000) sums up the flows of uncertainty, complexity and porosity that casts us, individualized consumers in an ever-changing era of globalization, into living episodically. What institutions (religious, political, recreational, economic and so on) there are, calling for commitment or adherence, are unstable and permeable. Or, if they are secure, they compete with other institutions for our attention and affiliation. "Choice" is the slogan, logo and brand of the moment. As noted earlier, it seems "we are becoming the species best fitted to the capitalist world" (Steinberg 2005: 143) in its current unstable and nightmarish form.

In another sense, however, the cosmos is and always has been liquid, streams of flows; uncertainty occasionally generating temporary and localized clusters of association. Bodies (sub-atomic, microbial, fleshy within skin-bags, pithy within bark, or conglomerated minerals) are always permeable and dynamic. There is, as Ingold (2011) insists, no barrier between earth and sky, soil and air, or between bodies and the media through which they move. Things are permeable; living is flowing through acts with others.

Within these flows, some religious institutions and authorities may proclaim certainty, but they are not alone. If an internet search for "religion and certainty" illustrates how commonplace this claim is, a similar search for "science and certainty" suggests a deep obsession with certainty cuts across the supposedly secure boundary between religion and science. Just like religion, science can be mis-presented as statements of facts about reality. Latour's assault on the *Modern Cult of the Factish Gods* boldly concludes that:

> Truth is not to be found in correspondence – either between the word and the world in the case of science, or between the original and the copy in the case of religion – but in taking up again the task of *continuing* the flow, of elongating the cascade of mediations one step further.
> (Latour 2010: 122–3)

Latour proposes "to suspend the belief of belief ... and iconoclastic gestures" (*ibid*.: x). He insists that the performance of science, like that of religion, must not be "freeze-framed". Neither science nor religion should "isolate an image out of the flows that only provide them with their real – their constantly re-realized, re-represented – meaning" (*ibid*.: 123). In short, Latour preaches a mode of doing science, being scientist, that flows with the liquid reality of the cosmos.

It does no good to complain that because evolution has no purpose, no pre-defined goal, it has no meaning. London too has no purpose or goal. These are not objects, but labels for freeze-framed cuts through the flow of all that happens. Such cutting may help us observe a moment in the flow, but as the flow will continue, the frozen cut necessarily becomes mute about the continuing process. If we seek meaning, we must do so elsewhere. Given that the flow of all that happens is a continuous intra-acting of relationships, of acts of relating, we must seek meaning by entering the flow, participating in the ongoing evolution of messy reality. Rituals might be a point of entry into engagement.

RITUAL EXPERIMENTATION

Ronald Grimes notes that "few people consider rites an effective means for saving the planet from environmental destruction" (2003: 31). Despite his doubts about the ability of religious liberals and ritual theorists alike to under-stand the possible connection between rituals and environmentalism, Grimes demonstrates that experimenting *as* ritualists and theorists is necessary: "We will not know what ecologically attuned rituals *actually do* apart from rit-ual experiment and critique. To wait, hoping for certainty *before* acting, is a greater risk than hoping to learn *by* acting" (*ibid.*: 44). This is, at least in part, a justification for the experiment of his "Incantatory Riff for a Global Medicine Show" called "Performance Is Currency in the Deep World's Gift Economy" (Grimes 2002).

Again, my purpose in this chapter is to bring into conversation multiple ways of engaging with, in, the real world. Thus, I bring Grimes in here not to agree with him and his sources of inspiration about the value of perform-ance or about the gift economy of the larger-than-human world (though I do). Rather, he is important here because his efforts to understand ritual are founded on a notion that the world is thoroughly relational. Ritualizing involves testing that hypothesis. If we do not live and act among relational others our rituals are really meaningless. It is possible that religious practi-tioners falsely attribute intentionality where there is none (as many cognitiv-ists seem to assume). If deities or hedgehogs are not truly intentional agents, they cannot interact or even react. Then, ritual acts will only make sense (albeit of a crazy kind) to those who understand that they are observing deluded people. But if the cosmos is thoroughly relational, there is a chance that some people get some rituals right because some persons of other spe-cies can and do intra-act and participate. The question for scholars of reli-gion living in such a world – one in which Grimes encourages scholars to do ritual with other animals – is whether we can stop obsessing about alleged anthropomorphic projections and recognize our kinship and similarity with other evolving Earth dwellers.

IMAGINING FISH AND GUESTS

Another take on the perennial and seemingly ubiquitous question of the rela-tionship between culture and nature involves the nested relationship between art and reality. From the many possibilities for rethinking these issues, I select only a morsel hooked out of Tim Ingold's essay "Ways of Mind-Walking: Reading, Writing, Painting". Ingold concludes his discussion of "the relation between the terrains of the imagination and of 'real life'" by drawing two conclusions:

First, we must dispense, once and for all, with the convention that the imagination consists in the power to produce images, or to represent things in their absence. ... [E]ven if they existed only as pictures in the mind, such decoys would belong – together with the missing thing they stand for – in the same outside world of appearances, of "elements", of programme music, of the figurative.

(Ingold 2011: 196–9)

[Second,] we must recognise in the power of the imagination the creative impulse of life itself in continually bringing forth the forms we encounter, whether in art, through reading, writing or painting, or in nature, through walking in the landscape. Remember: the line does not *represent* the fish. But the fish-in-the-water can be understood as but one of many possible emanations of line. (*Ibid.*: 208)

Methodologically, as the world has both fish-moving-in-water and fish-drawn-on-paper, in "nature" and in "art", we can attempt more imaginative ways of doing research and scholarship. Indeed, we must do so if the world is not constituted by a separation of nature and culture. Imagined fish and found fish both exist in the same world, both are real.

Seeking, again, to bring discrete debates, ideas and themes into dialogue and hoping that some strange juxtapositions might prove fertile, I read Ingold along with Byron Dueck's consideration of the interplay of imagination and intimacy. In research among First Nations and Métis fiddlers in Canada, Dueck (2007) sees "imaginative world-making" and "face-to-face intimacy" interact as a "broad public of strangers" (a global readership) encounters the intimacies of indigenous lives, concerns, fears, hopes and creativity. Here I find a language fit for use in a relational world. It enables us to speak more clearly about matters that, until now, have required seemingly endless struggles with unhelpful dualistic terms like representation and object, mind and matter, transcendent and imminent, faith and fact. Instead we may speak of imagining all manner of possibilities (musical trills, ritual encounters, epic meals, unified theories) as we take steps towards increasing intimacy with their actualization or materialization. We en-act possibilities and become intimate with the resulting world.

In later chapters concerned with the multiple religious matterings and performings (religion being nothing without matter and performance), I expect to see dynamic interplays between imagination and intimacy. Here though, I am interested in academic methods of being and doing in the real world. Imagination of a world separated by a Cartesian gulf has led scholars to constrain their practice of academia within boundaries deemed appropriately intimate by their peers. When we are being scholars we have attempted to bracket ourselves off from the world of senses, passions and emotions – with which we are only properly intimate in our time-off. But this division of ourselves and our world must mean that we have only partially engaged and partially understood reality. The very effort to be objective has resulted in partiality. Instead, we might experiment with the potential value of intimacy with the elsewhere world in which there is no Cartesian gap.

In my discussions of "guesthood" as a research method (Harvey 2003a, 2005b, 2011a: 227–8) I have been asking how we should do research in a relational world. Among Maori in Aotearoa, London, Alice Springs and Hawai'i, I have found that the possibility of being made a guest of local hosts is immensely significant. The entire cosmos appears to work together with local humans (members of ancestrally- and place-related communities) to realize imagined possibilities in more intimate communities. Strangers are called onto and across spaces, towards ancestor-houses (houses who are ancestors) and given the opportunity to be guests or enemies. Hosts and guests, mutually constituted, explore roles and vigorously debate issues. Within respectful relationships new possibilities emerge, knowledges are exchanged, challenged and evolved. This seems to me a fine model for pursuing better scholarship.

SUNRISE WORLD

In the real world in which humans live, where real bodies interact, the sun rises and sets. This is no less a scientific view than the secure knowledge that it is the turning of the Earth around the sun that gives the impression of sunrise and sunset. We cannot experience a feeling of Earth-turning – and our Earth-born languages (as spoken by humans or sung by birds) will continue to acknowledge the felt, sighted experience of sunrise and sunset despite our best rational science. Just as "we have never been modern" (Latour 1993), we have never truly been Cartesian or utterly objective. We have tried, and those efforts have yielded results – but understanding a world without hyper-separations is not well achieved by inserting divisions. Rather, the academic project has to take place in the real world. It would, in any case, be hard to study the ways in which religions are lived without doing so within this world in which the sun rises and sets. So many religions, after all, time ceremonies or orientate buildings or acts of devotion towards some point marked by the sun's relationship with the Earth.

The real universe is full of relating. There is nothing but relating, and no things that are not relating. There are encounters, connections, conversations, conflicts, consuming, communing ... and myriad other acts, intra-acts, which form the mesh of relational reality. We have fooled ourselves into believing in atomic individuals, discrete agents, accidental events and other players. Perhaps I mis-state the matter. There are individuals and agents. But they are not, and cannot be, separate or separable from others. But rather than trying to deny too much, I am trying, to start with, to emphasize something, namely that acts of relating are the key facts of the cosmos. They are what we experience and observe. In that context, we might find that our efforts to understand religion will be greatly enhanced if we retheorize it not as an independent object to be observed impacting people but as an activity performed within the ever evolving relational community.

This is not a definition of religion. It is an idea about reality. It needs stating only because scholarly activity has been going on in an imaginary (though utterly concrete and political) world. Academia in the mould of elite western European Christianity and Cartesianism has created phantasms and studied them. Just like psychotic, depressed and unutterably sad laboratory animals, torn from kin and kind, individualized, and unreal, the objects of atomizing studies are unlike beings in the real world. We need to act differently. We need to find ourselves in the elsewhere that is the real, relational world.

REAL WORLD RELIGION

In addition to knowing the real world in order to do research in the real world (which has been the chief topic of this chapter), we need to know the real world to know what hard work some of our words are doing. In particular, words like "natural", "social" and "cultural" are busy – but they can also be deceptive.

Armin Geertz has defined religion as "a cultural system and a social institution that governs and promotes ideal interpretations of existence and ideal praxis with reference to postulated transempirical powers or beings" (Geertz 1999: 471). Jim Cox offers: "Religion refers to identifiable communities that base their beliefs and experiences of postulated non-falsifiable alternate realities on a tradition that is transmitted authoritatively from generation to generation" (J. L. Cox 2007: 85). Steve Bruce settles for a substantive definition "as beliefs, actions, and institutions based on the existence of supernatural entities with powers of agency or impersonal processes possessed of moral purpose that set the conditions of, or intervene in, human affairs" (2011: 1). Ideas about nature, culture and society are embedded in these proposals. They express a nature/culture dualism that sets humans apart from the world and scholars apart from those they study. If the wording of these definitions is different, their meaning is not so far from Daniel Dennett's tentative proposal "to define religions as *social systems whose participants avow belief in a supernatural agent or agents whose approval is to be sought*" (Dennett 2006: 9). He continues, "This is, of course, a circuitous way of articulating the idea that a religion without *God* or *gods* is like a vertebrate without a backbone" (*ibid.*). This follows his note that for the purpose of laws against cruelty to animals "cephalopods – octopus, squid and cuttlefish – were recently made *honorary vertebrates*, in effect, because they ... have such strikingly sophisticated nervous systems" (*ibid.*: 8). Dennett asserts that people who believe in one or more deities are definitively religious and those who postulate other existences are, a bit like them, also religious. He acknowledges that his definition is rooted in Christianity but when he says "of course" he calls the bluff of colleagues who, perhaps, believe they have said something about non-Protestant religion.

Definitions like these ask us to define religion as a cultural error in interpreting nature. At the same time, we are presented with religion as a natural error that generates kinds of culture. As the postulation of a supernatural world inaccessible to the kind of science unaffected by Latour's challenge, religion must remain belief. To put things another way, such definitions propose that religious people wrongly socialize that which is not human. In finding social beings outside the human community, religious people are defined as "believers", as postulators of forbidden transcendence. But if scientific research in many disciplines shows that humans are not the sole agents acting in the cosmos, not alone in being conscious, discursive, reflexive, and not unique in our relational, social performance of culture, then religious people might not be falsely projecting human-likeness.

Sceptics may well be right that religious people are wrong about all kinds of things. Certainly religion is an evolutionary mechanism, a practice or way of being in the world which evolved in the real world. But if this world really is social, cultural and relational, then something else may be happening than the postulation of an anthropocentric error. What is that? What is it that people do when they do religion in a relational cosmos rather than an anthropocentric one? I do not mean that religions are not and cannot be anthropocentric. They may well be, but that is another matter. Here I mean that scholars who allege anthropomorphic projection, the false attribution of agency to inanimate objects or unself-conscious animals, are often anthropocentric themselves. It is their anthropocentric obsession with human exceptionality that prevents them engaging with the pervasive relationality of the world. This same obsession misdirects attention away from the experimentation and evolutionism of some religions, and causes some scholars to continue believing in belief or alleging either a comparability with or an absence of modernist constructions of religion.

If the world is inhabited only by social beings, and if we make the assumption that the world is relational rather than Cartesian, all sorts of things flow. I propose that a relational, performative, mattered account of religion ought to be plausible for four nested reasons: our world is pervasively social; our first need therefore is to negotiate with other persons (most of whom are not human); negotiation most passionately seeks either respectful or resistant outcomes; and the most significant outcome of negotiation is openness to further acts of relating. In the following chapters (albeit implicitly for the most part), I test these four themes in relation to observable phenomena that ought to count as religions.

BEYOND DESCARTES

To recap: the academic study of religions has largely been the Cartesian study of Protestantism. Scholars have studied Protestant Christianity, Protestant Buddhism, Protestant Hinduism, Protestant Shinto and Protestant Paganism. By studying I mean, of course, that they have invented, promulgated and polemicized about these intellectual phantoms, these systems of belief or postulations about transcendent, spiritual and otherwise alien unrealities. Being "objective" (i.e. deliberately, wilfully and with considerable effort disconnected, alien and uninvolved) themselves, they could not easily study anything other than figments of imaginations shaped by early and continuing modernisms. This is unfair – if only because it suggests that such colleagues are constituted as individuals. In the real world, this style of studying religion has a shared foundation and method. It remains the study of ideas, intentions and intellectualizing (texts and discourses) by modernist Protestant-like Cartesians of Protestant-like "believers".

Scholars of religion have not been unique in researching and teaching about unrealities. I believe there is a campaign afoot by which a few scholars of economics have begun sticking labels on economics textbooks, which say "Not to be used in the real world". That is, some economists object to the practice of teaching economics that imagines a world that is significantly different from the one in which we live. Similarly, just as most-modernity takes place in a world shaped in the post-Second World War redrawing of boundaries, allegiances and prejudices to benefit the colonialism of businesses and share-holders, so the study of religions takes place in a modernist artifice. It keeps on taking place in a world created in the aftermath of the European Wars of Religion and the individualizing reformation of what counts as religion. This imagined religion is carefully (intellectually but never in life) separated from politics and economics, and from bodies and places. Many commentators (e.g. McCutcheon 1997, 2001, 2003; Wiebe 1999; Fitzgerald 2000; Masuzawa 2005; Wiebe & Martin 2012) have said or implied that religious studies has been largely secure within the parameters defined by religionists. "Religion" is too often defined by what Luther, Zwingli and Calvin did with what Augustine, Paul and other Christians had set out as the key matters for discussion. Descartes hardly departed from this path; he only spray-painted his graffiti over their texts, changing "spirit" into "mind" and "bodies" into "*res extensa*" (material stuff). For some reason, the architects of the new (still Protestant) atheism have not noticed that they are still objecting to the agenda only of like-minded (religious) ideologues.

So the big problem that needs to be tackled is not really "religion" but "the study of". Happily, this is not a new claim. Unhappily, it needs to be pursued with more vigour. The path is open that should lead to an engagement with everyday religion – or what others have called vernacular religion (Primiano 1995, 2012; Valk & Bowman 2012), lived religion (McGuire 2008), and performed and material religion (Vásquez 2011). But it is time to go beyond opening a path. It is time to start elsewhere, and notice that religion in the real world requires scholars and scholarship in the real world.

6. Doing violence with impunity

Religious activity among Ngati Uepohatu has a purpose that struck me as surprising or even shocking when I first read Te Pakaka Tawhai's introduction to "Maori Religion" (Tawhai [1988] 2002). It became the major inspiration for this book when I found myself wondering whether Tawhai's statement that "the purpose of religious activity here is to … do violence with impunity" (*ibid.*: 244) applies to religious activities elsewhere. Perhaps it may even be true of religious activities *everywhere*. The entirety of Tawhai's article deserves a place in a shortlist of excellent discussions of religions. It exemplifies careful reflexivity, respectful engagement and clear analysis of data. It offers correctives to the ways religions are sometimes studied and written about. But, most significantly for the question of how religion might be defined, Tawhai's article takes us far from the Protestant and Enlightenment rooted treatment of religion as believing of hyperseparated individuals in transcendent deities. Instead, it attends to the performance of religion by relational persons in a participatory, material world.

TREES AND TUBERS

Tawhai illustrates his claim that (to cite the full phrase) "the purpose of religious activity here is to seek to enter the domain of the superbeing and do violence with impunity" by saying that this means "to enter the forest and do some milling for building purposes, to husband the plant and then to dig up the tubers to feed one's guests" (Tawhai [1988] 2002: 244). People in and around Ruatoria, near Aotearoa's East Cape, do not all engage in forestry or gardening.[1] Nor does everyone in Ruatoria carve ancestral style meeting houses, *wharenui* or *wharetipuna*. Some do. There are many fine Maori carpenters and carvers, and many excellent gardeners and cooks. This is true across the nation and in the global Maori diaspora. Carvers like George Nuku have built traditional style constructions out of modern materials like polystyrene in London's British Museum. As among other indigenous peoples, the knowledge and know-how associated with carving, especially of traditional-style meeting and community places, is a source of considerable pride among Maori. Similarly, skilled work within meeting houses is a central element of contemporary Maori cultural vitality. Hospitality too is of considerable importance, embraided as it is not only with knowledge of traditional horticulture, catering and oratory but also with the ability to host guests and to energize and promote culture.

Tawhai's point, however, does not depend on there being more carpenters or gardeners than there are. He has picked two activities that resonate with the *korero tahito* ("ancient explanations"), which he is using to introduce Maori religion to those unfamiliar with it. All kinds of quite ordinary processes may be the occasion and the focus of religious activities. However, Tawhai's choice of examples is far from random. Religious activities involving trees and tubers provide an unrivalled entry into much of importance about Maori religion.

Tawhai says that Maori "religious activity neither reaches for redemption and salvation, nor conveys messages of praise and thanksgiving, but seeks permission and offers placation" (*ibid.*: 244). People do not need to stop to praise divinities or seek redemption before, during or after tree-cutting or tuber-digging. They do, however, need to "seek permission and offer placation". These are, after all, acts of violence committed against living beings. The tree that one might cut down has its own purposes, desires and feelings. Perhaps it has fears and antipathies too. If so, these are likely to be raised by the threat of cutting. The tree also has kin and other relations in the forest. Similarly, *kumara* (sweet potatoes) have kin. They are not here in the world purely so that they can be eaten. They are sweet potatoes before they are food. To do violence to trees and *kumara* is not a neutral act. Properly undertaken, it requires that permission is gained – and this is not automatically given just because someone says "please". Placation is also required and may involve the

---

1. Much of the forestry locally is controlled by multinational corporations that give little time or space for traditional concerns. But, for now, let's overlook this and focus on acts closer to those discussed by Tawhai.

making of apologies, the respectful treatment of trees and tubers (including those parts not required for building or eating), and addresses to the kin of those cut down or dug up. What Tawhai identifies as "religious activity" is what someone does to make threatened beings (e.g. trees and *kumara*) less hostile and perhaps even happily willing to give up life to others.

Often, the consequence of violent acts is more violence. Assaulting a relational being implicates perpetrators in further confrontations with the relations of that being. In the ebb and flow of cause and effect, there are penalties for taking life. Religious activity is an intervention in those processes. It seeks, uncertainly but hopefully, to create, maintain and enhance mutually healthy relationships between species or groups. Everyday acts of consumption are, inescapably, moments of predation. Religion, in this context at least, is concerned with surviving such necessary acts of violence. It is performed in relation to acts of violence and rebounding violence (Girard 1986, 1988, 2004) in order to nurture the alternative dynamics of mutuality, survivance and intimacy.

If it seems that this chapter elides words (oratory, prayer or sermonizing) with acts (tree felling, *kumara* gardening), it is necessary to note the salience of Thomas Csordas's (2008) strategic attribution of corporeality to language. This ought to be especially clear when we consider a Maori *karakia*, prayer, spoken to locate people in renewed relationship with a river. To speak is to act, words are not merely expressive but sensuous, not merely representational but presencing:

> Speaking is a kind of sonorous touching; language is tissue in the flesh of the world. Or, to be more graphic, think of language as a bodily secretion; and if there is a suspiciously erotic connotation to this proposition, I can only remind you of how we refer to speaking as intercourse, and the double meaning contained therein. (*Ibid.*: 118)

Religious speeches are among the actions in which humans engage with the world. Thus, Tawhai's speech-act may seem all the more resonant.

COSMIC GENEALOGY

Tawhai's thoughts about violence, impunity, permission, placation, trees and sweet potatoes arise while he is making use of his oratorical skills to develop his tailoring of "ancient explanations" to the novel purpose of defining "Maori religion". His chapter begins:

If you ask a Maori in, for example, a settlement such as Ruatoria where Maoris constitute a majority of the population, what he under-stands by religion, expect him to scratch his head in thought, before at length replying, "Whose religion?" Religion and Christianity may be synonymous words for him but what they mean will vary between "a human recognition of a superhuman controlling power", on the one hand, and "the preaching of one thing and too often the doing of something else", on the other.   (Tawhai [1988] 2002: 238)

Setting aside the association of religion with hypocritical preaching (of colonial Christianity), this opening might suggest that Tawhai would agree that "religion" really should be defined by reference to metaphysics. Despite the temptation to do so, it would be disingenuous to claim that although beings that might be considered divine are involved in the activities Tawhai alludes to, and although he calls them "superhuman controlling powers", he is interested in their presence *as* trees, birds and sweet potatoes. He writes, for instance, "Tane manifest as Tane mahuta (trees and birds) is invoked by those who have business in the forest. Rongo manifest as Rongomaraeroa (sweet potato) is invoked during the cropping season" (*ibid.*: 244).

But, while it is true that Maori "superhuman controlling powers" are expe-rienced in forest trees and garden vegetables (as well as in many other ways), there is a better foundation for arguing that Maori religion is not "belief in deities" but an intra-activity of an interspecies kind. That foundation is the recognition that deities, sweet potatoes, humans and trees are all participants in a pervasively relational cosmos.

Tawhai provides a short *korero tahito* (ancient explanation or traditional narration) that speaks of the evolution of the reality in which we live:

Te Kore evolved through aeons into *Te Po*. *Te Po* also evolved through generations countless to man to the stage of *Te Ata* (the Dawn). From *Te Ata* evolved *Te Aoturoa* (familiar daytime) out of which in turn evolved *Te Aomarama* (comprehended creation). The state of *Whaitua* emerges (the present tense is used to animate the narra-tive) with the recognition of space. There are several entities present. Among these are Rangi potiki and Papa who proceed to have off-spring namely: Tane, Tu Matauenga (Tu for short), Rongomatane (Rongo for short) and Haumie tiketike (Haumie for short). The *korero tahito* ends.   (*Ibid.*: 242).

This is a genealogy. Or, rather, it is a fragment of the genealogy of endlessly procreating and diversifying life. Tawhai makes good use of it to develop his discussion of contemporary Maori religion. For my present purpose of seeking material (elsewhere than the currently dominant norms) relevant to defining religion (not only Maori religion, but religion wherever it is done) there is far more in this quotation than we need to know. However, it is important to understand that life (and lived religion as part of it) is more intimately propelled by closer rather than distant relations.

Tawhai explains that *Te Kore* is an ambiguous "The Nothing" or "Not The Nothing", while *Te Po* is "The never-ending beginning" (*ibid.*: 242, citing Arnold Reedy). From these mysterious, pregnant and remote states or persons, evolution continues until, in "familiar daytime", we recognize space, and in space we recognize Rangi, Father Sky, and Papa, Mother Earth. Although Earth and Sky are acknowledged and relied upon, it is their children who are first thought of by "the Maori on the street in Ruatoria" on hearing the phrase "superhuman controlling powers". As the *korero tahito* of cosmic *whakapapa* (genealogy) continues, these are the persons who have become the deities addressed in ceremony and implicated in the life of the world. They are superhuman but not supernatural (if that means separate from the nature-culture matrix). They are cosmic in a communal cosmos. They are powerful in relation to other beings, but remain kindred.

MAKING ROOM, LIVING SPACE

Although I strongly recommend that you read and consider Tawhai's well crafted words, I will summarize what he says happens next, what keeps on happening next. In abbreviating Tawhai's narrative even further, I acknowledge that he did not wish his purposeful telling of his people's knowledge to be treated as something fixed or (and he is absolutely clear about this) as a replication of a traditional way of teaching about religion. His full and fluid performed narrative is rich with complexity, rife with flexibility and charged with potential. Although applied to a new purpose, the fact that he offers us local knowledge to address a current purpose is itself entirely traditional. Ancient explanations are always told and considered for specific, contemporary reasons or needs. So we, now, are invited to learn and expected to demonstrate our learning by responding and growing.

Anyway, to paraphrase Tawhai (himself paraphrasing Arnold Reedy): after the many aeons in which the cosmos slowly evolved into community, becoming increasingly like the reality we experience, as space opened up for both vast and intimate dramas of life, among the myriad performers were Papa and Rangi. Their love making kept them in close embrace. The children born of their passion existed between the parental bodies, cramped and in darkness, seeking space but hardly able to imagine growth or fulfilment. Eventually, despite considerable dispute within the family, one of the children undertakes the monumental task of pushing Rangi away from Papa, in the process changing their relationship to each other and to all life. Rangi gains the name Rangi nui as Father Sky and Papa gains the name Papa tuanuku as Mother Earth. Tane (who is to become trees and birds, deity of forests and minister with the forestry portfolio in the cosmic parliament) achieves the task. His effort allows for the continuation of the evolutionary expansion of space and the unfurling potential of life. Genealogy continues. *Aroha* (love, sympathy) continues – between Earth and Sky as much as between the parents and their children. *Aroha* fills the expanding space between all the myriad others who can now flourish. Spaces between persons, places and moments are always filled with acts of relationship, of varying degrees of intimacy, because "spaces" are never empty but always a medium of movement, contact and being.

This summary of how things have come to be as they are is significant not as a "just so" story but as the foundation for knowing, deciding, dialoguing. In defining "the purpose of religious activity" Tawhai alludes to trees because Tane is not only the divine minister for terrestrial forestry but also the tallest tree in the forest. Tane as tree and as forest continues to push Sky from Earth, making space by making height, and making place by standing tall. What happens, then, when one proposes to cut down a tree? If the tree is Tane who separates, who makes space, whose act allows other actions, what happens when he is removed? Isn't the cosmic process of expansion and differentiation (of which that between Earth and Sky is representative and initiatory) endangered? This is not only another good reason for asking permission and for placating those involved. Rituals at this juncture might alert more powerful persons to the need to keep the Earth-Sky separation (the loving relationship that gives descendents room to live) in place. Religious activities may also maintain and perform the knowledge that foresters and others must restrain their violent acts/axes, limit their (human) intervention in the cosmos to that which is necessary, and seek to live within the constraints and obligations imposed by life in a social, relational world.

There is more. Trees are cut down for a reason. The purpose named in Tawhai's discussion is building, but he means more, so much more, than constructing everyday habitations. His introductory transcription and translation of Arnold Reedy's speech is said to invoke "the imagery of the tribal myths, with apt gesture, and with references to the symbolism, for example of the art and carving of the meeting-house" (Tawhai [1988] 2002: 239). The felled tree continues Tane's cosmos-changing, world-making, place-creating work when it becomes a meeting-house, and especially its central, roof-supporting post. As Tane separates Earth from Sky, and as trees separate land from sky, so house-pillars separate floors from roofs. Separation, as Tawhai says, "is physical only" (*ibid*.: 243); *aroha* maintains connections, constructs intimacy and strengthens relations. This is differentiation really, not separation. It is change, not break. In each and every case, the making of space allows, encourages and demands expansion on the part of those who move between and within space's media, performing in-between acts of relationality. Sky may be above Earth, but trees and humans and all Earth-dwellers exist in air, with air, with shared breath, rooted in soil, absorbing nurturance, permeating putative boundaries.

There is a point to all this story-telling for understanding religion. It is not only that religion can involve the telling of cosmological myths. It is not only that religion can be defined as the maintenance of tradition among groups of people. It is not even the recognition that religious narratives can be about evolution (however radical that thought might seem). It is that religion is also about what happens in forests and meeting houses when people (children of Tane, in the Maori case at least) act towards others to seek to make use of the spaces that separate-and-link them. It is an aspect of respectful consumption. Since this involves food and guests, more must be said about those sweet potatoes.

INTIMATE EATING

Sweet potatoes are not indigenous to Aotearoa but migrated there in the same ocean-crossing fleets that brought Maori to their new land. Maori and *kumara* sustained one another (the former experimenting with modes of horticulture). The culturing of both emerged over the centuries of co-inhabiting Aotearoa. For any gardener there could be an intimacy with the plants they nurture towards fruition. Digging them up or cutting them down can seem violent but is often encompassed by expressions of gratitude and pleasure. How much might this be magnified when the plant and the human descend from ancestors who migrated together? There is a history here. But it is a history of regular, intimate, cultivated violence. Thus, in defining the "purpose of religious activity" as "doing violence with impunity" towards *kumara* as well as trees, Tawhai points us towards religious activities grafted into the tending and harvesting of one species by another.

His article, however, is not about the rituals of gardening that occur with planting, weeding, cultivating or harvesting. Nor does it mention cooking. But it does mention feeding guests. It keeps us at the meeting house. If a carver makes trees into meeting houses, the rest of the local community stands at the meeting house to make guests. More precisely, locals stand out in front of their ancestor-house and call to strangers (and their ancestors) to come and be remade as guests. In speeches and etiquette of greeting and meeting, the potential violence of strangers (who may be enemies) is redirected into the dialogical encounter of hosts and guests. Hosts and guests speak together, seeking more intimate relationships of place and ancestry than those of strangers. They share breath together, recreating each other as hosts and guests rather than strangers. Then they find that eating together trumps eating one another. The imagined other becomes an intimate guest. And then the business of negotiating over which element of the many potential futures will be most beneficially brought or worked into reality.

A meeting house is the standing place of Tane and of local people. It is a breathing place of conspiring (breath- and expression-sharing) hosts and guests. It is an eating place where respect is given and received in hospitality and guesthood. The rituals here are not those of the meditative self-realization of individuals "following their breath", but the realization of relational-selves as intra-acting bodies share air and food while seeking a mediation of distinct and sometimes conflicting desires. Thus, when Tawhai throws tubers into the mix of his explanation of Maori religion, he alludes to the ways in which the effort of Tane in making place is continued in Maori hospitality and relationality. Importantly, though, what is sought on the *marae*, the meeting place where locals stand to make guests from strangers, is not sameness. There is no return to such flatness and constriction.

GIFT AND RESTRAINTS

What happens when a tree is cut down? Carpenters take Tane/tree and raise roofs above floors. Guests can be sheltered. Meetings can take place. Speeches and conversations can evolve. Tubers rather than enemies can be consumed. New possibilities can be brought from potential into the lit space of the still-evolving, still genealogical world. Rather than conflict, another round of imagination, arising from new intimacies, can be confronted and collaborated upon. Negotiations, mediations and decisions can be explored. All this requires careful attention to the obligations inherent in seeking to construct and sustain relationships, especially because not all relationships are the same and not all acts are equal. Peoples, places and activities are valued differently and may need to be separated and/or embraced with appropriate degrees of restraint.

This is a world in which chippings from a felled tree's wood are not discarded unceremoniously as if the act of cutting was simple, uncontentious, a mere manipulation of inert matter. No such object as "inert matter" exists, no such act as "mere manipulation" is moral in a relational world. Each and every separate-but-embraced person has a *mana* which requires respect. Too many publications mystify mana as a magical energy, flowing from a powerful, transcendent source and endangering mortals. Perhaps this is an interpretation generated by a nineteenth-century enthusiasm for electricity. Without that distraction, in a less mechanistic context, mana can be represented as being somewhat like charisma or gift (Mataira 2000: 101–2). Every body has an ability, a gift for something. That ability, construed as a benefit, is the mana inherent to the able person. However, some abilities are valued above others, and their performers gain prestige and worth from the skilled enacting of their giftedness. In this sense, mana does have the connotation "powerful", e.g. in the greeting "*haere mai te mana te tapu me te wehi*" ("Welcome to the powerful, the privileged and the awesome"; Tawhai [1988] 2002: 245). As a social power or authority, derived from and expressed in giftedness, mana is embraided in definitions of personhood and also in social processes.

In these social processes, differentiation is a cause of separation but never of modernist hyperseparatism. The act of carving a meeting house, being distinct from other acts (as all acts are) is to be differentiated from other acts (e.g. socializing or cooking). It is to be actively and demonstrably valued as is appropriate to its worth. Some other acts are to be kept separate from this act. Even acts that might be fine in their own context and time are placed apart from other acts. Restrictions that maintain proper relationships and proper distances inherently enforce proper behaviours.

The Maori dialect of the Polynesian word for these processes of restrained separation is *tapu*. Peter Mataira says that "Tapu is perhaps comprehended most clearly in the use of the biblical term 'holy' or 'sacred'" (Mataira 2000: 102), but he can only say this because he has not been infected by the moralizing of the terms "holiness" or "sanctity" (see Chapter 9 for more about

107

this). The word *tapu*, in various Polynesian dialects but primarily as *taboo*, is used many times in the record of Captain Cook's Pacific voyages of 1769–79, and thereby entered the English language. For instance, Cook writes: "When dinner was served, not one of them would even sit down, or eat a morsel of any thing, as they were all *taboo*, they said; which word, though it has a comprehensive meaning, generally signifies that a thing is prohibited" (Cook [1777] 1967: 3.1:129).

Cook also notes that his scientists were given a "potato field" adjoining a *morai* in which to erect their astronomical observatory (one purpose of these journeys being to observe planetary movements). He notes of this space allocated to them that:

> to prevent the intrusion of the natives, the place was consecrated by the priests, by placing their wands around the walls which inclosed [*sic*] it. This interdiction the natives call *taboo*, a term frequently used by the islanders and seemed to be a word of extensive operation.
> (*Ibid.*: 3.1:157)

Food, people and places can be "tabooed", restricted or set aside from ordinary use. Even in these first English uses of the term (and many others noted in the journey volumes), it is grasped that the "comprehensive" meanings of taboo require translations as variable as "forbidden", "interdicted", "prohibited" and "consecrated". The term seems to have rapidly gained acceptance and wide usage in English. Indeed, it is hard to imagine how English-speakers spoke of taboo processes and activities prior to learning from those who returned from these Oceanic journeys. Even now, an internet search for the earliest use and spread of the word in English is complicated by its continual use to mark the fact that other words (often of only four letters) and a remarkable array of acts are deemed impolite or improper. Nonetheless, taboos are not only and always negative, or applied in relations to matters that are considered negatively. In discussions of Maori and related languages and cultures, it is common to read that *tapu* is the equivalent of "sacred" (i.e. an adjective defining persons, places or things that are so powerful and highly valued that they are to be kept apart). Equally often, *tapu* is the equivalent of the verb "consecrate", to make, declare and treat someone or something differently from others.

As Cook said, this is "a word of extensive operation". The difficulty in translating it is not only that it came from a different culture but that the culture in which the English language developed intervenes to impose new resonances and applications. Specifically, European linguistic cultures typically inculcate dualism so that "taboo" comes to label "bad things" or "bad words". However, in order to correct this it is not sufficient to insist that good things or acts can be taboo in relation to others. Even though Cook rightly says that the process of making a place taboo is like consecrating it (just as particular behaviours are expected of those who enter religious buildings), taboo is richer still than this. Just as mana can be identified in all kinds of persons, things and acts, so the differences between the mana of one thing and that of another can be thought to require their separation, their tabooing. Carving is simply different from gardening. Constructing a meeting house is different from orating within a meeting house. But when the different acts are separated by particular acts and things (e.g. rituals in which, as Cook says, "priests" place "wands" to demarcate a space's differentiation) the simple difference becomes complex. It is marked out, concretized, objectified, established and made public or publicized.

Crucially, however, these are negotiated separations. When the gifted work of carvers ends, *tapu* is lifted or removed. This is not automatic but requires deliberate acts and acknowledgement. The finished house is made available to a wider community. In front of and within the house, protocols can then direct further mediations between different kinds of person, thing or act expressive of different kinds of mana and therefore enveloped in other kinds of *tapu*, restrictions, boundaries or appropriateness. In short, things are separate from one another until they are brought together. The breathing and eating together of hosts and guests removes *tapu* and makes further intimacies and conversations possible. The plain fact of difference is vital until it ceases to be important. Difference places constraints, restraints and obligations on people until those differences are deemed uninteresting or superseded by other important matters. Eventually, difference becomes the cause of encounter and, if negotiated respectfully – "carefully" and "constructively" in Mary Black's (1977) gloss – results not in uniformity but in mutuality. These are dynamic and relational terms for social processes in a multi-species cosmos in which expressive separations train people for cooperation and other modes of interaction.

TRADITION/*KORERO TAHITO*

When Tawhai tells us what "religious activity" among his people, in and around Ruatoria, is for, he talks about trees and sweet potatoes, cutting and digging, housing and feeding guests. On first reading the "ancient explanations" Tawhai retells, it is possible to give too much attention to those "superhuman controlling powers". But it becomes clear that his *korero* (talk) is really about the ability of people (human and other-than-human, tree and other-than-tree, potato and other-than-potato, deities and other-than-deities) to act in the world, enabled by the varied giftedness, and constrained and obliged by their inherent, fluid and always dynamic relationships. Inherited and learnt knowledge is expected to help people decide between different possibilities that present themselves when they act (as they necessarily do) with, among and towards others. Religious stories may be about "superhuman controlling powers" but they are told within the context of religious activity, which is about relationships among the persons of the larger-than-human world (in which humans are not hyperseparated out).

Tawhai most certainly says that religious activities are performed by Ngati Uepohatu when they cut down trees and use the timber to make buildings and when they tend and dig up sweet potatoes to feed guests. Thus, religion is an activity braided into the living of worldly life. In doing it, people seek permission and offer placation for doing what needs doing. Religion is taught by the narrating and debating of traditions (verbal or performative) that entail myth, memory, repetition, authority and a community in which these are handed on. In Maori terms, this might be spoken of as ancestral *korero tahito* (ancient explanations), and justify Danièle Hervieu-Léger's working definition of religion as a "chain of memory" (Hervieu-Léger 2000, 2008) or Jim Cox's contention that religion is partially defined by "a tradition that is transmitted authoritatively from generation to generation" (J. L. Cox 2007: 85). Indeed, there is more in Tawhai's exposition of ancestral narratives (which are normally told for other purposes than introducing or defining "religion") that resonates with understanding religion as traditional and communal.

Nonetheless, when he has a chance to speak of the purpose of religious activity, Tawhai does not speak of beliefs or postulated alternate realities. He does not speak principally of transcendence or sacrality (as hyperseparated domains). Nor are the humans who perform religious acts hyperseparated from other beings or species. Rather Tawhai addresses the acts of violence necessary to living life in this world. He speaks of religion as those acts which enable perpetrators of everyday, unexceptional and necessary but still forbidden or dangerous acts of violence to survive and thrive. He uses tradition for the non-traditional purpose of defining religion. He should not be mistaken as retelling stories that are religious rather than social, environmental or practical. In fact, he writes of social acts, of behaviours that make the cosmos, world and locality liveable by relational beings of many kinds. Religion is about cutting down trees and digging up *kumara* because without religious activity no one would survive the cycle of violence. Instead, the processes of mutuality and dialogue can take place, make place, establish spaces in which people can stand, make guests out of strangers, share breath and food, and go on to seek further ways of relating.

RESTORING RELATIONS AND RIVERS

An invitation to participate in an historic moment on the slopes of Mount Ruapehu, rising from the central plateau of Aotearoa's North Island, provided me with an opportunity to see if Tawhai's ideas applied elsewhere. He is clear that he wants to speak of his people's knowledge and practice. Nonetheless, if there is a chance that his assertion that "the purpose of religious activity [is to] do violence with impunity" might apply more generally, then it ought to be relevant among Maori communities beyond Ruatoria.

In March 2011, Ngati Rangi (the indigenous community living around Mount Ruapehu) signed an accord with Genesis Energy. For some time, all the water from twenty-four water courses arising on the mountain has been captured and fed into Genesis Energy's hydroelectricity-generating scheme. Following lengthy negotiations, the power generator and supplier agreed to begin releasing some water into some of the original stream beds. Water would once again flow from the mountain springs to the sea. Marking the accord, a day of events began in a meeting at a *marae* that reinforced the lines of communication between locals and their guests and further tested the authority or (social) power relations between "ordinary" people and the directors and representatives of a utility company. Then a convoy of busses and cars took everyone part way up the mountain, to the banks of one of the water courses, at a point where the water trapping takes place. Here, following further speeches, a document setting out the agreement was signed and witnessed.

It would be entirely possible to describe this event with little (if any) use of standard (Euro-Christian) "religious" terms. It could be presented as a political and cultural encounter in which indigenous people's rights to livelihood and lifestyle were recognized. A full description would need to record and discuss moments of prayer or blessing in the analysis of inter-cultural events. Such prayers were not merely cultural packaging of an otherwise secular intercultural event. The event did not only publicly mark an agreement that water resources would be handed from the control of Genesis Energy to Ngati Rangi and their neighbours. It was not only a moment expressive of Maori treaty rights being honoured. Differences of mana, mediated by *tabu* protocols and practices, were significant in all that happened – but these too could be treated, rightly, as social processes. Is there any sign of religion that needs consideration here? A standard discussion of indigenous culture could discuss a Maori evocation of the mountain and its water-courses as sacred, of ancestors' observance over the proceedings, and of the more-than-mundane importance of water. But, without rejecting these possibilities, it is possible to discern more than a little of Tawhai's "doing violence with impunity" here.

The multi-species symbiotic community that is a living river, flowing from its springs to the sea through a course that provides and requires diverse habitats and habitus, can be subject to violence. It can be disrupted and dominated, treated as a resource rather than a relation. Its internal cohesion as a community can be destroyed as constituent species find it impossible to survive canalization. Its external relations with others (birds, mammals, plants) can be curtailed. When the water was first trapped to become an industrial technological tool (the motivating driver of electricity generators), it is unlikely that any official ritual act or address was made to the river or its members, or even to local Maori traditional custodians and users. We will not find any record of an official act that "seeks permission and offers placation" (Tawhai [1988] 2002: 244) in the initiation of this act of violence. Indeed, recognition that it was an act of violence seems unlikely. Possibly someone thought of the increase of electricity as a "reaching for redemption and salvation", and possibly the labour of diverting so much water inspired someone to "convey messages of praise and thanksgiving" to a deity.

On the day that we stood on the mountain and signed the agreement (since everyone present was invited to sign as witnesses at least), I recognized more than echoes of Tawhai's themes. More than one Maori involved in the agreement that would see some water returning to its accustomed stream mentioned to me, quite casually, that the partners to the day's agreement were not only Ngati Rangi and Genesis Energy, but also the rivers themselves. In the casual, joyful entry of many people into the part of the stream still flowing freely, above the water-trap, it seemed possible to observe a restoration of intimacy between local humans and local water. If Tawhai's article drew attention to acts of violence as the occasion for religious activities, on the mountain that day, as local Maori came back to a violated river, religious activities were understated. If the agreement between the two human communities was indicated by speeches and signatures on paper, an agreement between Maori and river was also indicated by intimate contact and addresses. I am not asserting that everyone who paddled in the mountain stream was deliberately engaging in a religious act, offering placation for past wrongs or reaching for renewal of respectful intimacy. Nor am I asserting that the river – flowing over feet, between fingers, into mouths – visibly or audibly expressed a preference for one mode of existence over another. All things are possible. Here, I am only seeking to apply a definition of religion to a series of acts, some intentional, some casual, that might justify the extension of Tawhai's claim that "the purpose of religious activity here is to seek to enter the domain of the superbeing and do violence with impunity". It seems possible that "violence with impunity" might sometimes mean that religious activity is required in the restoration of right relations long after the first violence has occurred.

A more explicit resonance with Tawhai's discussion can be found in the *karakia*, prayer, orated by Che Wilson during the proceedings. Commencing "*Mai ara rā!*" ("Let us return to our origins!"), it situates the speaker and those who stand with him not only in proximity to the river sources but to the cultural (re)sources of intimacy with local mountains and rivers. It declares a clan/totemic relationship (Rose 1998) between humans and other-than-human persons, finds a more fundamental energy than electricity in knowing one's being-with others, and seeks to draw on those cosmic energies in generating more respectful relationships and activities. The effort to correct what has passed between rivers and humans establishes a precedent for further efforts to address and redress acts of violence that have not, until now, been the cause of religious acts. Religious acts, then, are not about isolated "doing violence with impunity" but are concerned with building and maintaining respect across species boundaries. Or, more sociologically, the purpose of religious activities is to create and continue cooperation in multi-species communities.[2]

BRONZE PRINCESS IN WAIKIKI

In order to further test the validity of Tawhai's statement beyond the homeland of Ngati Uepohatu, I was able (with the generous support of the British Academy and the hospitality of the Mataira *whanau*) to spend a short while in

---

2. For more interventionist resonances with these ideas, see Rappaport (1999) and Grimes (2000, 2002, 2003).

Hawai'i. If *tapu* structures social relations within the larger-than-human community as Maori understand it, I wanted to understand how similarly processes might be evident on the opposite side of the Oceanic Polynesian world.

Historically, the Hawai'ian kingdom (before annexation by the USA) rejected the *kapu* system (cognate with *taboo* or *tapu*). This deliberate dismantling was one aspect of wide-ranging social and political changes between 1810 and 1850. It was not uncontested but it was pervasive. Nonetheless, reference to *kapu* is still made in various contexts and is perhaps growing. I will only note two examples that illustrate two possibilities in ongoing experiments in the relation between Polynesian and European originating cultures.

In the grounds of a hotel on Waikiki Beach there is a bronze statue of Princess Bernice Pauahi Bishop (1831–84) reading to a schoolgirl as both sit on a shaded bench. A sign next to the sculpture reads: "KAPU: Your respect for the statue of Princess Bernice Pauahi Bishop and the Native Hawai'ian garden is greatly appreciated. Please keep a distance from the statue, the planted areas and the water feature. Mahalo!" Bishop's legacy established the Kamehameha School system (among other things) and is honoured in this public artwork.

The globally popular practice of rubbing selected parts of bronze statues so that hands or feet (or scrotum in the case of the Andras Hadik's horse in Budapest) shine seems not to be followed here. The *kapu* request seems honoured in that way. But both the Princess and the girl wear *lei*, garlands, that are regularly renewed and fresh. Someone evidently touches the *kapu* statue. Given what has been said about *tapu* as a negotiable restriction of contact until it is permitted or required to make contact, the garlanding of this statue does not negate the *kapu* request. Instead, perhaps, it reinforces the performance of ritual or etiquette in which differences are maintained and celebrated as causes rather than barriers to relationship.

The *kapu* sign might seem parallel to British "keep off the grass" instructions rather than an invitation to consider a whole world or cosmos of changing relations. However, perhaps restrictions on walking on grass signal an otherwise unacknowledged British taboo system. In Chapter 9, I will note another taboo system in Jewish *kashrut*. Regardless of how seriously we take this suggestion, other references to *kapu* in Hawai'i evidences the continuing salience of traditional knowledges, know-how and lifeways. An annual lunar calendar made available through the *'Aha Moku* website (www. ahamoku.org) furthers the group's encouragement and enabling of traditional resource management protocols and practices. These always at least note that particular places, times, stages of lifecycles (e.g. breeding periods of fish) are *kapu*. This can be glossed as "sacred", expanded as "take care not to disrupt these cycles" or implicit in the note "each month required strict ceremony" or involve particular restrictions. Efforts to restore land and sea use (given traditional management of areas "from the mountain to the ocean") include restoring physical structures (e.g. fish ponds), cultural expertise (e.g. marine and botanical knowledges and management) and educational and consultative styles (e.g. protocols of local consultation and the inculcation of "respect"). As with Tawhai's discussion of forestry and gardening, so this website and calendar refer to deities. In this case, deities are participants in the ecological and cultural systems of interest to those interested in fishing.

The 2011–12 calendar provides a brief introduction to Lono as "one of four main deities. Lono is associated with peace, fertility, agriculture, rainfall and music". In Honolulu's Bishop Museum, it is now possible to visit statues of Lono and other deities which have been removed from their original locations and placed on more public, less restricted view. In one sense, their *kapu* has been removed – perhaps because their prestige, mana, was diminished with widespread European and American influence in the nineteenth century. They are not, however, merely museum displays now. In the calendar, and elsewhere, Lono is an active member of a multi-species community. The absence of the word "religion" here seems significant in indicating that a reference to deities is not a reference to a separable realm of supernatural transcendence. Rather, religious activities (e.g. speaking of deities and structuring the year according to ceremonies involving deities) pervade and permeate "mundane" acts. Religion, as Tawhai indicates, is an aspect of everyday human relations with others.

BAHÁ'ÍS, CATHOLICS AND LATTER DAY SAINTS

Before concluding, I note that the people I have benefited most from in my attempts to understand religion among Maori and Native Hawai'ians are not all self-identified "traditionalists". They most certainly celebrate ancestral knowledges and encourage practices of respect that recognizably arise from ancestral lifeways and teachings. However, they include Anglicans, Bahá'ís, Catholics and Latter Day Saints. They do not compartmentalize religious complexes, performances or identities so that anyone could unequivocally say "this is traditional, this is Catholic". Their self-presentations and activities are, in various ways and with varied stresses and benefits, a blend and sometimes a fusion of ideas and lifeways evolving from different origins. As with many contemporary indigenous people, a preference for the word "spirituality" rather than "religion" is sometimes expressed. For instance, I have often been told that there is a "Maori spirituality" that underlies all manner of Maori cultural practices. Many undoubtedly devout Christian Maori speak of and to ancestral deities without ever considering that they have transgressed a boundary. Religion does not exist or operate in neatly boxed packages (McGuire 2008). Not only do we (scholars of religion) need to consider religion as a fluid phenomenon, we need to demolish the overly policed boundaries of many of our categories – including the names of seemingly discrete religions and the terms of our critical enquiries.

WHEN A TREE FALLS

When Tawhai notes the possibility that religion could be associated with "the preaching of one thing and too often the doing of something else" (Tawhai [1988] 2002: 238), he does not allow this to affect his definition of religious activity as "doing violence with impunity". Religion is not about trying to get away with rule breaking. Rather, Tawhai's chief claim is that religious activity begins in the acknowledgement that violence is necessary but dangerous. Religion does not occur when people excuse themselves by imagining their violence is without impact. Rather, religion occurs when people face their victims, fully cognisant that reciprocity is integral to relationality, and seek to enhance intimacy with others despite violence. Religious activity is undertaken when, in ritual and etiquette, in restraint and celebration, and in honouring mana and taboo, people seek permission and offer placation either for necessary but nonetheless wrongful acts of violence. If a tree falls in the forest, philosophers may wonder if anyone hears it, but religious studies scholars might wonder if religion was involved.

7. Respecting relations

Columbus and his collaborators and successors in the European imperial conquest of the Americas frequently declared that they could find nothing like religion, or nothing like Christianity, among indigenous peoples. Given the charter documents of their project – in which the conquest, enslavement and despoiling of "discovered" peoples is predicated on their failing to have a "Christian prince" (see Newcomb 2008) – this was perhaps a fortunate failing. It seems unlikely that people who were busy resisting, surviving or succumbing to the European onslaught would have much time or interest in inviting Columbus and company to many of the myriad ceremonial complexes of the continent. Mostly, however, the cry "no religion" seems disingenuous. At another extreme, more recent interpreters have claimed to find that beliefs in supernatural and/or transcendent entities are widespread among Native Americans. Here, the effect of adopting a theological approach to religion seems evident. Neither view is particularly helpful in understanding either Native American religions nor in defining "religion" for academic purposes.

In Chapter 6 I pondered how Europeans managed without the word "taboo" prior to Captain Cook's Oceanic voyages. Now I ask what the word "totem", originating among speakers of Algonkian languages in what is now North America (but also remains indigenous homelands), might contribute to a redirection of our gaze towards non-transcendent, non-metaphysical but thoroughly empirical evidence about something we might call religion. In doing so, I follow the lead of Ken Morrison (1992a, 1992b, 2000, 2002, 2013) who argued for the need for a different, "non-supernaturalistic", understanding of religion and a different, "post-Cartesian", approach to doing academic work. With him and other colleagues, I build on the research of Irving Hallowell (1955, 1960, 1992) because it has inspired so much of the new approach to "animism" (Harvey 2005a, 2013) and I am confident that its trajectory contains keys to retheorizing "religion".

Because I will follow Hallowell's lead I will also follow his spelling, "Ojibwa", for the name of the indigenous nation that is the focus of the majority of the chapter. Sometimes, however, I will use "Ojibwe" or "Anishinaabe(g)" where these are more typical of local self-identifications. I have been privileged to spend some time among Anishinaabeg in the Midwestern USA and in southern central Canada trying to ascertain the relevance, validity and application of Hallowell's arguments and conclusions in relation to present day people. However, my first visit to indigenous North American lands and people took place at Miawpukek, Newfoundland, so I propose to introduce matters of importance by summarizing an experience there.

KITPU!

Eagles are quite common along Newfoundland's Conne River. They live among the forested rocky crags across the river from the Mi'kmaq town of Miawpukek (a First Nations reserve recognized by the Newfoundland and Canadian governments). They often take salmon or trout from the community's fishery in the nearby Bay d'Espoir. Local people see them every day. However, when the people of Miawpukek held their first traditional, non-competitive powwow in 1996 an eagle flew one perfect circle over the central drum group during the final "honour song" (in which only elders and veterans dance), and then flew back to its treetop eyrie across the river. Everyone, locals and visitors, noticed. Cries of "*kitpu!*" ("eagle!") simultaneously greeted the eagle, expressed pleasure at its beauty and presence, and declared that its flight demonstrated approval for the event. The flight of this eagle, in this way, at this moment, continues to be celebrated as an encouragement to the Mi'kmaq community to continue the process of gaining or regaining confidence in traditional knowledge and its relevance in the contemporary world.

Soon after it happened, one young man told me, quite spontaneously, that this was the first time he had felt proud to be native. Several people told me that what was happening at Miawpukek was not a "revitalization movement" because traditional worldviews and lifeways did not need revitalizing, the eagles and bears had always maintained them. A representative of the eagles was honouring those in the aboriginal human population of the area, and of the island more generally, for their willingness to experiment again with traditional ways of life and traditional understandings of the world. The eagle participated in the powwow because the humans were participating in local culture again. In the seventeenth annual powwow in 2012, the event was remembered fondly as inspiring more steps along the new/old ways.

Much that is important is contained in this short moment: it can be summed up as animistic with hints of totemism (both of which terms will be discussed below). It occasioned spontaneous expressions of respect and thanksgiving, and is embedded in reciprocal and mutualistic relations across species boundaries. The honouring of powerful persons (elders, veterans, drums and eagles) was braided into a social event, a spectacle with nested ceremonies. But is this "religion"?

Powwows are not religious. Their participants might be members of many different religions or none. What ceremonial aspects there are in pow-wows flow between honouring elders and veterans, nationhood, "tradition" and presence in modern market economies (i.e. the fishery business) and much more. It is possible that some of the participants in 1996, including those who are Roman Catholic Christians, addressed prayers to their deity but, if so, this would not make the whole powwow or the eagle's flight religious. Similarly, some "traditional" people may have addressed words or acts towards "the Great Spirit" as well as exclaiming "*kitpu!*" or "eagle!", but did not think of the whole powwow as a single religious ceremony.

Throughout this and other powwows, such people maintain sacred fires and conduct sweat-lodge ceremonies. Nothing dramatically transcendent or supernatural is involved here, and no one has ever hinted to me that the 1996 eagle might have been a symbol, a metaphor, a spirit, a message or anything. Rather, it was an eagle communicating approval. Is all this not just people seeking the well-being of others (human or other-than-human) around them – for example, encouraging young people to respect themselves, perhaps by honouring traditional values and knowledges? Are powwows any more than vibrant social events or happenings? To understand how the remarkable but not supernatural flight of an eagle might be helpful in defining "religion" it may be helpful to dive deeper into debates about supernaturalism, and to move further west.

THE SOLIDARITY OF KIN

In surveying the (plural) histories of French and Algonkian religious encounters in the seventeenth century, Ken Morrison's *The Solidarity of Kin* (2002) perceptively explores and often contests recent interpretations and approaches to knowledge. Although the phrase "the Solidarity of Kin" is meant to sum up the foundations, generative acts and ambitions of various Algonkian peoples (i.e. the inculcation of closer, more respectful relationships), it might also hint at a key problem in the European project from colonial times until now. (Some of my indigenous friends insist these days in which we live are the most-modern and most-colonial of times – so now I've explained an ironic allusion to temporal periodization.) The solidity of European obsessions, frameworks and traditions regularly prevent many scholars from escaping the box which keeps them associating "religion" with beliefs and transcendence. Happily, and in some significant degree because of Morrison's publications, the construction of "religion" as "belief in god" now looks far more flimsy than it once did. Thus, a new solidarity, association or assemblage is emerging in which "religion" is taken to refer to far more interesting matters than the peculiar eccentricities or follies of irrational or ignorant people.

In order to take us (fellow academics) from the cage of established Christian theological and modernist approaches towards a more appropriate framework within which to understand indigenous religious knowledges, Morrison leads us "Beyond the Supernatural and to a Dialogical Community" (K. M. Morrison 2002: 37–58). In his chapter by that name, he makes use of Åke Hultkrantz's article "The Concept of the Supernatural in Primal Religion" for the first stage of this liberating process. Hultkrantz writes that "Empirical investigations have guided me to the conviction that an assumption of a basic dichotomy between two levels of existence, one ordinary or 'natural,' the other extraordinary or 'supernatural,' conditions man's religious cognition" (Hultkrantz 1983: 231).

Far from being an empirical observation, Morrison argues, this insistence on the definitive nature of "the supernatural" (and of "man") is "a widely held assumption about the unconscious existential principles in relation to which we think erroneously that all people shape their lives" (K. M. Morrison 2002: 37). It is an assumption rooted in a particular cultural system (Saler 1977), which might not accurately describe the reality in which even its proponents dwell. Later, Morrison argues that Hultkrantz's essay

> not only wrongly describes Native American cosmologies, it also subverts the possibility of achieving new, cross-cultural insights about American Indian life. An exalted, vertical superiority does not describe empirically either the Ojibwa or other Native American religious systems. ... Seventeenth-century French Jesuits could find no

evidence that Algonkian peoples had any notion of a god, or God,
or, for that matter, worship.   (K. M. Morrison 2002: 41)

Similarly, Morrison criticizes James Axtell's *After Columbus* (1988) for con-
taining a devastating self-contradiction. Despite noting that Native Americans
(prior to European "contact") did not make a distinction between natural
and supernatural, Axtell still contends that "spiritual or supernatural power,
supernatural talismans, and a monotheistic belief in an 'ultimate being'
characterized Native American religious orientations to the world" (K. M.
Morrison 2002: 159, discussing Axtell 1988, especially 16, 118, 278).

Axtell does not claim that Native Americans manage such a characterization of the cosmos while lacking the language to make the distinction.
Rather, an ingrained European-originated characterization of religion as
"supernaturalist" has improperly intervened between empirical data and
scholarly analysis.

I have followed Morrison in emphasizing some exemplary faults in
studies of these religions – and, by implication, others.[1] Perhaps it would
have been better to start more positively by outlining what facets of Native
American knowledge(s) demand a rethinking of scholarly categories and
approaches. However, I am concerned throughout this book with two related
problems. The first is about wrong understandings of religion. The second
is about wrong approaches to studying religion. With Morrison, I propose
that although there is now a wealth of data about particular religions that
could challenge and improve on our existing definitions, categories and
sub-categories, it is our approaches that most need radical attention and
adjustment. For that reason, this brief summary of highlights of Morrison's
criticisms of two approaches to Native American religions seems justified.
What, then, does Morrison offer to replace the supernaturalist definition and
the approaches that assume and, unsurprisingly, find it almost everywhere?

Morrison cites an "origin account of the Ojibwa shaman, Hole-in-the-
Sky" of a response from the Great Spirit to a request from Shell (a "great
person" from "the bottom layer of the earth" "who is the Great Spirit's equal"
and the one who "envisioned the *Midewiwin*, a major Ojibwa religious rite,
in order to empower the Ojibwa people"):

---

1. That implication is already partly addressed in a special issue of the journal *Religion*,
   guest-edited by K. M. Morrison and including essays not only about Algonkian peoples
   but also about Hopi, Oglala, Yaqui and Zuni – see Detwiler (1992), Fulbright (1992) and
   K. M. Morrison (1992b).

Ho! Thank you for your plan for the Indian. Actually you are just ahead of me, for I was intending a similar thing, practically the same but a little different. This will be good for the Indian. Call all the manitos [personal beings] of Earth; tell them of this that we plan. And I, too, will tell those up there with me.

(K. M. Morrison 2002: 42, citing Landes 1968: 98)

The Great Spirit, Shell and "the Indian" here are differentiated by power or ability but not by ontology: they are all relational beings who share responsibility for the well-being of others. Expanding on this by considering the origins and evolution of indigenous relationships with the idea of "the Great Spirit", *Kitche Manitou*, Morrison demonstrates that the Ojibwa have not succumbed to a Christian theological belief or to a system of cosmic hierarchy. Rather, "power/knowledge … is constituted in the exercise of interpersonal ethics and responsibility", "politics emerges in the dialogical give-and-take of personality, power, and persuasion", while the cosmos remains consensual and relational (*ibid.*: 42–3; see also 79–101, 186 n.26). Indigenous knowledges and protocols have continued to structure and encourage the adoption, absorption, accommodation and/or adaptation of novel ideas and activities (see also Soyinka 1976: 53–4; Garuba 2003 – suggesting that this is a pervasive element of indigenous animisms worldwide).

Morrison's publications demonstrate the importance of relational ontology, epistemology and ethics for Algonkian people. Confronted by the powerful danger and powerful attraction of European missionaries, traders and others, those who survived the colonial assault were continuously "propelled [by their cultural norms] toward constructive alliance, a religious socialization of selfish, individualistic, and authoritarian (and thus non-Indian) others" (K. M. Morrison 2002: 79). A pervasive relational expectation proved robust enough to keep Algonkian people seeking to incorporate Europeans and their deity into social networks even when faced with what could only seem utterly antisocial, hyperseparated beings. Elsewhere, Morrison (2013) cites contemporary Navajo as saying that European Americans "act as though they have no relatives". Resonating with Lévi-Strauss's ([1952] 1973: 384) discussion of indigenous Caribbean and Spanish Catholic approaches to determining the humanity of strangers – played out in enquiries about definitive materiality or immateriality (as discussed already in Chapter 3) – the perennial question raised in inter-hemisphere "contacts" has been "are they human?".

However, in a quest for a "post-Cartesian anthropology" informed by historical encounters between peoples with differing ontological assumptions and expectations, Ken Morrison (2013) advances Hallowell's demonstration that the question "are they human?" is a sub-species of the larger question, "are they persons?" To understand this we will listen in on conversations that are expressive of Anishinaabe animism.

CATCHING THE MEANING OF THUNDER

Hallowell writes:

> An informant told me that many years before he was sitting in a tent one summer afternoon during a storm together with an old man and his wife. There was one clap of thunder after another. Suddenly the old man turned to his wife and asked, "Did you hear what was said?" "No," she replied, "I didn't catch it". My informant, an acculturated Indian, told me he did not at first know what the old man and his wife referred to. It was, of course, the thunder. The old man thought that one of the Thunder Birds had said something to him. He was reacting to this sound in the same way as he would respond to a human being, whose words he did not understand.   (Hallowell 1960: 34)

He comments that:

> The casualness of the remark and even the trivial character of the anecdote demonstrate the psychological depth of the "social relations" with other-than-human beings that becomes explicit in the behaviour of the Ojibwa as a consequence of the cognitive "set" induced by their culture.   (*Ibid.*: 34)

After a lifetime living as animists this couple assumed that thunder is an act of communication. Acceptance of not having "caught" what was said indicates another vitally important assumption: not all communication is about us (humans in general or the hearers specifically). The elderly couple could carry on talking with their visitor while the thunder engaged in a separate conversation nearby.

In another key passage in his increasingly influential discussion of "Ojibwa ontology, behavior, and world view" Hallowell describes asking an unnamed old Ojibwa man, "Are *all* the stones we see about us here alive?" (*ibid.*: 24; emphasis original). He could ask this because in Ojibwa grammar the addition of a particular plural ending *-iig* indicates that stones, *asin*, are grammatically animate (Nichols & Nyholm 1995: 14). In much the same way, tables are marked as "female" rather than "male" in French grammar. Actually, not really "in the same way", as it turns out. If you ask a native French speaker if they treat tables differently because of this use of "feminine" gender terms, they are likely to treat you as mad or foolish. French linguistic gender assignment is a figure of speech, and probably has no other sense or significance (see Sedaris 2001: 185–91). However, Hallowell's question about rocks received a more helpful (if still enigmatic) response.

Hallowell's question, unpacked, is whether the Ojibwa treat grammatically animate stones as animate persons. Do they speak with stones or act in other ways that reveal intentions to build or maintain relationships? If all stones everywhere are grammatically animate, did the old man actually think that *particular* rocks around him were alive? Did he treat them in some way that showed them to be alive? The old man answered, "No! But *some* are". He had claimed to have witnessed a particular stone following the leader of a shamanic ceremony around a tent as he sang. Another powerful leader is said to have had a large stone that would open when he tapped it three times, allowing him to remove a small bag of herbs when he needed it in ceremonies. Hallowell was told that when a white trader was digging his potato patch he found a stone that looked like it may be important. He called for the leader of another ceremony who knelt down to talk to the stone, asking if it had come from someone's ceremonial tent. The stone is said to have denied this. Movement, gift-giving and conversation are three indicators of the animate nature of relational beings, or persons.

In the old man's full response and in the other narratives Hallowell includes, it becomes crystal clear that the key point is that stones engage in relationships – and not just that they might do things of their own volition (however remarkable this claim might seem). For the Ojibwa the interesting question is not "how do we know stones are alive?" but "what is the appropriate way for people, of any kind, to relate?". This is as true for humans as it is for stones, trees, animals, birds, fish, and all other beings that might be recognized as persons. Persons are known to be persons when they relate to other persons in particular ways. They might act more or less intimately, willingly, reciprocally or respectfully. Since enmity is also a relationship, they might act aggressively – which is the chief reason why animists employ shamans (Harvey 2009b). The category of "person" is perhaps only properly applicable within such thoroughly relational worlds when beings are actively relating with others. There, "person" is not a nominal category but a performance, and one that is both corporeal and corporate. This is quite different to the understanding of most European-derived cultures in which personhood is an interior quality, a fact about an individual (human) who is self-conscious. Hallowell recognized this by insisting that we are not talking here about different "belief-systems", epistemologies, but about different ontologies, different ways of being in the world. Indeed, we could say that the Ojibwa elder lived in a different world from Hallowell's until the latter learnt to see the world as his teacher showed it to be.

Once he saw the world in which Ojibwa elders and local rocks might actively relate together, or share gifts and ceremonies, Hallowell had to find new ways to use the English language to write about what he had learnt. To talk of animism may have suggested a discussion of life (animation) versus death. To talk of persons may have implied notions about human interiority (belief, rationality or subjectivity). He has, in fact, been misread in both these ways. However, the "animate persons" Hallowell introduced were relational beings, actors in a participatory world. His question is phrased in a way that indicates he had already appreciated some, at least, of what it meant to live in the old man's world: he did not ask "are all rocks (universally) alive?" but inquired about nearby rocks.

Hallowell was already recognizing the importance of relationship and participation. Then, having learnt from his Ojibwa hosts, Hallowell coined the phrase "other-than-human persons" to refer to the animate beings with whom humans share the world. He was not privileging humanity or saying that what makes something a person is their likeness to humans. He is clear that "person" is not defined by putatively human characteristics or behaviours. The term is a much larger umbrella than "human".

All beings communicate intentionally and act towards others relationally: this makes them "persons". All persons are expected to give and receive gifts, and to act respectfully (to mutual benefit or communal well-being) and, if they do so, this makes them "good persons". It is useful for us (humans) to speak about "human-" and "other-than-human" persons only because we are humans talking to humans (if we were bears we might speak of "other-than-bear persons"). This is also useful for speakers of English because we are preconditioned to hear the word "person" as a reference to other humans. The word "person" should be enough, without the additional "other-than-human", and would be if English-speakers had not learnt to privilege humanity above other beings.

125

Animists live in a different world: a community of persons of many species, all of whom are deemed to be capable of relationship, communication, agency and desire. Humans are not the unique possessors or performers of something called "culture". There is no mute or inert "nature", no inert and value-free "environment", but only the many competing conversations of a multi-species cultural community. Some of these conversations cross species-boundaries. Ceremonies are regular opportunities for different kinds of person (e.g. humans, bears, eagles, rocks, sun) to interact for the benefit of the widest community. Paying respectful attention to these implications of animist knowledge might also further promote the deliberate transgression or effective demolition of the boundaries by which the "natural" and "social" sciences, as well as the "humanities", seem to treat different subjects or objects. Our scholarly ancestors have bequeathed us a world in which humans are separated from "the environment" in contrast with animals which are integrally placed in their environments. While we may not live fully in an animate cosmos (despite our habit of naming cars, begging computers to work properly, and perceiving some weather systems as "aggressive") neither do we live fully in the scientific world that Darwin too has revealed to be thoroughly relational.

In brief, then, the term "animism" is now being used not as Edward Tylor used it – to sum up his definition of "religion" as "belief in spirits" (Tylor [1871] 1913) – but in a way that listens respectfully to Ojibwe discourse. Animism labels those efforts to live well in a world which is a community of persons, most of whom are "other-than-human". It refers to varied relational ontologies and epistemologies, and challenges the too-easy allegation that to speak of animals or birds communicating is to project human-likeness or to commit anthropomorphism. Rather, many denials of the likeness of humans and other species commit the larger errors of hyperseparatism and androcentricism. There is more to be said about the animist world introduced into academic debate significantly by Hallowell's publications. In particular, it is time to revisit another Ojibwe word, one that has already entered academic vocabularies but has been misinterpreted.

TOTEMS

As Darwin showed, all beings are related. We share a genealogy and a history. We can expect multiple similarities in our physicality and our performances. The radical inter-relatedness and myriad interactivity of species within the traditional Ojibwe world may be labelled "animism" but something more specific and intimate is vital. Perhaps Hallowell's elderly interlocutor paused before replying "No! But *some* are" because to him the interesting question was not precisely the one that Hallowell had asked. What his answer, as he expands upon it, taught Hallowell and his heirs, is that the aliveness of the world can be assumed, taken-for-granted, relied upon. The really interesting matter is particular relationships and their activation. For that reason, within the broad, cosmos-wide animism (which did not need a label until an alternative lifeway was forcefully asserted), the Ojibwe have a word for specific interspecies relationships. That word is "totem".

Among the Ojibwe, *totem* refers to clans that include humans and particular animals and plants. It has been used by academics in theorizing about how people imagine and relate to (other) animals. Claude Lévi-Strauss established the notion that totem-animals are chosen because they are "good to think" (1969: 89). This is a great advance on James Frazer's (1910) view that people selected particular animal or plant species as totems to magically aid their quest for sustenance and protection, and that of Bronisław Malinowski (1948) that what is selected relates to the ease with which "totems" become food. However, a richer understanding (and a provocative invitation to improve human relations with the world) could be gained from taking seriously the plain Ojibwe use of the word *totem* (or -*doodem*-) to refer to clans. As Chris Knight says, "Totemism is … embedded in animism as an aspect of sociality" (Knight 1996: 550). It is a more immediate and intimate mode of relating than the all-embracing relationality indicated by "animism". It does not refer, principally, to animals or plants but to associations or social assemblages of persons of different species who are treated as more intimate kin groups within the larger animate world. Animals and plants, in this context, are good as relatives.

In writing of Aboriginal Australian traditional knowledges, Debbie Rose's *Dingo Makes Us Human* (1992) points (by its title and its contents) to the central importance of totemic relationships in making human people what they are. The job that clans are supposed to do within the wider, inclusive, cross-species community posited by animism is to animate the privileging of respect, cooperation and interaction, and locally enact the bias towards resolving differences amicably rather than destructively.

This should not be mistaken for romanticism. Elsewhere, discussing Aboriginal Australian relationships with their lands and other-than-human neighbours, Rose uses the term "totemism" in writing about the possession by all species of "their own rituals and law, and … they too [alongside humans] take care of relationships of well-being" among all the inhabitants of an area or "country". All related beings share rights and responsibilities, and are expected to be committed to and concerned for each other's "flourishing in the world" (*ibid.*: 7, 11). Totemic/clan kinship involves high degrees of mutual care. An absence of care or an irresponsibility in consumption creates "wild" places (Rose 2004) – that is, places damaged by hyperseparation or dominance. The policing of correct, balanced or careful action and consumption is undertaken across species boundaries and illustrated in the taking of lives. It is interesting, in this context, to read Val Plumwood's (2000) account of being attacked by a crocodile, in which she recognizes that she had been in the wrong place. The vast differences between Ojibwe and Aboriginal Australian cultures should not be ignored, but in their understandings of "totemism" there is a confluence of ideas about kinship, mutuality, care and responsibilities.

CANNIBALS AND MEDICINE PEOPLE

Just as Plumwood and Rose are clear that relationships and co-habitation are not always harmonious but can lead to tension, conflict and competition, so the Ojibwe relational world has its dangers. In the following passage, Hallowell begins with a reminder about the shared nature of "persons" and then brings out an implication of differences in power between them:

> Speaking as an Ojibwa, one might say: all other "persons" – human or other than human – are structured the same as I am. There is a vital part which is enduring and an outward appearance that may be transformed under certain conditions. All other "persons," too, have such attributes as self-awareness and understanding. I can talk with them. Like myself, they have personal identity, autonomy, and volition. I cannot always predict exactly how they will act, although most of the time their behavior meets my expectations. In relation to myself, other "persons" vary in power. Many of them have more power than I have, but some have less. They may be friendly and help me when I need them but, at the same time, I have to be prepared for hostile acts, too. I must be cautious in my relations with other "persons" because appearances may be deceptive.
>
> (Hallowell 1960: 168)

As Morrison notes:

> [Mary Black] calls this uncertainty [in knowing the intentions of others] "percept ambiguity," and so emphasizes people's need to position themselves both cautiously and constructively ("respectfully" is the usual contemporary Ojibwa gloss) towards other persons.
>
> (K. M. Morrison 2002: 40, citing Black 1977)

Indeed, the globally prevalent indigenous term "respect", is everywhere a good summary of the appropriate and necessary positioning of persons towards others in an animate world.

Persons are not all alike. Not only are they of different species, they are also differently powerful. Some are socially powerful, such that younger people are taught to treat elders (of whatever species) with respect (see McNally 2009). But not only do some socially powerful people not act with regard to the benefit of others, there are also persons who have achieved the ability to change appearance. Not all such persons do so for negative or aggressive purposes. They too may be ambiguous. Remember that this is a pervasively relational world and acts have to be observed carefully before it can be determined whether a "good person" is involved. Powerful individuals may lead communal ceremonies or share the produce gained in hunting to benefit others. However, Algonkian peoples narrate an exemplary danger of the social world as the possibility of cannibals. These ultimately antisocial beings are definitively obsessed with consuming without regard to kinship, sharing or the rites of thanksgiving. The process of growing up, therefore, involves learning to seek mutuality and to share with kin and neighbours. If seventeenth-century Jesuits worried whether Algonkian peoples had god-ideas, their indigenous interlocutors worried that Europeans were antisocial, all-consuming cannibals. Still today, alongside positive communal virtues, Algonkian culture teachers encourage taking care, being cautious, and approaching situations with an eye to being constructive but safe.

Additionally, this remains a world in which people regularly seek the aid of more powerful persons (human or other-than-human). People who might be compared with "shamans" of other cultures are typically identified as "medicine people" in many Native North American contexts. "Medicine" here is not solely a reference to the knowledgeable use of healing substances and techniques, but indicates expert ability to draw on sources of support and aid both for healing and for other needs. Medicine people, like shamans, might be able to address animals or those who control them, seeking to gain permission for hunters to do their job. They might know how to expertly divine the causes and solution of many problems. As in the Amazon, medicine people may be expected to know how to recognize dangerously predatory persons (human or other-than-human) or those with cannibal tendencies. Seeing past the shifts of apparent "natural" form, the medicine person perceives allies or enemies, prey or predator (compare Viveiros de Castro 1998, 2004). As elsewhere among those identified (rightly or wrongly) as shamans or sorcerers, medicine people might exhibit such individual prowess or eccentricity that their singularity makes them, in turn, suspect of being antisocial and dangerous. Nonetheless, the chief need for medicine people arises from the ambiguous fact that in an interspecies community (with significant interspecies kinship) some species are necessarily, but not ungraciously, food. Thus, again as elsewhere among shamans (see Harvey 2003b; Harvey & Wallis 2010), mediation and diplomacy can be required between species to maintain food supplies, to prevent excessive violence, and to mitigate insults.

SILENCE IN THE WOODS

It is not only the medicine people who engage with powerful other-than-human persons. Everyone walking in the woods or along a shoreline is already in the domain of the larger-than-human world, in the home of bears, deer, eagles, fish and other persons. Larry Gross, therefore, says that "a traditional way of life in the woods found Ojibwe people 'immersed in silence,' 'taking in the world around them'" (Gross 1996, cited in McNally 2009: 298). Perhaps this is a "matter of survival" (as Gross and McNally suggest), especially when it is hunters out in the forest. Then and there they follow locally appropriate rules, or maintain taboos, that are comparable to those described by Rane Willerslev (2007) in relation to Siberian Yukaghir hunters. Or, as Richard Nelson wrote of the Koyukon approach, "the environment is like a second society in which people live, governed by elaborate rules of behavior and etiquette, capable of rewarding those who follow these rules and punishing those who do not" (Nelson 1983: 226).

This is to reinforce points made earlier, that the world is pervasively social, a community of persons (not all of whom are human), in which terms like "natural" and "supernatural" have no meaningful or appropriate use. Differences between persons do not generate significant hierarchies but energize cautious relationships. In relation to hunting and the consumption of animals, it might be said that in grateful return for offering their lives as sustenance, animals are offered respect by humans. Respect here carries the meaning of "appropriate behaviour" as well as "gratitude" and careful, constructive action. In turn, this exchange of gifts (of nutrition and respect) is enveloped in the expected practice of gift exchange.

BIMAADIZIWIN

Writing about the "existential postulates" or "principles" of "the concepts Person, Power and Gift", Morrison concludes:

> If, on the one hand, positive powerful persons share, then, on the other, negative persons withhold and act in self-interested ways. Thus the power of both the individual religious specialist and of those collective ceremonial societies extend co-operation micro- and macrocosmically.
> (K. M. Morrison 1992a: 203, building on Blackburn 1975)

Reciprocity and restraint are virtues inculcated within Ojibwe communities by sharing stories, by participating in ceremonies and by observing the habits of elders. This being so, an extensive quotation from McNally's *Honoring Elders* is insightful:

> This [the Ojibwe conviction that moral relations extend beyond the human community] is crucial to understand about Ojibwe "religion," a term that most Anishinaabe people I've meet have rejected as a representation of what they have consistently preferred to call "our way of life" or "our way." Indeed the this-worldly focus of Ojibwe beliefs and ceremonial practices has proved a stumbling block for missionaries and scholars of religion alike. Rather than starting with "religion" or simply "nature," let's begin with the indigenous category that has served anthropologists, historians, and community people alike, as a coherent organizing concept of this Ojibwe way of life: *bimaadiziwin*. *Bimaadiziwin* is a substantive form of a verb that indicates to "move by" or "move along" and that serves as a verbal root for terms that refer to things and people that are alive. *Bimaadiziwin* can be rather flatly translated as "life" or "living," but a richer rendering shows it to be a window into the traditional goal of Ojibwe religion: to

131

live well and live long in this world … *Bimaadiziwin* orients the natural ordinary workings of this-worldly existence to an ultimate order of things. Translating it as "the good life," A.I. Hallowell placed the concept of *bimaadiziwin* at the centre of the Ojibwe religious project, noting the moral, aesthetic, and spiritual connotations carried by the term. "Ojibwa religious behavior," he wrote, "can be identified as any activity by an individual or a group of individuals that helps to promote a good life for human beings by making explicit recognition, direct or indirect, of man's [*sic*] faith in and dependence upon other-than-human persons".

(McNally 2009: 48–9,
citing Hallowell 1992: 82)

McNally goes on to write about the "hard work" of living so that "ordinary life" really does match up to "an ultimate order of things". It is not poetry or romanticism that leads Anishinaabeg to note human "dependence upon other-than-human persons". The claim of Tawhai ([1988] 2002: 244; and discussed in Chapter 6) that "the purpose of religious activity is doing violence with impunity" similarly honours the need of humans – and all other species – to take life but to do so within the appropriate boundaries of respectful, reciprocal and always negotiated communal living. This, in turn, requires a cultural context in which life taking and food consumption can be performed "properly" (whatever that might mean in local contexts). Elders teach by example (especially by living and by silence) what it might mean to live a "good life" – both as "living well" and "living long". Other-than-human persons (such as the eagle at the Miawpukek powwow in 1996) help humans to recognize when they are – or ought to be – acting respectfully within the wider-than-human community. Humans are, then, aided with sustenance and guidance in the ways of living in the world.

In the end, the rejection of terms like "supernatural" from definitions of "religion" or *bimaadiziwin* is not because indigenous people live "natural" lives in "nature" but because both members of the duality ("supernature" *and* "nature") are alien imports. Experiences are not separable into "supernatural" and "natural" any more than the world is divided between "culture" and "nature". Rather, there is a richly pluralistic community of species, co-inhabiting places-as-societies. Religion cannot be about transcendence because nothing transcends this vibrant worldly community. We can find religion here *within* the interactions of persons, human or other-than-human.

SAGE PICKING

On one research trip within the midwestern United States, I was invited to join a group of Ojibwe and Lakota people who were going to pick sage. They use sage in their prayers throughout the year, burning some when they seek purification, and making up small bundles to offer as gifts to helpful other-than-human persons. We drove out of the Twin Cities towards a location where sage grew plentifully. On the way, the driver of the first car in our *ad hoc* convoy noticed abundant sage growing along the verges of the highway. He pulled over and we all followed. We began, some more hesitantly than others, to pick sage.

When the police arrived a discussion ensued as to whether this was a legal or good activity. Native Americans may have the right to benefit from state property (as perhaps wild plants may be), but picking sage beside a busy highway could be deemed dangerous as well as illegal. The police were persuaded to let us continue our journey. Reaching our intended destination, we paused and before even entering the field, everyone took pinches of sage left over from the previous year and held it to their hearts while introducing themselves – not to each other but to the plants. Everyone, individually, sometimes silently, sometimes vocally, requested permission to cut new sage for the following year. After a pause each person placed their sage on the ground. Once these gifts were given and one of the elders had indicated that permission was given, everyone gathered sage, being careful not to destroy entire plants and expressing gratitude each time they cut.

The people I was with on this occasion were mostly Ojibwe or Lakota, with a couple of Euro-Americans. Apart from myself, this was primarily a Roman Catholic Christian event. In the preceding church service, tobacco smoke and water were included in blessings and purifications, and the otherwise unexceptional Mass included prayers for sun-dancers and other "traditional" ceremonialists. When we returned to the church, the new cut sage was to be dried and some of it made into small bundles to be hung around the sweat-lodge style framework that served as the place for the sacramental bread/body and wine/blood to be housed between services.

I note this complex of events and the fact of these people's religious affiliation to point out that, as is true elsewhere among indigenous people, these Native Americans seek to live well in the world and to maintain "tradition", to some degree at least, as well as to honour traditions and knowledges originating elsewhere. The accommodative habit of animism and the syncretic habit of Catholicism seem to have fused here. Here they may address a

133

transcendent deity, they may believe in other-than-natural miracles, but they also request the help of ordinary, natural, proximate but powerful other-than-human persons in their efforts to live good lives. Like the eagle at the Conne River powwow, it is not only humans who are expected to participate in religion or to encourage others to live well. Accounts of respectful acts of inter-relationship between aboriginal North Americans and birds and plants help us redefine religion.

8. Things full of meaning

A stroll through any Yoruba town will reveal the highly public presence of religions. As noted in Chapter 2, many of the shops in Abeokuta in southwestern Nigeria display their owners' affiliations in names like a "Holy Family" bookshop or "God is Great" photographic shop. Several shrines – especially that of the orisa Igun, maintained by a group of priestesses – are located in caves or overhangs under Abeokuta's Olumo Rock (comparable to Stonehenge and the Vatican as a fusion of heritage, sacred and tourist site). Christian and Islamic groups are represented within this religious built environment not only by churches and mosques but also by schools, clubs and the offices of charitable institutions that declare their affiliations. Then, as Afe Adogame points out:

> It is not uncommon for a casual observer walking on the streets of a traditional Yoruba town or village to confront certain objects such as cooked or raw food, a decapitated bird or animal, eggs, cowry shells, coins, candles, etc., in a clay bowl or pot, conspicuously displayed at a road junction, road intersection, or at the foot of a gigantic Iroko tree. (Adogame 2009: 75)

He identifies these as offerings or sacrifices, ritually offered to avert calamity, request help, fulfil vows, and/or ensure cosmic balance and social cohesion.

Quite what this diversity of religious presence and practice means requires careful consideration. A number of people in Nigeria told me that commonly cited national statistics for religious affiliation are misleading. At least in part this is because religions are treated (everywhere, not only in Nigeria) as monolithic blocks with secure boundaries and known effects on people's behaviours.

This, in turn, follows from defining religions by the imaginations or preferences of elites, codified in rhetorics and writings. So the statistics quoted in Chapter 2 that contest whether ten per cent or ninety per cent of Nigerians are adherents of "traditional African religions" rely on contrasting notions of religions. If people can only be members of one monolithic and securely bounded identity group, then Nigerians must be Muslim, Christian or traditionalist. On the other hand, if religions have porous boundaries at best, and if people can participate fluidly in seemingly distinct practices with degrees of ease, then Nigerians can be Muslim, Christian and traditionalist at the same time. Indeed, they are likely to transgress the religion/secular boundary too and perform their lives in much more complex and interesting ways than these labels seem to require.

While various censuses count the self-identifications and declared affiliations of a population, they fail (as they generally do everywhere) to account for multiple memberships and fluid practices. What the "ninety percent" statistic indicates is that although an Abeokuta shop-front may declare the owners to be Christian, Muslim or (seemingly less commonly here, but somewhat more commonly in places like Ile Ife) "traditional", somewhere within the shop there are likely to be protective amulets or signs that indicate recourse to putatively different religions. In response to my questions about the dynamics indicated by these practices, I was told that when confronted with illness, job loss or other difficulties, any Nigerian would probably visit a leader within the religion of their most immediate affiliation. If prayers or offerings within that tradition or community seem ineffective, the needy person will seek help or support from the next leader, ritual practice or amulet maker that they hope will be useful. Christians and Muslims resort to one or more of the various divination experts of traditional culture.

Meanwhile, "traditionalists" are not only willing to seek the support of the Christian or Muslim deity or saints, they have also adapted their ritual practices to match the increasingly popular "Pentecostalist" style of service. A pragmatic philosophy that encourages the adoption, accommodation and/or adaptation of whatever seems helpful is definitive of what Harry Garuba (2003) defines as "animist materialism". This will be the chief focus and contribution of this chapter: the contribution of contemporary African religioning to the attempt, made necessary by an unwarranted focus on interiority and transcendence, to redefine "religion" with reference to matter and mattering.

As a further illustration of the kind of thing (or mesh of interacting acts) which I seek to bring from "elsewhere" into this conversation about defining religion, allow me to allude to some uncertainities during my fieldwork in Nigeria. In the Yoruba city of Ibadan, I was taken to visit Esu. I had seen Eshu dancing in Havana, Cuba, and I had read about Exu in Brazilian Candomblé rituals, but I was not at all sure what to expect of this meeting. My host and guide while I was in Ibadan, told me that this Esu is the oldest one and that a house had been built for him. I wondered what a Yoruba deity looks like when they are not incarnated in a human dancer. Then other questions occurred to me: What kind of house does a deity want? What is the appropriate behaviour here for meeting this deity? What is expected of academic researchers visiting deities? What does it mean to say "this Esu"? If there is more than one, how many are there? How should I explain my research interests both to Esu and to his devotees, if that's the correct term?

How many mistakes can be made in writing about Esu? Never mind that I have just typed three spellings of the name Esu (as it is written in Nigeria); I have just called Eshu a "deity" rather than an "orisa" (or its variant spellings). Is this correct? Does it suggest a similarity between orisas and deities which, in turn, misleadingly suggests that I know what "deity" means? What kind of taxonomy do these beings belong in? Are they transcendent, supernatural, non-empirical? Or are they something else, something more everyday, local, and/or material? Perhaps what will concern some readers more than these worries about classification is that I have not used words like "representation" in relation to these beings. Some might ask whether it is good religious grammar and/or good scholarship to say that I have seen an orisa at home in Ibadan and dancing in Cuba rather than that I have seen symbols or representations of orisas. The resolution of my various uncertainties about Esu (and other orisas whose presence I found myself in) revolves around a strengthening of the certainty that "representation" and "symbol" are indeed the wrong words. They encourage a wrong approach, a misunderstanding and a misrepresentation of important matters concerning not only Yoruba religions but all religions. Thus, the justification of this chapter is the mattering of religion and its ambition is to present ways in which Yoruba religioning contributes to the "material turn" in our discipline.

ANIMIST MATERIALISM

In discussing what may appear to be "merely ... extended metaphors" in African and African diaspora literature, Garuba demonstrates the great value of paying attention to "animistic aspects" and "material details" (Garuba 2003: 274). He means far more than that if we attend to such matters we will gain a better understanding of African novels. His article is about African culture, society, modernism and postcolonialism. An animism vitalizes and/or is mediated within these varied domains, but does not (necessarily) conflict with modernization. It is an animism in which concepts or ideas have material form, expression or phenomenal implications. They are things or even actors. The literary and ritual forms of "animist materialism" are aspects of something so pervasive that Garuba identifies it as resolving an uncertainty in understanding Africa. He cites Patrick Chabal's statement that "There is undoubtedly something going on in Africa but ... we (outsiders) are uncertain what it is and, especially, what it means" (Chabal 1996: 32, cited in Garuba 2003: 265).

"What it is", according to Garuba, is "continual re-enchantment of the world" or a culturally pervasive and deliberately performed animism. (Perhaps it needs saying that, as in earlier chapters, this "animism" is not that of Tylor and colonial "progressive" and "intellectualist" anthropology. Neither is this an attribution of any kind of primitivism.)

Among the literary examples cited by Garuba are the opening of Wole Soyinka's *The Interpreters*, "Metal on concrete jars my drink lobes" (Soyinka 1970: 7), and the episode in Toni Morrison's *Beloved* concerning Paul D having "a tobacco tin lodged in his chest", tightly sealing in the memories of his slavery experience until it is explosively opened in response to Sethe's horrors (T. Morrison 1987: 113). It is this last example that leads Garuba to write that "It is tempting to see this merely as an extended metaphor, but we need to pay attention to the concentration on the animistic aspect of its realization and note the careful rendering of the 'material' details" (Garuba 2003: 274). This, he argues, is more than the "magical realism" of Latin American and other literatures. It requires the employment of the term "animist realism" as a description of "this predominant cultural practice of according a physical, often animate material aspect to what others may consider an abstract idea" (*ibid.*). Concepts are not (merely) mental abstractions but materially, physically affective actors in social situations.

Garuba writes not only of literature, but also attends to the animist materialism and "continual re-enchantment" of postcolonial African political and social domains. His article begins with an evocative description of a "larger-than-life statue of Sango, the Yoruba god of lightning, clad in his traditional outfit, presiding, as it were, over the offices of the major power generation and distribution corporation of the country" (*ibid.*: 261).

A variety of other elements of social, political, economic, material and performance culture which utilize "traditional" themes and motifs are engaged in the article. Garuba's point is not merely that "tradition" survives in modern postcolonial Nigeria. That would be almost uninteresting. That more is at stake is indicated by the fact that the "Sango statue was particularly meaningful to the new 'educated' leaders who were supposedly alienated from their traditions by their Western education" (*ibid.*: 262). This Sango symbolizes a meeting point between "tradition" and "modernity". The new elites stand at that same intersection as they seek to "bolster their authority and legitimacy" by manipulating pervasive animist tendencies. Meanwhile, even as traditional elites maintain their position "by incorporating the instruments of modernity into traditional ritual practices ... an animistic understanding of the world applied to the practice of everyday life has often provided avenues of agency for the dispossessed in colonial and postcolonial Africa" (*ibid.*: 285).

Thus, a wide range of Nigerians fuse elements of "traditional culture" into their particular, plural and evolving forms of "modernity". Despite some modernist rhetorics of "progress", there has been no linear process which has made "tradition" something of the past, obsolete or superseded, while "modernity" emerged as an anticipation of a globally unified future. In contrast, Garuba claims that:

> Animist culture thus opens up a whole new world of poaching possibilities, *prepossessing the future*, as it were, by laying claim to what in the present is yet to be invented. It is on account of this ability to prepossess the future that continual re-enchantment becomes possible. (*Ibid.*: 271; emphasis original)

This is not a resistance by a putative primitivism towards a singular modernity, but an illustration of the paradoxical situation that while there are many modernities, "we have never been modern" (Latour 1993). Disenchantment is rarely complete – only some institutions and some individuals have successfully persuaded themselves of their separation from the relational world.

Within that context of multiple modernities, none of which securely banish enchantment, Garuba's article invaluably makes present to us the dynamics of West African animist materialism in many social and cultural domains. He points to "The 'locking' of spirit within matter or the merger of the material and the metaphorical, which animist logic entails, then appears to be reproduced in the cultural practices of the society" (Garuba 2003: 267).

Knowing that this may sound like a capitulation to or reinsertion of an alien (European-derived) dualism, he offers a note here: "It is important at this stage to note that the mind/body dualism that appears to run through this essay is highlighted only to foreground it as a metaphysics and an epistemology that animist thought rejects" (*ibid.*: 267).

Garuba is wise, then, to make so much of African and African diaspora literature. Although his article begins with an orisa, Sango, it is not so much "religion" (as usually conceived) but economics, politics or society that is in focus. The device of the metaphor is enabled to contribute significantly to our rethinking (not only about religion but also about literature, discourse and power) because Garuba is clear about materiality. Thus, regarding Soyinka's previously quoted sentence, "Metal on concrete jars my drink lobes" (Soyinka 1970: 7), Garuba writes: "The idea of an imploring calabash in somebody's stomach intrigued me for a long while until I came to understand that this *materialization* of ideas, this habit of giving a concrete dimension to abstract ideas was a normal practice within the culture" (Garuba 2003: 273). Religion, like literature, and not only in or from Africa, might make more sense if we follow this lead and attend to the materialization of religion too.

MAKING DEITIES

I have seen deities in their homes. I have learnt how to prostrate in the presence of deities. I have learnt how to offer things when seeking guidance from deities. I have seen (but not really understood) how deities use things to communicate to humans. A visit of only a few weeks in the Yoruba homeland can be profoundly educative. It would be untrue to suggest that I was unfamiliar with material deities, object persons or venerated things. I have, after all, lived and researched among Pagans for many years. Similarly, I have visited Shinto shrines, Buddhist temples, Catholic churches, Maori *wharenui*, Hindu mandirs and many other places where statues, carvings and other things are honoured. Even reading scholarly books has reinforced the lesson that things are not always rightly treated as inert receptacles of human meaning-making (see Latour & Weibel 2005; Henare *et al.* 2007; Latour 2010; Ingold 2011; Spretnak 2011; Whitehead 2012).

Nonetheless, not only do researchers need to learn locally appropriate ways of acting in the presence of other people's deities, saints or teachers, we also need to learn new languages for conceptualizing and conveying significant matters. Therefore, in previous chapters I have considered the value of words like mana, taboo and totem for revisiting data about religions and for retheorizing religion. Some "–isms" that might help or hinder our scholarly project have been encountered, such as dualism, hyperseparatism, Cartesianism, Buddhism, Catholicism, Judaism and Protestantism. Animism has been a focus of attention in several chapters. The contribution of "totem-ism" as a way of understanding animist relationships was a theme of the previous chapter, while this one, guided by Garuba, has advanced considera-tion of animist materialism and the dynamic tension between modernism(s) and traditionalism(s). Now it is time to attend to another contested "-ism": fetishism.

Unlike the terms mana, taboo and totem, "fetish" is not drawn from within the complex linguistic cultures of indigenous peoples but from a European language. Conversely, just like the terms mana, taboo and totem, "fetish" is drawn from relational encounters between people with significant differences from one another (Johnson 2000: 247). Among the various mat-ters that could have attracted the attention of fifteenth-century Portuguese merchants in west Africa (particularly in what is now Ghana), it seems to have been the made nature of venerated objects that inspired them to create a new word.

"Fetish" derives from *feitiço*, "to do" or "to make", and is part of a fertile semantic field that has produced words like artefact, fabricate, factory, fact, fixation, obsession, artificial and form. That is, "fetish" emphasizes the artifi-cially and artefactuality of things. Initially at least, "fetish" was used to refer to made rather than found things: to cultural construction rather than natu-ral occurrence. Perhaps little has changed in the obsessions of the modern (European-originated) academy in which the constructed nature of this, that or another cultural item or act is tediously asserted to no-one's edification or enlightenment. Conversely, the endless repetition lulls us into accepting that a duality of nature and culture is and ought to be generative and taxonomic. Despite this, "fetish" has long escaped these policed zones and labelled all manner of physical and material stuff, only needing someone to act with desire towards them. Even the invention of the term "fetishism" signalled that escape as Charles de Brosses, who coined "*fetichisme*" in 1760, somehow managed to associate it not with construction but with "fate" and "the fey" (de Brosses 1970; see also Latour 2010: 3).

Scholarly and popular uses of "fetish" and "fetishism" have been accessi-bly, admirably and provocatively traced by authors as various as Pietz (1985, 1987, 1988), Hornborg (1992, 2013), Pels (1998), Johnson (2000), Latour

141

(2010), Masuzawa (2000), Whitehead (2012, 2013) and Olsson (2013). Among other things, this wide-ranging literature demonstrates that relationships with and imagination (or fear, loathing, desire and obsession) about materiality are vital components of the evolution and performance of modernity. In its engagement with or assault on its "others", modernity's ideologues and troops have made it difficult to understand assemblages of things and assembled things.

For example, in Latour's (2010) imagined conversation between an African "fetishist" and a European "anti-fetishist", the problematic imputation of "belief" to the former and arrogation of "knowledge" by the latter is clearly set out. The European interlocutor is prevented from understanding how someone else can both make and venerate an object, indeed how precisely the making of an object is deemed sufficient cause for its veneration. Things, as imagined by Europeans of many eras, seem to require humans to impute or attribute meaning to them. Things have to be symbols or representations in order to be anything but inert "natural" substance. This in turn, however, is not a "natural" inclination but arises from the varied efforts of and aggressions between different kinds of Europeans about matter (e.g. statues). In all of this, the promulgation of separations between nature and culture, given and made, faith and fact, objects and ideas, resonate (but not harmoniously) together.

Garuba's article points a way beyond the impasse of this conflictual history, but requires us to remember his warning against reading dualism in his words:

> Perhaps the single, most important characteristic of animist thought … is its almost total refusal to countenance unlocalized, unembodied, unphysicalized gods and spirits. Animism is often simply seen as belief in objects such as stones or trees or rivers for the simple reason that animist gods and spirits are *located* and *embodied* in objects: the objects are the physical and material manifestations of the gods and spirits. Instead of erecting graven images to symbolize the spiritual being, animist thought spiritualizes the object world, thereby giving the spirit a local habitation   (Garuba 2003: 267)

If, as he goes on to say, objects such as rivers gain "a social and spiritual meaning within the culture far in excess of their natural properties and their use value", then we might add that made-objects ("fetishes") take on increased significance as relational actors within ever-ramifying webs of relations. Thus, to understand what happens in Africa when people make deities and houses for deities, and seek their protection by making offerings and talismans, we need to heed Johnson's reminder that "the fetish is a fluid, mediating term, an idea about objects, not an object itself – a mode of action, 'to fetish'" (Johnson 2000: 260). This expands his argument that:

> Fetish may be best viewed as a mode of action rather than a kind of object itself. It is a condensation of social powers onto an object in order to reconfigure them. "To fetish" would therefore be more apt than "fetish." Viewed in this broad sense, it is a structuring technique of human consciousness in time, not an evolutionary stage of the false attribution of power to objects, a stage now surpassed. (*Ibid.*: 249)

It is neither "surpassed" nor "other" because it is among "us" since we are wearers of wedding rings, carriers of photos and collectors of memorabilia.

In many Yoruba places, there is no need to have faith to see deities. They are made present in things and dancers. They are housed in shelters but also in flesh. They act with those who prostrate and those who seek guidance (even if somewhat surreptitiously because sometimes the boundaries between religions are policed). So although I have devoted attention to the orisas in physical form (not fully explaining how they look, only saying that they are recognizable, tactile, present, mattering), and although I have devoted attention to reclaiming "fetish" for academic purposes, only now can I get to important matter of definitive Yoruba religious acts: divination and sacrifice.

DIVINING AND DEFINING

I have noted that deities are venerated, and this is not wrong but neither is it the primary way in which humans engage with deities. Or perhaps it would be more accurate to say that veneration often precedes and follows more significant acts in which people make requests and respond to divine instruction. In West Africa and its diaspora, the former of these is most often conducted by means of divination while the latter generally involves sacrifice.

A number of systems of divination have been experimentally developed among the Yoruba and their neighbours. For the purposes of bringing matters from "elsewhere" into dialogue with what we think defines "religion", I do not propose to describe in detail any of these (or the myriad other global possibilities). A short statement about what divination can look like will be sufficient, but those who want more depth should see Curry (2010), Holbraad (2007, 2008, 2010) and de Aquino (2005), and follow their leads.

In Ibadan I was taken to visit a *babalawo* (diviner in the Ifá system) in his consulting room. In Osogbo I was invited to approach diviners at both the forest and town shrines of the goddess Osun. I attended services which included divination at temples in several places. From what I have heard and read, what I experienced and observed is similar to what happens throughout West Africa and its diasporas. (That it may be similar to what happens in many other locations and among many other communities is important to its use for theorizing, but so too are the specificities and differences. I make no claim here to cover all forms of divination, even among the Yoruba.)

Divination may be said to begin when initial introductions and general chattiness fade into a more focused attention on the business in hand, and a serious atmosphere is developed. The specific encounter between humans (diviner and client) and orisas becomes the only matter of interest. People take turns to prostrate in front of the orisas. Most of the latter, in these contexts at least, are housed in decorated bowls and covered in the dried palm oil and other offerings that have been poured over them. Even when more figurative or representational artwork is used, these are "not taken to 'represent' the deity, but rather to *be* it, and are hence fed with blood [and palm oil, and other substances], spoken to and generally taken care of in ritual contexts" (Holbraad 2007: 203). After some further suitable preparation, such as words addressed to the relevant orisa, the divination proper takes place.

For instance, in several places I was instructed to address a question directly to a whole kola nut, wrap some money around it as an offering, and hand this package to the diviner. The diviner would place the money near to the *orisa*, divide the nut into quarters, and cast these onto a mat, cloth or tray. The parts fell in different positions (e.g. making their outside or inside more prominent) and the diviner examined the resulting pattern, and delivered a message in response to the query.

This is obviously a simple summary, but it should convey something of the flavour of divinatory events. Other uses of kola nuts, cowry shells, divining chains and/or powder, and the knowledge of the *odu* (256 possible configurations of the divining objects, each associated with a particular poetic stanza or story) may be more complex but are recognizably part of the same repertoire. Deities speak through objects. Meanings are recognized in what some others might interpret as random events. (Note that "randomness" is as much an interpretation as "there is meaning here",

THINGS FULL OF MEANING

both notions arise from cultural training.) Some diviners spend years learning the craft, being shaped so that the deity can work through them. Afe Adogame (2009: 80) indicates that diviners are consulted for all manner of situations. In addition to those who approach diviners about life crises and transitions, decisions and worries, I have been told that politicians regularly consult diviners, e.g., about the success of their election campaigns. However, more is involved. Adogame approves of Kamari Clarke's assertion that "Divination represents the central organizing mechanism through which the world of Yoruba practitioners is understood" (K. M. Clarke 2004: 20, cited by Adogame 2009: 80). So, it is not only advice that people seek, and not choices that they are offered.

In a powerful critique of "attempts, no matter how ingenious, to accommodate divination without any significant changes in what 'we' already 'know' … describing and adjusting conditions of native error (regardless of who the natives are)", Patrick Curry (2010: 6) encourages us to move beyond the "you believe/we know" duality. Instead of imagining ourselves as already expert enough about the world (i.e. the reality which "believers" falsely interpret), we are invited to join in an unstable and exciting project of seeking understanding that challenges and enriches knowledge by taking the tested experiments of "others" seriously. This, you will recognize, is another way of challenging the "belief in belief and believers" which forms a significant part of our discipline's general misunderstanding of religion as "belief-systems" and of those who do religion as "believers". Hopefully, bringing matters from "elsewhere" into the debate should be more effectively educative than "explaining away".

Martin Holbraad advances Curry's argument:

> Hence, from the practitioner's point of view, to wonder why people might "believe" that divinatory verdicts are true is just to misunderstand what divination is – a misunderstanding equivalent to wondering why children in Britain "believe" that 4 is a number, or, later, when they become of marrying age, why they "believe" that bachelors are unmarried men.　　　　　　　　　　(Holbraad 2010: 269)

If the knowledge that "bachelor" is a definitive term for an "unmarried man" is not about belief, neither is the knowledge that "divination" is "communication from deities to humans" about belief. At the very least, to make these things "beliefs" (and thus automatically to contrast them with "what we know") does not help us understand them or their use any more clearly.

How, then, should we define "divination" if not as "the curious ways in which other people believe they can get advice"? Holbraad provides a necessary clarification here. To approach a diviner is not like seeking advice from a friend. Divination does not result in advice that one might chose to accept or ignore ("try this and you will succeed") but in the shaping of the world, such that one must act. Engagement in divination (by those who approach diviners as much as by the diviners and deities) is a process of definition, of defining. By asking a deity a question through a diviner I am defined in relation to that deity, that diviner, that act of divination. I will be further defined by following through on the deity's edict spoken in the falling of kola nuts. Divination does not only suggest possibilities and solutions for contemplation and consideration, it defines. It tells the enquirer who they are, what the problem is, and what must be done. Divination casts the enquirer as a person *who is* (e.g. an enquirer, worried, sick, needy, intrigued, related) and a person *who ought* (e.g. to work, to study, to leave, to devote); "Thus construed, divinations are true, precisely, *by definition* (since they just *are* definitions), and are therefore indeed indubitable, much like analytical truths such as 'bachelors are unmarried men'" (Holbraad 2010: 274; emphasis original). Divinatory diagnosis and remedies carry obligations because they are part of the continuing process of creation (implying all that might be considered cosmic and social, natural and cultural – though, once more, since these should be taken to refer to a single reality: a pervasively personal, social or relational cosmos).

It seems possible that Yoruba divination *could* be treated as a psychotherapeutic or self-help technique. Just as ceremonies in many religions across west Africa have adopted a broadly "Pentecostalist" flavour (illustrated in singing and preaching styles, "temple" layouts, excitation and authority patterns), possibly divination could be treated as advice not definition. When Christians, Muslims and academic researchers consult diviners, are they defined in the same strong way that Ifá devotees are? I think we must answer affirmatively. Christians, Muslims and researchers are defined in the act of approaching diviners. They are people who, not ignoring their other affiliations, epistemologies and ontologies, deem it useful (for whatever reason) to approach diviners and their deities. The world is made in such a way that "Christian" can function as an identification for someone who might ask an orisa, through a diviner and through cowry shells, for instruction and/or remedies for their situations. "Religion", then, must be defined as performance, embodiment, materiality, and as fluid, accommodative and permeable. It might be the definitive role of some religious leaders, and of some structuring systems (such as *tabu* and *kashrut*) to construct and then to police borders. But it is the necessary permeability of boundaries, the everyday fact of their transgression, that is more truly definitive of lived religion than any elite (academic) imagination of fixed and secure boundaries between, say, "Christianity" and "Yoruba traditional religion". This certainly seems true not only of religion among the Yoruba but, like the materialization of ideas discussed by Garuba, seems pervasive in all parts of the culture. Thus, a sign on a clothing store in Ile Ife (the heartland of Ifá divination) reads, "Highest Fashion at the lowest prices. Men. Ladies. Children. Define Yourself."

SACRIFICE, OFFERING, GIFT AND RESTRAINT

According to Adogame, "In almost every case, divination ends in the prescription of sacrifice". This follows from his summary statement that:

> Sacrifice may be enacted during individual rites, family feasts, or communal festivals and is usually partaken of first by the divinities or ancestors and then by the individual, family, or community of worshippers. Thanksgiving, communion, votive, propitiatory, preventive, substitution, and foundation rites characterize virtually all indigenous African religions. Through divination, an individual finds out what type of sacrifice will ensure that a predicted good fortune will actually come to pass or, alternatively, mitigate the worst effects of a predicted bad fortune. (Adogame 2009: 78)

The statement that different forms of sacrificial rite "characterize virtually all indigenous African religions" indicates that a key component of any definition of "religion" that might perform useful work in relation to African religions must include sacrifice. As with other religious technical terms that have become academic critical terms, the danger exists that the protocols and programmes of one religion may be taken to define those of other or all religions. Whether "sacrifice" should be defined everywhere in relation to words like "sacred" is problematic, especially when that word, in turn, is taken to indicate transcendence of some kind.

Perhaps the seemingly less technical "offering" or "gift" carries less baggage. Or, rather, there being a significant literature on "gift" that expands from the work of Marcel Mauss ([1923–4] 1954), perhaps these words carry

147

a different baggage. Nonetheless, the crucial point is that, whatever word we chose to refer to this array or diversity of acts, human relations with the larger-than-human world often include giving and receiving (sometimes reciprocally). Sometimes a life is taken with the intention that it, or the previously living being's blood or flesh, should be given to another being. Sometimes objects are offered, and they too might be broken or damaged so as to remove them from circulation among humans. However the act of offering is undertaken, the intention might generally be considered to be the increase of intimacy or healthy relationships.

Acts of offering take place in the wider context of social systems in which a dynamic balance of restraint and consumption is negotiated. Where deities or ancestors are thought to require all of that which humans offer them, those who make the offer may give up their own ability to consume. Not everything is available or permitted for humans. However, the kind of sacrificial acts that Adogame calls "communion" include shared acts of consumption. Religion might definitively include this blend of "giving up" (restraint) and "giving out" (sharing). The extreme case of child sacrifice (evidenced in some archaeological sites and religious texts) illustrates a more general sense that what is deemed acceptable as an offering might be sacrificial in the sense of "giving up something vital, something without which life is less tenable or pleasant" (see Levenson 1993). If there is any room for the discourse of "faith" in studies of religion, it might be in relation to the hope that the recipient of such extreme acts will respond with exceptional generosity and recompense. This is to echo Ruel's (1997) insistence that "belief" (in religious discourse) is a synonym of "trust", a relational term, rather than an antonym of "knowledge". All of this might be to say that acts of sacrifice materialize the possibilities inherent in relationships. Like divination, they are mechanisms by which imagined outcomes are worked towards and intimacy is enhanced.

PREPOSSESSING DEITIES

Somewhat playfully (because he is clear that animism is far from a systematized belief-system), Garuba sums up the "basic creed of animist belief" as being "made up of two basic tenets. One, that things possess a life of their own and, two, that when their souls are awakened their breath is freed and may migrate into other objects" (Garuba 2003: 272). If things are alive and possess some element that is able to "migrate" this is because all persons (human or

148

other than human, thing or being) are capable of acting in this way. The orisas might be conceived of as supremely skilled in relocating at least aspects of themselves in other persons or material forms. For brevity's sake, this might be labelled "possession" – another term undergoing critical revisitation (e.g. Schmidt & Huskinson 2010; Johnson 2002a, 2013).

There are religions in which the official teaching is that deities cannot be seen or touched. They are, however, almost always contradicted in real life when practitioners engage with persons (priests, diviners, mediums) and things (statues, drums, relics, staffs, stools and other "made things" or fetishes) as audible, tactile, visible, consumable, and otherwise material divinities. To ease the difficulty of the juxtaposition of imagined transcendence and intimate immanence, the idea of representation or manifestation may be discursively employed. The priest holding a food item and speaking significant words is supposed to stand, speak or act for or otherwise represent a deity or ancestor. The statue or musical instrument is supposed to symbolize the real presence of the invisible or inaudible other. But these interposed mediums are so often treated as less important than the beings that they allegedly allow to become manifest that they transgress neat distinctions and separations. In lived reality, some humans and things do not merely act *for* but act *as* their deities. Simultaneously, some deities sometimes "migrate into" persons and objects through whom they act. Concealment and revelation combine in what Michael Taussig (1998: 359) identifies as "the performance of hiddenness", illustrated by initiation, healing, sorcery and, supremely, by possession.

In the Yoruba Cultural Center in Havana, Cuba, tourists and conference delegates can be treated to the performance of traditional drum and dance acts modelled on orisha trance dances. That the dancers and the orishas sometimes fuse so that a cultural excursion becomes more like an audience, séance or initiatory encounter, shows that "make believe" sometimes trips up the playful "suspension of disbelief" and creates a new reality. That this is always a possibility is revealed elsewhere in the building. Traces of regular devotion are evident in offerings laid in front of museum-like displays of the orishas (or *santos* since they are fused with Catholic saints in the various Cuban Creole religions – see Fernández Olmos & Paravisini-Gebert 2003). Indeed, it seems likely that mats are provided for those devotees who wish to prostrate before those they venerate. Beyond the permeable and transgressed boundaries of the Cultural Center, similar dances and statue devotion occur in homes and churches throughout the city and throughout Cuba, the Caribbean and the African diaspora.

Deities materialize in the physical spaces and embodiment of their devotees and, especially dramatically, in the bodies of the initiates they "possess". An understanding of African-originated religions points to the value of considering how matter (places, objects and persons) is "spiritualized" in two contradictory senses. In too many studies of religion, matter is objectified, assumed to be inert, and only allowed to symbolize or represent something deemed properly invisible. "Spiritual" here is definitively glossed as "non-physical" or "non-empirical".

Thus, religion is metaphorical, a device for revealing interiorities. However, in an alternative move which resists both dualism and its inherent separatism, matter *is* spiritual in the sense that what appear to be metaphors and symbols are the necessarily localized and embodied vitalities. It is difficult to speak or write about this, in large part as a corollary of the difficulty even Roman Catholic Christians have, after the European Reformations and Wars of state-making, with the liturgical phrase, "this is my body". They, and Protestant Christians even more so, tend to interpose additional words or thoughts, emphasizing the spiritual (transcendent) nature of "this" and its priority over the mere matter of bodies or bread. Nonetheless, even the majority of Protestant Christians have not stopped consuming the bread in their rituals. They might be at one end of a continuum from their neighbours who gladly and passionately venerate "made-things", but it remains a single continuum. Religion, not only in Africa, is a matter of things and relations, substances and meetings, bodies and movements. Possession is not an aberration in which (paradoxically) matter overwhelms spirit, but it reveals the pervasive performance of religion and its deities, ancestors and spirits as bodies and things. Deities and religion are prepossessing, attractive, and seductive not as escapes from reality but as engagements with its most mundane elements: the need for health, happiness and other goods.

VISITING ESU, MATERIALIZING RELIGION

In Ibadan, the shrine guardian considered my request to take a photograph of Esu, and said "yes, first we'll sacrifice a goat". I decided that a goat's life was more valuable than a photo, and that sacrifices should be for more important matters than photography. The shrine guardian seemed unperturbed and even uninterested. Sacrifice rather than photography would have indicated that I wished to seek a more intimate relationship with Esu or other orisas. Instead, I had clearly stepped back and become a passer-by who imagined that Esu's abilities were not needed. However, my failure to relate appropriately (in the terms expected by Esu's shrine guardian and devotees) has led me to reflect on those expectations and experiences. Rereading the work of colleagues involved in the reconsideration of animism, fetishism, divination and gifting has reshaped my understanding of the materiality of religion. It is not only that materiality, things, are used by people in religious acts. It is no longer of interest that some scholars interpret the primary significance of the use of things to be the expression of belief. We have moved on. We have found that religion matters. Is it a materialist pursuit.

Yoruba religionists may affiliate with named religions but few of them live as if their religion was a set of ideas walled off from other aspects of their lives. They resist the apparent transparency of statistics by adopting, adapting and accommodating the putative elements of "other" religions into the experiment of their living. They seek definition by relationship with powerful but not necessarily transcendent others. Their relationships are empowered by gift exchange, by restraint in some circumstance and the ecstasy of excess in others. In this chapter, particularly following the lead of Garuba, Holbraad, Olsson and Curry, I have explored the materialization of ideas in African religions. The conclusion that there is no necessary separation between concepts (metaphors, interpretations, teachings, divinations, deities) and matter is required.

As Holbraad concludes in relation to the power which is powder or the powder which is power in Cuban Ifá divination, "All it takes is to stop thinking of concepts and things as self-identical entities, and start imagining them as self-differential motions" (Holbraad 2007: 218–19). If for a moment we allow ideas and things to be separate, just as Garuba temporarily allowed matter and spirit to seem separate in his writing but not, finally, in his analysis, then we might conclude that the practised and ingrained habit of separating and atomizing each and every idea or thing hinders our efforts to understand, theorize and define. We who have allowed ourselves to adopt the habits of separatism and atomism, rather than those among whom we research, have created problems for ourselves. If instead we revise our perspectives, approaches and imaginations, we might understand not only the animist materialism of contemporary African and diaspora cultures, but also the (still not entirely, despite considerable effort) modern culture of academia. That, in turn, may enable us to reach a better understanding of the performative and materialist nature of religions.

9. Purity and pilgrimages

What facets of life are indicated to Jews when, talking to one another or addressing others, they use the word "Judaism"? What is the relation between that and the word "religion"? If "religion" (the term) had originated among Jews, to what kind of acts would it refer? What words in Jewish religious discourse (whether in Hebrew, Yiddish, English or any other language) are used for similar purposes when Jews talk with Jews?

It is commonly stated in books introducing Judaism that this is a religion of observance, encouraging orthopraxis more than orthodoxy, and best seen in everyday acts such as keeping meat and milk separate in meals. Judaism is a religion for living today; its concerns are not with immortality. Its questions are about human living and it insistently focuses attention on bodies, movement, materials and relationships. Its leadership models generally encourage facilitators rather than unquestionable authorities. It ought then to be the perfect model for any argument about vernacular, lived, material, performative religion.

I have no intention of contradicting that claim. Rather, I intend to emphasize it by arguing that Judaism is definitively religion in ways that Protestant Christianity is not. I will acknowledge that Judaism has its Protestantism/modernism too, but even that is affected by the gravitational pull of a well-established performative tradition. For most of this chapter, however, I want to go elsewhere. This is not to negate a prevalent or textbook view of Jews and Judaism but to say something about one popular Jewish event which both confirms and complicates common (re)presentations of Judaism. By visiting one Jewish event, I initiate a consideration of Judaism as a way of forming habits of behaviour deemed appropriate to a community. Following some descriptive introduction, further sections will discuss the text-reading and food-traditions that are utilized by Jews as they pass habits of disciplined life, observance, from one generation to the next.

RABBI SHIMON'S *HILLULA*

Picking a place that might be recognizable (by name at least) to many people, this visit "elsewhere" begins near the Sea of Galilee (*Yam Kinneret* or *Bahrat Tabariye*). The town of Tiberias stands on the lake's western shore and has been a significant venue for religious activities by members of different religions for millennia. It has been an important place of Jewish learning and study, attracting many leading rabbis over the centuries. Maimonides, the great twelfth-century philosopher and codifier of Jewish law, is buried here. We won't linger; this is really just a geographical orientation. However, a number of significant things are obvious even to the most casual visitor to the cemetery.

The tomb of Maimonides and those of several other important rabbis are the focus of considerable attention. People come to pray at the tombs. Signs clearly point women and men to different sides of a large screen so that they can perform their prayers and other liturgical acts separately. The entrance lobby to the otherwise open air cemetery contains pictures of the deceased rabbis. People touch the actual tombs as they pray. I keep saying "pray" here, but that word might normally indicate "talking to god" in Judaism. Officially, Jewish authorities vehemently reject the idea that someone might ask a deceased rabbi to intercede on their behalf, to carry prayers to god, or to act to the supplicant's benefit in some practical or spiritual matter. But this clearly happens at these tombs. This is already an aspect of Judaism that gets little if any coverage in most books about Jews and Judaism.

About twenty kilometres north-northeast of Tiberias is the small village of Meron. It is on the lowest slopes of mount Meron and near the larger town of Zefat – which is internationally famous for its association with Jewish mysticism. Meron, however, is the focus of an annual event in which many thousands of Orthodox Jews make pilgrimage to the tomb of another rabbi. Rabbi Shimon bar Yohai died and was buried at Meron during the Roman occupation of Palestine. He is claimed to be the composer of the Jewish mystical text, *The Zohar*, although historical and literary evidence makes it clear that this is a much later work (i.e. about a thousand years later). Regardless of that (and momentarily adopting acceptance of that understanding), the revelation of divine mysteries to and through him, as recorded in *The Zohar*, inspires many people to celebrate at Meron.

For at least a week before the main night and day of the festival or memorial celebration (both good translations of *hillula*) pilgrims arrive and pitch tents all around the village. Internet searches provide varying estimates of the numbers attending in any year – certainly, though, a small village rapidly becomes a small city. In recent years, pilgrims' attempts to reach Meron have caused traffic jams all across the country. These journeys might be mere adjuncts to the celebrations and transformations that occur in Meron itself, nonetheless considerable effort is expended in getting there and getting back, and these journeys may entail various forms of preparation for actually being there. (I say this because "pilgrimage" can be defined as a journey, as getting somewhere, as being elsewhere for a significant event, as going and returning from somewhere significant, or as circulating among significant locations, usually with defined purposes in addition to "being there" – see Pye 1993, 2010.)

My own experience of visiting the *hillula* at Meron in 2008 entailed some moments in which I felt that I was part of the flow and drama of the main night's events. But there were longer moments, minutes even, of acute awareness of my difference and outsiderliness. As I joined the men and boys in trying to get into the room that houses the rabbi's tomb I was alarmed by the increasingly competitive approach taken by a far from passive or welcoming crowd. The unity of purpose – to touch the rabbi's tomb – shared by everyone but me (I only wanted to see what was happening!) in that confined space was matched by vigorous attempts to push everyone else out of the way.

Suddenly I was ejected into the next room, having only glimpsed the front row, who seem to be grabbing a moment of the rabbi's attention before they too lost their place and were forced away and onwards. We all ended up in a room that seemed immensely more spacious than the previous one even though it was physically smaller. The mood was completely different, much lighter, more inclusive. Nobody shoved or elbowed anyone. People insisted that I joined in a dance. Different styles of orthodoxy, originating in different places and/or periods in the Jewish diaspora, which might sometimes have caused antagonism, seemed forgotten. Even obvious outsiders like me were brought into the circle and told "we are commanded to celebrate not to watch". Smiles in the direction of the latest person to be ejected from the tomb room suggested that the crushing competition was, for them, a kind of initiatory ordeal or camaraderie. But there had been no smiles or accommodating easing of space, only a rib-crushing struggle to be in touch with the beneficent Rabbi's tomb. Beyond the building, in the square and streets outside, the festive atmosphere restored a sense of pleasure.

It is possible that full participants, pilgrims rather than academic tourists, felt that the liminality of being in the rabbi's presence now melded them into the sense and experience of the corporate body that is Victor Turner's *communitas* (V. Turner 1973). In describing the welcome she and other anthropologists were offered into the generally male, Hasidic enclave of the roof top of the main building, Edith Turner quotes Barbara Myerhoff as saying, "Though we took their [Hasidic boys'] places, they let us. The communitas paradigm reigned" (E. Turner 1993: 245; also cited in Ross 2011: xxxvi). Given the varied antipathies expressed among differently affiliated or identified Jews (e.g., allegedly, Hasidim towards Sephardim) that Edith Turner writes about, it seems more likely that it was not so much communitas as disinterest or entertainment that gained these anthropologists access. As evident outsiders and non-participants they were perhaps uninteresting, undeserving of confrontation, or practically invisible. But as strangers not subject to Jewish regulations they could be allowed where others (non-Hasidim or non-males) could never have entered. Perhaps this is unkind. Perhaps liminality-plus-communitas temporarily swayed the Hasidim to bypass their own normative restrictions and exclusions in favour of a more encompassing tendency to hospitality and the anthropologists to drown their knowledge of exclusions and conflicts beneath their desire to contribute to festivity.

Meanwhile, those restrictions may be behind the absence from YouTube and similar sources (as far as I can tell, today) of film or photos from inside the tomb rooms during the *hillula*. They provide views of the processions from Zefat, the campsite, the market stands (selling everything from snacks to scriptures), the roof-top fires, the courtyard dances, and the first haircuts given to Hasidic boys. It is probably true that the vast majority of participants are not there to record the event or their presence. Also, most camera-wielding visitors are aware that religiously motivated people often object strongly to the filming of their most significant activities or even of themselves. Signs about dress codes and other required observances are posted in many places (including the internet) for potential and actual visitors to see. The words "holy" or "sacred" in this context openly announce boundaries, separations and restrictions. Anyway, an elbow in the ribs would probably ruin recording in any media! Nonetheless, if one were to judge Shimon bar Yohai's *hillula* at Meron by what YouTube displays of it, it would be easy to miss a key moment for most pilgrims: people enthusiastically touching a tomb.

Yael Schwartz contributes significantly to paying attention to the lived realities of the *hillula* as religious culture, particularly by summarizing many women's experiences:

> The women also crowd around the tombstone in the women's section and stand in the courtyard. Women from the Oriental communities hand out refreshments: sweets, sugared cakes and salted snacks. Orthodox Ashkenazi women usually stand on the second-floor balcony of the building and watch the [male] dancers. During the festivities there are different customs: people fulfil vows made during the year, give charity to the poor or to institutions, offer food and drink to the participants, and throw sweets, candles or coins onto the gravestones. The coins are later collected and given to charity. Some women pour rosewater onto the tombstones. Some people draw a thread around the stone, which they then use as a charm to cure an invalid: the thread is drawn around the patient's bed, and this is thought to create a link to God through the grace of bar Yohai who, it is believed, will plead with God to save the ill person.
>
> (Schwartz 1999: 55)

Schwartz ends her article by quoting a saying: "Someone who has never seen the rejoicing at Meron at Lag baOmer, has never seen rejoicing at all" (*ibid.*: 59). That might be true, though one might also see exclusion, division and even hostility there. However, the point of my devoting so much space to this event that is hardly if ever mentioned in textbooks introducing Judaism, is that the *hillula* is revelatory of a range of significant matters for defining the religion that is Judaism as people live it, and therefore for redefining "religion" as a critical, scholarly term. Possibly, then, this is an event (among others) that might deserve a new saying: "Someone who has never seen the *hillula* at Meron, has never seen Judaism fully".

OF CRUSTACEANS AND CRABS

According to normative Jewish teaching, crustaceans are *treif* – not kosher, not acceptable for eating. They are unlikely to be publically offered for consumption at Meron during the *hillula* (things are different in Tel Aviv and Eilat). My point in mentioning this is not to introduce a discussion of food and purity rules. That comes later. Instead, I mention crustaceans in order to play with William James's consideration that "Probably a crab would be filled with a sense of personal outrage if it could hear us class it without ado or apology as a crustacean, and thus dispose of it. 'I am no such thing,' it would say, 'I am MYSELF, MYSELF alone'" (James [1902] 1997: 9).

In response to this, Thomas Tweed writes "of an experience my nine-year old son Kevin and I had at the beach ... we realized that crabs could be both crustaceans and just themselves alone" (Tweed 2009: 446). Like Tweed and his son, we too should seek to understand the taxonomic equivalents of "crustaceans", "crabs" and "*myself* alone", not as bounded or fixed categories, but each as a more or less helpful, more or less fluid, more or less transgressed or transgressive term. In seeking to understand what the *hillula* tells us about Judaism we engage with one (albeit annual) event that attracts many but not all Jews. What analytical weight should be placed on particular aspects of the festival? How do we distinguish between core and eccentric, definitive and accidental (f)acts? What conclusions can be drawn that might contribute to an understanding of religion? Perhaps we should see the *hillula* and its constitutive participants and activities, as an entry point into a fluid heterotopia in which we might learn to

> appreciate, and ultimately account for, the idiosyncratic or singular features of the complex traditions and communities we study, yet without describing them, in James's terms, as entirely "*sui generis* and unique." It [a social antireductionist approach] encourages us to explore the transgressive or elusive – even ineffable – dimensions of our everyday lives and imaginations, yet without attributing them to a transcendent space lying somewhere beyond the social world.
> (Goldschmidt 2009: 567–8)

It seems unlikely that anyone casually or accidentally visits Meron during the *hillula*, so two key motifs must be obvious: whatever else defines this event – while also defining Jewishness or Judaism – place and time are central. Researchers, then, might look for data about the meanings and performances of location and time as they consider how to categorize and theorize this event and its Jewishness. How these matters contribute to an effort to understand, define and theorize religion (or culture or whatever other categories seem helpful) will be considered later.

It would also be immediately obvious to any participant or visitor that a number of differentiations are important during the *hillula*. Soon after arriving in the burgeoning festival tent-city, the majority of people divide into fairly distinct neighbourhoods or communities. Most evidently, culturally defined costumes and musical styles indicate that there are Jews of Moroccan and other Sephardic origin, and Hasidim of eastern European origin. In central locations and moments, but also within tents and trailers, people either separate along gender lines or perform distinct, culturally gendered, tasks (cooking, praying, blessing, bartering, dancing or sweet throwing).

On the main night and day, at *Lag baOmer*, even without the aid of prior knowledge or a local guide, a visitor might find themselves swept along by the crowd and both pushed and pulled into the presence of a tomb that is the focus of intense activity. A blazing fire on the flat roof of the buildings attracts everyone's attention, and some important men are seated as near to it as is comfortable. Others, usually younger men, seem attentive to their needs. There is a continuous ebb and flow of people around the fire, and also within the courtyards where people dance. Groups of men dance together. Groups of women dance together. Gender seems important. A short but noticeable distance away, there are stands from which food and drink is distributed. Then, a much larger commercial market area is at some distance from the main buildings and spaces. Nonetheless, although this area is clearly identified as a market, there are continuities between the music near the fire and that sold on CDs in the market, between the snacks given as charity and those sold for profit, and between the mystical impetus of the whole event and the religiously inflected literatures and DVDs on sale further away.

A little time spent milling around within these only partially demarcated spaces provides the opportunity to begin recognizing further subdivisions. There are contrasting kinds of Hasidim, once again differentiated by costume. In the market, some have PA systems to advertise their groups, traditions or products, and perhaps to drown-out the sounds produced by competitors. Notices at food stands advertise compliance with the standards required by particular Rabbinic authorities. Once alerted, one notices other indicators of Jewish purity systems in relation to food, costume and gender. Classificatory systems structuring gender relations are less evident but not entirely absent at the event itself. It is assumed that generally *mitzvah*-observant women will abide by regulations that prescribe avoidance of contact during menstruation. There are reminders about this on websites that might be consulted prior to making the pilgrimage – perhaps less-observant potential visitors are their intended addressees. Similarly, descendents of temple priests, *kohanim*, are reminded that as they are expected to stay well away from tombs and the dead, the central focus of the *hillula* is not a good place for them (e.g. Chabad-Lubavitch Media Center 2012).

So, there are different kinds of Jews (e.g. male and female; communities with different geographical, ethnic or cultural backgrounds; affiliates of different systems or degrees of observance; mystics and merchants) and different activities to participate in or avoid. These and other matters noted above make up the complex of the *hillula*. If some Jews touch tombs which others avoid, and some Jews purposefully touch red threads to tombs (to gain healing and protective benefits) while others decry this as "foreign" magic or idolatry, what is Judaism? There are activities that might happen only at Meron during the *hillula*, and similarly there are probably activities that only happen at Meron during the event. Some things (charitably sharing food, celebrating first hair cuts, dancing with leading rabbis) might happen in other places and times, but they seem intensified by happening here and now. Meron and the *hillula* are distinctive as a complete package (or as packages, given the varied emphases, expectations and experiences of participants) but also make sense because of connections with other times and places. Recognizing what is of taxonomic or classificatory significance in deciding what defines Judaism or Jewishness, and/or what defines religion is not straightforward. We do now need to know a bit more about Jews and purity.

IMAGINING A TEMPLE, TEXTING INTIMACY

Traditionally Jews present the Torah (their corpus of authoritative law-and-lore) as having been given to Moses on Mount Sinai in written and oral/aural form. The written form is the biblical text, especially the Torah as Moses's Five Books. The oral form is collected and texted as the Mishnah and Talmud. This, however, would be far from obvious to a naïve or unguided reader of these texts. Mishnah and Talmud texts read, to a large extent, like the recorded debates of rabbinic authorities in late antiquity. This too, however, is no more true than that the texts record what Moses heard on the mountain. They are a curious double fiction in which they are claimed as Mosaic and read as if early rabbinic but are in reality a deliberate project of later rabbis. Nonetheless, to understand the Torah, in both forms, it is important to inhabit the fiction, to suspend disbelief and work on gaining intimacy with its world.

There is more: against archaeological and historical evidence of plurality the biblical Torah asserts that there is properly only one temple for the people of Israel. The Mishnah and Talmud almost completely ignore the fact that this temple had been destroyed centuries before they were written. A literal reading would indicate that temple services continue to be performed – and continue to generate almost all matters of importance in everyday Jewish life. In many important respects, Israelite religion and its successor Judaism, are the imagination of a temple and all that a temple entails. Rules for the behaviour of a priestly caste are elaborated and offered for effortful habituation and inculcation. Biblical texts circulate around the (fictively singular) temple.

What makes them different from other ancient west Asian texts is not an insistence on devotion to one deity (polytheists regularly build close relations with only one among many deities) but their focus on the minutiae of temple provisioning and performance. The appropriate costumes, diets and relationships of temple functionaries and ritualists – and the wider society in which they operate – are exemplary generative themes. Without a temple, not much of the (written) Torah makes sense. (This is, of course, only partially true: Jews, Christians and others have created a different world in which to read and make sense of the texts.) However, after the second destruction of the temple (in the year 70CE), these rules for priests became the foundation for a lifeway of non-priests. In the face of disastrous efforts of resistance to Imperial Rome, imagining national life circulating around a temple became the means of what Gerald Vizenor (thinking of other imperialisms and genocides) calls "survivance" (Vizenor 1998). This is not mere survival but the finding of ways to celebrate local cultures without provoking further devastation by the powerful; it resists victimhood (understandable as that would be) but reaches for more promising traces of vitality.

Jacob Neusner is a prolific author (Wikipedia attributes over 950 authored or edited books to him, and does not mention his journal articles). In the library he has published, a single theme is reiterated and ramified. This begins with the argument that, following the return of exiles from their Babylonian exile:

> All Judaisms to come would in some way or other find in the priests' paradigm the model to which either to conform or object. The priests' Torah, the Pentateuch in its final statement, constituted the first and enduring Judaism, with its paradigm of exile and return for all to follow. (Neusner 2002: 59)

It continues:

> Judaism maintains that humanity finds God in books through the act of learning. [In previous chapters] we have examined encounters

161

> with God that correspond to those afforded by other religions, for
> rites connected with eating and public worship are commonplace.
> But it is not ordinary for religions to equate prayer with reading and
> discussing books, and Judaism does just that. ... Torah-study (in
> Hebrew, *talmud Torah*) in the here and now recapitulates the encoun-
> ter at Sinai. That is meant concretely.   (*Ibid.*: 115–16)

The religion of priests (who conduct sacrifices in a temple) transmogrifies
into the religion of readers. There are scholars of these texts but at the heart
of the normative (if occasionally contested) way of being Jewish from the
Roman period to now, it is neither academics nor an elite class who maintain
the system. Rather, every Jew who reads texts is both the foundation and the
current embellishment of Judaism.

This leaves only implicit the reason why it can be claimed that the Judaism
which began to be formed after the Roman destruction of the temple (and
the failure of a subsequent revolt against Roman rule) served and performed
a means of survivance. Indeed, it was less the conditions of Roman tolera-
tion than the rise of Christian persecution that mobilized and energized this
Judaism of priestly-text readers. That is, when Christianity became the official religion of the Roman Empire, its claim to ownership of the texts and
trajectories of Israel's story required a vigorous but not provocative response.
It could certainly not be a military response. Rather, as Neusner sets out
(e.g. *ibid.*: 69–72), Jews were encouraged to study Torah (in biblical and rabbinic textual forms) to find in them the means to achieve sanctification in
everyday life. Redemption at the end of time could be hoped for, but it too
would take the shape of a studious rabbinic messiah, not a militaristic one.
Nonetheless, the insistent focus of Jews and Judaism was towards the here-
and-now of worldly, if sanctified, life.

In short, Jewish religious and cultural life was reformed around the continuous practice of studying Torah. Certainly, Jews attempted to live by the
things found in the texts. But they survived by making studying central. Two
absences in rabbinic texts are revelatory: first the absence of the destroyed
temple and secondly the absence of an army. Jews were to survive by studying rules written by and for priests concerned with sacrifices in a temple,
regardless of the absence of that temple and of the impossibility of sacrifice,
and by studiously avoiding remilitarization and revolt. Selflessness became
the "highest virtue of all" (*ibid.*: 126).

Abiding systems of observance were generated by and in intense debates
about what constitutes "work" forbidden on Shabbat, about what size bits

of leaven might be unproblematic when unleavened bread is prescribed at Pesach, and about the kind of water that might purify people ritually. All cultures have these: the English require people not to walk on some areas of grass and refuse to eat horse-flesh knowingly even though they sell horses to the French for that purpose.[1] Without texts neither the priests before the temple was destroyed nor the scholars afterwards could have successfully elaborated what has become the normative Jewish system (as indicated by both observers and opponents). This could not be an entirely oral culture. Instead, it encouraged each Jew to gain intimate experience of dwelling a double life: imagining a functioning temple and living everyday without one.

PURITY AND DANGER

It will not have escaped notice that in this chapter I have been circumambulating around the work of Mary Douglas. Since we are discussing the veneration of ancestors, it is appropriate to spend a bit more time in the publication monuments that are her lasting memorial.

In *Purity and Danger*, Douglas (1992) opens up the logic of *Vayikra/Leviticus*, demonstrating that it constructs boundaries and distinctions for temple priests and, if derivatively for the most part, for their lay neighbours. She does this in comparison with the Lele pangolin cult and other rich data. In short, she finds in these examples a pervasive concern with pollution and disorder, with boundaries and order, and with rites and habits that are generated by seeking "purity", where relevant, by either avoidance or engagement. She determines the likely existence of these "purity and pollution" systems in other cultures, cults and texts.

In lived reality boundaries are permeable. People move across borders. They do not always act as expected or required. There are, perhaps, teachers, preachers and promoters of texts and cults to insist on boundaries precisely because boundaries are rarely natural, obvious, or universally agreed upon. What disgusts and outrages some people appeals to others – so moral systems need teachers, thought and debate (Midgley 2004: 105).

In discussing biblical texts, Douglas engages with ritual systems rather than moral ones. Or, perhaps, morality is a secondary theme within those systems. This is important, but not the chief focus of attention here, because

---

1. Melanie Joy's *Why we Love Dogs, Eat Pigs and Wear Cows* (2010) provides an impassioned presentation of the peculiarities of typical American foodways.

words like "pure", "impure", "clean", "dirt", "right" and "wrong" sound to many of us now like moral terms and seem objectionable in relation to matters that we find natural or normal. Menstruation, for example, is "unclean" in the purity system of the bible, and its inheritor religions, because it is deemed out of place in the temple. Of course, women would be in the wrong place if they penetrated too far into the temple, according to these texts which are concerned to regulate the activities and experiences of an elite group of men.

The undoubtedly male authors of these temple texts imagined themselves to be the standard for what is normal. Then they imagined that acts which they could undertake would make them and their families, nation and world, derivatively, holy. Once more, "holy" is not, here, about morality but ritually correct behaviour. They imagined a system establishing a polarization between beings, matters and acts associated with life on the one side and death on the other. The deity is fully the statement of life; dead bodies of death. The structuring of reality follows from that duality. The temple (associated more with "God" than "sacrificing/killing animals") is contrasted with tombs. Sheep (associated with the temple *per se* more than with "sacrifice") are contrasted with pigs (because they are never associated with the temple). Healthy bodies are contrasted with diseased or blemished ones. This is, however, simplistic and too static. Questions obviously have to be asked about blood and death since the temple rites would be full of them. But let's delay that consideration and ask, just why are pigs unclean?

Douglas is clear that we must find reasons for the placing of beings, matters and acts *within* the system, which is after all quite explicit in offering reasons. It may seem arcane that *Kashrut* (the system of purity rules that organized the life of temple officiants and now organizes everyday Jewish life) declares sheep "clean" or "normal" because they chew the cud and have cloven hooves. That other animals are declared "unclean" is not because they cannot (physically) be eaten nor because they might cause disease or somehow symbolize bad behaviour. The authors of these texts could have said such things if they had wished to. Instead they categorize some animals (which chew the cud and have cloven hooves) to be different to others. They are different because the system needs them to be different. Their status means that they can be eaten by humans or offered sacrificially to the god.

But not all sheep are equal. Some sheep are blemished, their skin imperfect, or their legs damaged. They could be eaten but never sacrificed. This is a significant clue to a vital aspect of this system: it is not about boxed entities, eternally hyper-separated from others. It is a dynamic system in which sheep that get injured can play different functions in the cosmic system to healthy sheep. Indeed, the body of a sheep killed by a "wild beast" rather than a human slaughterer is to be associated with "death" and kept from Israelite tables as well as the priestly altar. This exemplifies but does not exhaust the dynamism that is missed when people misread the key texts as speaking (metaphorically or otherwise) about morality. Choices are being made, but not between beings, matters and acts that do not relate. The dynamic system is, as Douglas notes in her title and throughout her book, about taboo. It is a complex of negotiations and shifting associations, assemblies or relations.

Just when the idea that blood is polluting is accepted, then it is insisted that blood sanctifies. It is all a matter of what is deemed to be in the right place at the right time, with the right companions, contexts or activities. Jonathan Smith's *To Take Place* (1987) adds to this by attending to the ways in which ritual definitively structures not only places but other acts. It is Douglas, however, who points to the power of text and thereby anticipates Neusner's work.

Without a temple, the biblical system cannot operate or be operated. But the texts survive and the effort to imagine, emplace and empower boundaries can continue. Again, the efforts are dynamic, not static. Taking a text that is not about them (because it is about temple priests), non-priestly readers picked up two seemingly minor themes and gave them sufficient attention to generate a new reading and a new construction. They read themselves into the story by emphasizing that if some sheep were taken from flocks to the temple altar, the majority went to tables to be eaten. This, in turn, indicated that decisions about differences, choices and intentions, matters of will, were vital. Fittingly, such innovative insights or developments generated a new text to study: the Mishnah (later claimed to be the written expression of the oral Torah). Neusner writes:

> The Mishnah's evidence presents a Judaism which at its foundations and through all its parts deals with a single fundamental question: What can man do? The evidence of Mishnah points to a Judaism which answers that question simply: Man, like God, makes the world work. If a man wills it, all things fall subject to that web of intangible status and incorporeal reality, with a right place for all things, each after its own kind, all bearing their proper names, described by the simple word, sanctification. The world is inert and neutral. Man by his word and will initiates process which force things to find their rightful place on one side or the other of the frontier, the definitive category of holiness. (Neusner 1981: 282)

FOOD, SEX AND STRANGERS

In Judaism, then, Jews inherit a purity system of imagined boundaries and behavioural norms. They take the rules home to their tables and other home-spaces, but especially to the places in which they read, study and debate. They structure the world (as their deity is said to have done) by placing things in order. They maintain separations that order temple ritual life but do so dynamically and paying attention to the present, worldly needs for surviv-ance as well as sanctification.

COUNTING BARLEY AND AVOIDING THE DEAD

At Meron during the *hillula* of Rabbi Shimon bar Yohai imagination and intimacy, fiction and reality, time and space, text and life come together. The main event or high point of the gathering occurs at Lag baOmer, the thirty-third day of the counting of barley offerings between the festivals of Pesach and Shavuot. It is somewhat staggering that nearly two thousand years after the destruction of the temple, and thus the cessation of the practice of offer-ing god freshly-harvested barley, people are still counting these days. But, again, there is more.

The time between Pesach and Shavuot also involves an imaginative reca-pitulation of the time between fleeing Egypt and receiving Torah at Sinai, a shift from "we were slaves" to "we were chosen", a flight from imposed con-ditions to an acceptance of rules for living. Simultaneously, observant Jews at the *hillula* stand at Sinai, in the temple in Jerusalem and at a rabbi's tomb in Meron. They receive Torah, offer barley and share sweetness and light. As women throw sweets and men light fires they materialize the enrichment of mystical traditions, further intensifying imagination of the past (creation, Sinai and temple-times) and the future (redemption) while committing to a present in which charitable giving and the observance of appropriate habits and behaviour are of all-consuming importance. It is not enough to imag-ine that the temple and agriculture continue uninterrupted from antiquity, or that a nation's relationship with their deity continues to be honoured in the bringing of barley to the temple. It is necessary that ordinary meals are conducted as if they, rather than temple sacrifices, were the focus of divine interest.

However, at the *hillula* it is also declared to be necessary that the descend-ents of priests, despite the absence of that which defines priesthood (temple and sacrifice), avoid contact with the dead and their tombs. This key plank of Levitical/priestly *kashrut* is maintained. Another plank of the evolved system is indicated by the ubiquitous but unremarked "*kosher*" signs at market stands so that sanctification by proper (*kosher*) meals is possible for ordinary people in ordinary conditions on ordinary days. (The *hillula* is ordinary in the sense that it is not a biblically mandated pilgrim festival but a day between two festivals. It is extraordinary as a pause in the restrained waiting for the denouement that is Shavuot. It is also extraordinary as the day on which Rabbi Shimon bar Yohai taught his final mystical lesson.) What, then, does it mean that some people are so eager to touch a grave?

Mark says in relation to the graffiti "*na, nah, nahma, nahman meiUman*" (נ נח נחמ נחמן מאומן) that an alien visiting the country might think that this is the core of Judaism (Mark 2011: 101). The same alien arriving in Meron at Lag baOmer might well conclude that Judaism is a system of ancestor veneration. Seeking information about the spatial and temporal coordinates of the event in relation to other places and times (shrines and calendars) might lead the visitor to conclude that the annual cycles of the region's agricultural year constellate around the world-making myth-telling of a famous ancestor. Observing the touching of the tomb (and the elbowing of others away from the tomb), hearing about the powers attributed to red threads that have been in contact with the tomb, and/or being drawn into ecstatic dances near a bonfire of candles that have touched the tomb, what could a visitor conclude but that Jews expect some ancestors to benefit the present generation powerfully. It is hard to say that any of this is a wrong interpretation of what people at the *hillula* do or think. Some religious authorities do, certainly, insist that people would be wrong to do or think like this. But they are imagining (and wishing to inculcate their imagination among others) a different way of doing or understanding Judaism. In the lived reality of many of those who participate in the *hillula* the textbook version of "Judaism" is too constrained.

What is missing from the textbooks about Judaism that declare that a separation of life and death is the chief organizing factor of kashrut and therefore of Judaism? What is Judaism if it includes public and enthusiastic efforts to make contact with a dead rabbi's tomb? What is missing when people insist that Judaism is strictly monotheistic? Douglas concludes *Purity and Danger* by noting that:

> If anyone held the idea that death and suffering are not an integral part of nature, the delusion is corrected. If there was a temptation to treat ritual as a magic lamp to be rubbed for gaining unlimited riches and power, ritual shows its other side. If the hierarchy of values was crudely material, it is dramatically undermined by paradox

FOOD, SEX AND STRANGERS

and contradiction. In painting such dark themes, pollution symbols are as necessary as the use of black in any depiction whatsoever. Therefore, we find corruption enshrined in sacred places and times.

(Douglas 1992: 178–9)

Paradox is important. Douglas is aware that while the delusion that death is not natural is corrected in ritual, it is also contested; while ritual may not result in riches and power, people do seek physical improvements by doing ritual; and while materialism may be devalued, it is far from negated among the aims of ritual participants. That is, at the *hillula* and elsewhere, Jews can seek to benefit from contact with the dead in a range of ways. They are not solely focused on divinity, transcendence and spirituality. These are, finally, not generative. Rather, living well among others (of one's kind certainly, and avoiding strangers where necessary) is enhanced, apparently, by performing deeds that do not seem strictly monotheistic. People at least flirt with other persons and anticipate good results.

WHAT DOES A NON-RELIGIOUS ISRAELI LOOK LIKE?

It is a major error to imagine that in order to describe a religion it is sufficient to survey the contents of religious texts, so I have attended to the uses to which texts are put. It is also an error to imagine any event as monolithic, monovalent or monothetic; so I note here that "secular" Israelis attend the *hillula* too. Unlike the Hasidim, they do not wear long coats, fur hats or *peyot* (uncut hair from in front of their ears). They might not be as keen as the religiously enthusiastic Sephardim to touch red threads to Shimon bar Yohai's tomb. These are just a couple of surface differences. "Secular" (*hiloni*) Israelis might visit Meron at Lag baOmer to enjoy the music or the atmosphere, or to see an impressive spectacle. Some might be motivated by desires or intentions precisely paralleled by those of people in North America who have begun labelling themselves as "spiritual but not religious" (i.e. seeking self-understanding, personal fulfilment and/or holistic well-being). Usually, however, there is something more distinctively Jewish about Israeli discourses of "non-religion".

There are Israeli atheists of the kind that decry anything which might be called "religion". There are philosophically astute Israeli Humanists. But equally, there are and probably always have been religiously observant Jews who see no need to "believe in god" or to theorize the existence of any deities.

This understanding might be summed up in a suggestion that the existence of god is assumed, taken-for-granted and largely uncommented upon in roughly the same way that the existence of gravity is assumed, taken-for-granted and largely uncommented upon. Everything can carry on regardless of the attention given or not given to such matters.

Goldschmidt cogently states matters in parenthetically explaining that when a "newly orthodox Lubavitch yeshiva student" glosses his own use of the word "secular" as "non-religious", he means "non-observant" (Goldschmidt 2009: 563). When Israelis and diaspora Jews refer to other Jews as either "religious" or "not religious" two things are important for this consideration of what "religion" might mean. First, being religious means being observant to some degree. Usually that means "looking like it" too – wearing at least some kind of head covering (skull cap or scarf if not hat or wig), lighting Shabbat candles even if the rest of Shabbat is only minimally observed, and keeping at least some semblance of a kosher home. This last might mean keeping meat and milk separate, or being vegetarian so that when more observant relatives visit they need not worry whether meat and milk have been mixed inappropriately. There may well be questions about whether Progressive Jews are appropriately observant, but they are recognized as at least somewhere on a continuum of "doing things that Jews do". In fact, Reform and Liberal Jewish movements encourage more observance than their reforming ancestors did in the nineteenth century.

Second, in typically Jewish discourse, "religious" need indicate nothing about interests in, obsessions with or devotion to transcendent beings or metaphysics. It might not even be equivalent to "spirituality" as used by those influenced by Protestant Christian piety and modernist subjectivity. Religion is about human living, alongside others, in the world. It is about who one eats with, and who one avoids eating with. This, again, may be determined by who one trusts to have a kitchen or shopping habits in which foods are properly treated. As "religion" is not the opposite of "atheism" so it is not defined by theism.

Jews can be thoroughly religious atheists because "religion" and "theism" refer to two separate domains. My argument is that this is true not only for Judaism but also for other people. We have been mislead by the generative obsessions of Protestant Christian preachers into mis-identifying religion with believing in deities. Had we sought, instead, to understand religion from within Judaism we would have noted the prevalence of words like *halakah*, way or walk, and sought to understand "religion" as observance, performance or lifeway. We would have attended to casual, habitual, everyday acts alongside dramatic, ritual and occasional acts. Our textbooks and teaching would be more focused on taboo and purity systems than on interiority and cognitive processes. Instead we have interpreted Judaism as a sub-set of Christianity and Christianity as the definitive religion. These trends are evidenced by the somewhat ridiculous terms "Judeo-Christian" and "Abrahamic religions" and the utterly ridiculous term "world religions". It is now time to start again from elsewhere, even from the seemingly familiar "elsewhere" of Judaism. If the *hillula* of rabbi Shimon bar Yohai at Meron at Lag baOmer helps us see Judaism differently (even if that is because it is in some respects eccentric as Judaism), perhaps it will help us see new/old possibilities for defining, understanding, theorizing, researching and teaching about religion.

vs. worlds religions

10. Enchantment and emplacement

Paganism is a new religion that is evolving within the modernist West, drawing on older repertoires to engage with contemporary concerns. These facts generate some basic questions in the prehistory of this chapter: are tradition, hierarchical authority, unified ideology, and community definitive of religion? Is it legitimate to claim membership of something that should be identified as a religion while knowingly inventing cosmologies and rituals, developing individual practices, and not committing to an agreed creed? In what ways do the disparate practices and interests of Pagans cohere into a recognizable unity? Given that Paganism undoubtedly began in the matrix of modernism, how has it become something other than another kind of Protestant modernism (i.e. something disenchanted and ideas-focused)? If questions like those underlie this chapter, what is it about Paganism that justifies its use as a lens through which to approach the larger question of redefining religion? Taking cues from and following clues in the work of colleagues, I will argue that Paganism is more deserving of the label "religion" than Christianity-as-belief-system is.

I propose that observing Pagans doing what they do can provide valuable data for redefining religion. Precisely because this religion has evolved within modernity but refuses disenchantment, it encourages me to consider whether enchantment is a feature of all religions. Because Pagans experiment with different ways of assembling together, while also experimenting with different assemblages of sources and performances, I am inspired to wonder about the role of fluidity, hybridity and experimentation in all religions. Because Pagans have ritual practices, protocols and orientations in common and care little about defining beliefs (let alone "correct beliefs"), it points to inadequacies in existing definitions of religion. If Paganism were proved to be exceptional it would not help us think more about our scholarly categories and approaches. However, it is the fact that many of the dynamics made visible by studying Pagans are also evident among other communities which justifies this chapter. For example, given the prevalence of accusations of syncretism levelled against "ordinary" members of many religions, and even against some of the priests, preachers and other leading proponents of religious institutions, it is more likely that Pagans are unexceptional and therefore interesting.

Alongside the question of whether our ideas about religions are flawed, it is equally important that we consider further whether our common definitions of modernity are flawed. If, for example, the progressive disenchantment of the world is illusory, contested or merely temporary, this might make the continuity of enchantment less remarkable. Simultaneously, perhaps it would require the adjustment of the rhetorics and performances of academia. Some of the work has certainly begun. It is, for example, now less common than it once was to approach religions as discrete, boxed and bounded objects, separate from other religions and from other facets of life (e.g., economics, catering, sport, politics, ethnicity, gender and sexuality).

But whenever the idea that religion is a discrete, *sui generis* thing misdirects some of what passes for the study of religion(s), then it fails to account for the ways in which Paganism and all other religions are performed or lived. For that reason among others, in discussing the ways in which Pagans learn from others, this chapter will engage with the cliché of the "spiritual supermarket". This chapter, in short, aims to do something a little different to the previous ones. It offers thoughts about how Paganism might be a religion and how it might aid redefinitions of religion, while also querying both the facticity or givenness of modernism and the academic approaches it has encouraged. First, however, an outline of the origins and evolution of Paganism will provide a descriptive orientation.

SOURCES AND TRAJECTORIES

From 1976 (when I first went to Stonehenge People's Free Festival) until now, most of my engagement with Pagans and Paganism has taken place in Britain. But significant encounters in continental Europe, North America, South Africa, Australia, Aotearoa, Israel and Japan have also shaped my understanding. In the last few decades a steady increase in academic research, initially provoked by the interests of students, has enhanced the opportunities for debate about both descriptive and analytical matters. Research among Pagans has become vibrantly interdisciplinary with rich potential for dialogues about different perspectives. One result of this is that I can sum up significant points in the trajectory by which Paganism has evolved.

People have been valorizing "Pagan" and "Paganism" as positive terms for well over a century now. Since the 1950s increasing numbers of people have self-identified as Pagans. What had been (from late Antiquity until the early modern period, and often more recently) a largely derogatory accusation made against people for not being Christian, or for not being Christian enough, gradually came to be used to refer to noble and civilized classical (pre-Christian) Greeks and Romans. In the nineteenth century, Pagan began to refer to "celebrants of nature". In response to industrialization and urbanization, and in tandem with Romanticism and Transcendentalism, nature and wilderness began to be positively valorized in the nineteenth century. What Catherine Albanese (2002) calls "nature religion" became increasingly identifiable, if never as an organized or systematized tradition, but nonetheless gaining ground as a pervasive, largely implicit contributor to American civil and popular religion (B. Taylor 2010). Simultaneously, esoteric ritualism (or "high magic") diversified, proliferated and became visible to wider society, sometimes in "secularized" and "scientistic" forms (Hanegraaff 1996). Esotericism provided the structure and protocols for more exoteric religious ritualists, Pagans among them. The new self-identified Paganism grew verdantly from this fertile blended compost.

The trajectory of this emergence has been traced fully by Ronald Hutton (1991, 1994, 1996, 1999, 2003, 2007, 2009) and, in summary, by myself (Harvey 2006, 2011b, 2012a). Briefly stated, it involves a heady brew of classicism, romanticism, celticism, naturalism, naturism, anti-clericalism, ritualism, bardism, esotericism, individualism, communitarianism, evolutionism, feminism, anarchism, rationalism, different kinds of activism (from anti-war, pro-festivals, anti-globalization, and pro-justice movements to climate change and occupy movements) and some folk and rural traditions. Quite evidently, some of these conflict with each other and their mixtures do not always result in experiences or systems that seem coherent to insiders let alone to outsiders. It is unlikely that anyone involved in these wider cultural currents intended or could have predicted the current situation or style of the miscellaneous forms of self-identified Paganism.

However, within the accommodating diversity of groups and practices, a common theme and thread is regularly reiterated by Pagans and their

173

scholarly observers. This is the notion that Paganism is a "nature religion", a "religion of nature" or a "religion centred on the celebration of nature". Quite what "nature" means, beyond the religiously positive or even sacred tone with which it is invoked, is regularly debated among Pagans and those who research among them (e.g. Letcher 2000, 2001, 2005; Clifton 2006; Jamison 2011). Taking a cue from the late Chosen Chief of the Secular Order of Druids, Tim Sebastian, I note the resonances of "nature" and "nature religion" with both "countryside" and "wilderness", that is, those relatively close and relatively remote places beyond the largely human dominated urban realms, places where it is still possible for humans to realize their minority status and to be reminded to act more responsibly in the world (Harvey 2012b). Additionally, "nature religions" are this worldly rather than transcending the world, matter and bodies. They encourage people to celebrate seasons and locations, life cycles and mundane experiences.

In relation to varied senses of "nature", groups constellate around particular ways of celebrating, particular locations or particular heritages (putatively Celtic, Saxon, Hellenic, Craft and others). Typically, Pagan groups are fairly democratic and often egalitarian. Where dominating styles of leadership emerge, Pagans often leave to seek more intimate modes of association. They are highly literate, drawing on an eclectic range of sources to inspire and shape their practices and ambitions. Botanical guides share bookshelf space with Fantasy novels, anthropological texts and esoteric manuals. Academic histories and inspirational poetry nestle together. With other sources they blend with individual and group experiences to form traditions and communities that others can adopt and adapt or resist and reject in favour of alternatives. As a new religion with ancient inspirations, Paganism evidences many similarities with other religions in formation and evolution. It is, therefore, admirable as a lens with which to consider what makes a religion.

PERFORMING ENCHANTMENT

Among the defining characteristics of modernity, disenchantment is supposed to be central. The Protestant polemic against rituals – portraying them as futile repetitions of meaningless acts – laid a foundation for modernism's programmatic privileging of other ways of knowing. Max Weber explained that the "increasing intellectualization and rationalization" that defines our times does not, therefore, indicate an increased and general knowledge of the conditions under which one lives. It means something else, namely, the knowledge or belief that if one but wished one could learn it at any time. Hence, it means that there are no mysterious incalculable forces that come into play, but rather that one can, in principle, master all things by calculation. This means that the world is disenchanted. One need no longer have recourse to magical means in order to master or implore the spirits, as did the savage, for whom such mysterious powers existed. Technical means and calculations perform the service. This above all is what intellectualization means.   (Gerth & Mills 1948: 139)

This intellectualization fuses with increasing bureaucracy, specialization, individuation and other world-shaping activities to alienate and disenchant people.

However, despite the successes of the modern project, rituals have not ceased. People have continued to find performance significant and in doing so have resisted the impossible fantasy of disembodied intellect. Sceptical enquiry and managerial bureaucracy are rarely experienced as life-enhancing. This is not to argue that religion is definitively irrational or that its goal is necessarily life-enhancement. Rather, it is to indicate dissatisfaction with the rhetorics that denigrate embodiment, emplacement and performance. In ritualizing people seem to find ways to contest modernity's alienation and to maintain relational and participative enchantment.

Paganism initially evolved within the conflicted modernist world of the early to mid-twentieth century. Many of the sources that fed, and continue to feed it, are aspects of modernity. Pagans are, for instance, likely to insist on each individual's right to determine what style of religion is best for them. They commonly state that magical ceremonies are undertaken in an experimental manner, requiring careful planning and tested by results for effectiveness. Traditions or knowledges that might aid people in particular ways are also treated, by and large, as requiring no mediation. The individual determines the value of a text, speech, observed activity or other potential inspiration, and makes use of it as they deem appropriate. Other facets of modernity (showing signs of Protestant origins) could be adduced. Nonetheless, one obvious sign of tension with modernism more than hints at the existence of others. Paganism is ritual-centred religion.

Pagans could have chosen to disseminate their new and evolving religion in intellectual fora and media. They could have published manifestos or proclaimed sermons. They did, indeed, write books and other texts. They are often voracious readers, but the inclusion of fantasy fiction among the most commonly named books read by Pagans indicates something about their celebration of imagination and creativity. But, even so, text production and usage do not form the main activities of Pagans. For whatever reason (and it probably has something to do with the influence of esotericism), the choice of ritual performance as the core communal and individual activity of Pagans has shaped almost everything else about the emerging tradition. It can be interpreted as a contest with the "systematic creation and maintenance of estrangement from society and selfhood" (Mills 1951: 340) which is at the heart of modernity's project. The construction, maintenance or encouragement of relational selves and emplaced assemblages, moulded by embodied performance and creative imagination, have not been pursued "irrationally" or "mystically". Rather than the splitting apart which Weber presented as defining our "world robbed of gods" (Gerth and Mills 1948: 282), there is an interplay between rational experimentation and creative experientialism.

Patrick Curry (who has inspired much of my thinking about re-enchantment) writes, "What cannot be calculated, controlled, or bought and sold is at the heart of what makes us human and makes life worth living" (Curry 2011). This is undoubtedly true, and encourages careful thinking about modernism and its alternatives. Nonetheless, Curry's is not a naïve romanticism but a robust radicalism. It chimes with Pagan efforts, tangled as they are, to develop a modern life that values ritual, embodiment, emplacement, imagination and other contraries of disenchantment. In ritual and in the places (per)formed as people ritualize, imagination and reality cease to be opposites, but not because one overpowers the other. In Pagan ritual, at least, the imagined good world of larger-than-human co-dwelling and co-creation meets the reality of human efforts (perhaps partially imagined) towards domination. An alternative emerges into renewed imagining of more respectful relating *and* simultaneously into real-world efforts to enact respectful human lifestyles. It is not quite that "the imaginary is transformed into the real" because religious worlds are simultaneously "at once and indistinguishably mental and social" (Lefebvre 1991: 251). Imagination and intimacy mix to shape selves, relations, actions and the world. Whether or not this is a core aspect of religion, it suggests a less tidy process than the imagined "progress" of modernism towards disenchantment.

Engaging in "illegitimate activities that [mingle] the increasingly distinct [according to modernists] religious and material realms", Pagans refuse to "extricate religion from the material world" (Benavides 1998: 198). Perhaps this is true of all religionists. It seems to fit the "modern western shamans" discussed by Kocku von Stuckrad (2002). It may even fit those who claim to be partisans of "universal religions" but regularly meet it specific locations and build affection for those places. Certainly, however, Paganism is a modern but hardly modernizing attempt to rejoin and conjoin social and mental, imaginary and intimate, meaningful and spiritual possibilities by keeping religion firmly enmeshed in the material world. Its explicit and determined emphasis on performance and place make it ideal for testing some of the most interesting currents in recent and ongoing theorization of religions. In the following section I turn to another area of confusion about religion which might be disentangled by observation of Paganism.

SYNCRETISM

Far too many studies have been written as if religions and religion were properly thought of as discrete entities, securely bounded and separated from other phenomenon. Hard as they may try, colleagues who write about "syncretism" rarely escape implying that there is something improper or degenerate about adopting from or accommodating to others. There might be much to be said about the processes by which people learn from one another, and thereby change their cultures, religions, habits, knowledges and so on. But the first thing that needs saying is that these are normal and necessary processes. Anything else would be exceptional and require explanation. That which is called "syncretism" is ordinary and undeserving of a name with such a weight of negativity about it. The derogation of learning, borrowing or fusing is another hangover from elite theologies and creedal orthodoxies. In every lived religion the processes of change and exchange that follow from encountering others and alternatives are everyday.

Modernist rhetoric adds an additional twist (albeit one that turns out to be quite Protestant) to the imagination of religion as contained in boxes. If religious leaders preach against the ideas and practices of other religions, modernity encourages observers of religion to castigate those who mix religion with politics, economics, tourism and so on. In discussing the stubbornly resistant processes (especially to do with place-making) of religions, Vásquez sums up the work of de Certeau, Orsi, and Chidester and Linenthal: "Hybridization, in turn, mixes and scrambles what dominant strategies have tried to naturalize as taken-for-granted sacrality, transgressing the sharp

177

boundaries and distinctions made in the name of that sacrality" (Vásquez 2011: 279).

Peripheral matters and groups, in this analysis, keep taking centre stage, usurping attention normatively devoted to whatever is defined, by the powerful, as sacred. Seemingly secure knowledges about the focus of religious rites on transcendent matters, or of religious discourse on spirituality, become hybridized with putatively economic or political concerns. Life, especially in times of crisis and division, refuses to be trammelled within boundaries. Or, more likely, religion has been wrongly constructed as a discrete domain or activity.

"Hybridity" is perhaps the still elite but more secular synonym of "syncretism". What is theorized as hybridity is less the everyday borrowing of one ritual style into the repertoire of another tradition than the transgression of spiritual otherworldliness into politics. Following Giselle Vincett (2008, 2009), I propose that the term "fusion" might be a less polemical way of labelling people's deliberate choices to identify as "Buddhist Jews", "Quagans" (Quaker Pagans) or to integrate indigenous ceremonies into non-indigenous ritual complexes.

Publications concerned with vernacular religion are replete with examples, demonstrating again that fusion or sharing is normal and pervasive. These processes can be exemplified in the ways in which observers and practitioners think about sweat-lodge ceremonies that originated among the Lakota and other nations indigenous to north-central North America. Most commonly, worldwide, they are largely conducted according to protocols that evolved among the Lakota and their neighbours. As the practice spread among other Native Americans, and then among people of European ancestry and beyond, it changed, and it keeps changing.

In outline, the traditional Lakota-style sweat-lodge ceremony fuses purification with self-giving efforts to benefit others. In an enclosed and darkened space, usually made freshly for each such ceremony, after some suitable preparations (focusing on protocols and desired results), the ceremonial leader calls for rocks to be brought in. These will have been heated in a fire outside of the lodge, and when they are brought in they are placed in a central hole in the lodge's earth-floor. Water is then poured over the rocks to produce steam and increase the heat. Sweat-lodges are not intended to be endurance tests, though the heat, darkness and confined space is challenging. Each participant – including the rocks, named honorifically as grandfathers – gives up this effort and submits to this discomfort with that double aim of seeking self-purification and the good of others. Participants then join in rounds of prayers to powerful helpers, interspersed with the introduction of more grandfather rocks and the consequent increase of heat, steam and therefore sweat. If we were to define religion not as belief but as the performance of limitations to build community, sweat lodges would be archetypal.

The conduct of ceremony can vary among indigenous/aboriginal nations. It is vital to note this intra-indigenous diversification before considering the spread of sweat-lodge practice elsewhere. Although there have been considerable abuses of indigenous knowledges, many deserving identification as theft or appropriation, we should be wary of ignoring the agency of indigenous teachers, leaders and communities in the negotiated extension of ceremonies (Welch 2007). Intercultural teaching and learning, translation and enabling, are rich aspects of many indigenous cultures. Confrontation with ongoing colonialism does not prevent people seeking to disseminate indigenous virtues of reciprocity and respect, or indigenous knowledges about many matters, to a larger community. In addition, despite my sketch of a seemingly normative Lakota version of sweat-lodge protocols, we should not take a single case as evidencing what happens everywhere. Even Lakota sweat lodge practice varies (Stover 2001) and variations proliferate across the continent. Pagan adoption of indigenous knowledges is usually (if not always) predicated on efforts to relearn European ancestral knowledges. In the case of sweat lodges, archaeological evidence encourages some Pagans to think this may be a fruitful area for intercultural dialogue. However, my point in selecting sweat-lodges for discussion here is precisely that they have been adopted into a Paganism in ferment.

For brevity's sake alone, two poles of a continuum can be identified among the many other things that are happening within Paganism. A localizing animism has been emerging among Pagans in the last few decades, and perhaps was already inherent among the first self-identified Pagans of the past century. This animism is in tension with Paganism's foundational popularized or democratized esotericism (as identified by Hanegraaff 1996). As Ian Jamison (2011: 138–43) points out, these animist and esotericist trends parallel the "indigenizing" and "globalizing" trajectories identified by Paul Johnson (2002b) among Caribbean indigenous peoples.

They can be observed in the conduct and explanation of Pagan sweat-lodge ceremonies. An increasing emphasis on restoring good relations with the larger-than-human world has led some Pagans to value sweat-lodges as key entry points or initiatory reintroductions to that thoroughly relational, animistic world. They enter the lodges intent on communicating respect for and participation with other-than-human persons in world-making efforts.

They might conduct other ceremonies to express gratitude to animals and plants who have become food, or to seek permission to continue taking lives. In a more esotericist context, sweat-lodges can be significant moments in self-discovery and self-development.

Those influenced by modern Western shamanism, or "neoshamanism", might conceive of the ceremony as a way of accessing and engaging with deep inner, archetypal or psychological realities. This more esotericist Paganism is likely to have a more globalizing style and intention than the localizing, particularizing animist Pagan trajectory. While both ends of this continuum (neither of which exist in pure form isolated from the other) have adopted sweat-lodge and other practices from others, their adaptations are recognizably different. The resulting fusions evidence different relationships with modernism. More animist Pagans are typically seeking ways to resist and sometimes contest individualism, alienation, disembodiment and disenchantment. More esotericist Pagans are typically seeking ways to mitigate alienation by "seeing to regain a 'sacramental view of reality'" (von Stuckrad 2002: 792, citing Benavides 1998: 198). Their individualism and symbolic view of nature may explain the attraction of this and related traditions derived from earlier esoteric currents.

None of this is to say that one pole of the animist–esotericist continuum, or one style of sweat-lodge practice is truer to indigenous roots or, conversely, more modernist than the other. These are fusions of Paganism and a pan-Native American practice. They evidence some of the uneasy negotiations between modernity and its alternatives (indigeneity, re-enchantment, performative embodied emplacement, to name but three). As with other fusions, it is possible to trace some of the lines of influence and sometimes the fractures that indicate incomplete synergy. But to do so tells us little. Pagan fusions of contemporary Western yearnings for enchantment fuse with indigenous technologies for self-performance in ways that are similar to those polemically identified as syncretism among other religionists. These are everyday and ordinary processes in the evolution of religions, arising from communication and proximity between peoples. There are no absolute boundaries – and the effort to police those we imagine to exist (by labelling the result "syncretism") provides yet more evidence of academic efforts to replace religious authorities in maintaining orthodoxies.

SUPERMARKETS

The notion of hybridity is sometimes played out in allegations that one group of religionists or another treat "other cultures" as a "spiritual supermarket". Setting aside the spurious insistence that religion and economics should be categorically separated, the supermarket metaphor fails precisely by being untrue to anyone's shopping habits.

It is a fact that some of the Pagans who participate in sweat-lodges also celebrate northwest European seasonal ceremonies, create ritual working spaces following nineteenth-century protocols, play didgeridoos, venerate or invoke Greek, Roman, "Celtic" or other deities, and otherwise fuse performative materials from diverse sources. However, just like a visit to a supermarket, there are underlying factors that determine and make sense of the choices people make. Just as occasional random items might be added to a trolley because advertising pressure is ubiquitous and powerful, so new ideas might be added to Pagan repertoires, perhaps because a friend or a book suggest a possibility for experiment.

Nonetheless, by and large, people shop for things that they already know match their lifestyle and tastes, or their intentions for a particular meal. Certainly they might eat Italian-style pizza while drinking German-style beer and listening to American-style music. Fusion or eclecticism are commonplace in modern culture. Just so, there are some core themes at the heart of Paganism or its sub-traditions (e.g. Druidry, Heathenry, the Craft) which shape understanding of what resonates or might enhance life and rituals. These themes include a this-worldly spirituality or "nature veneration", a celebration (usually quiet, sometimes ecstatic) of embodiedness, and an encouragement of participation. It is entirely possible for Pagans to address the dead as now gone to another world – but the same Pagans will speak of the same deceased people as reincarnated, or as having reblended their material constituents into the cosmos.

Similarly, Pagans may talk about "spirits" and some insist that intention (putatively an inner, mental act) takes precedence over action. These discources, too, are matched by thoroughly physical and embodied acts: spirits exist as trees or in deity-statues, and intention is irrelevant if not enacted. Some Pagan events are open to all who wish to attend, but even the legally registered US Pagan "churches" or "congregations" typically involve greater degrees of participation than similarly named institutions. In these and other ways, implicit and learnt knowledges underlie the choices particular Pagans (individuals or groups) make when forming their celebrations, teachings and traditions.

In addition to the objections that the "spiritual supermarket" metaphor fails to recognize pre-existing conditions as determinants of shopping habits, it seems to treat religions as different from other activities undertaken in modernity. What is it about religion that leads some observers to think eclecticism (if that occurs) is improper among religions? Once again, the notion of boundaries between religions and between religion and the rest of culture is evident. Also, the "supermarket" allegation seems curiously divorced from debates about gift cultures (following Mauss [1923–4] 1954), which generally celebrate the ubiquity of exchange and cross-cultural learning or fusion. Just as studies of lived religion are likely to demonstrate that "syncretism" labels something so ordinary as to render it uninteresting (except to those who imagine religions differently), so they ought to propel us away from the inadequate polemic about supermarkets. This is not to disallow critiques of the ways in which people adopt and adapt from others any more than it is to approve of theft from supermarkets. It is, however, to indicate that not all learning is (negatively inflected) appropriation.

INVENTING TRADITION

With tedious regularity, scholars who become known for their interest in Paganism are approached by the print and broadcast media with questions that themselves define a tradition. Do Witches do bad magic to harm others? Did the use of mistletoe at Christmas originate in an ancient Druidic fertility rite? Are people who venerate Odin and Thor always racist? As with other traditions there is a annual cycle to the asking of questions like these. Midwinter and midsummer are times for a funny story about Druids, preferably in white robes at Stonehenge or another stone circle, and preferably bearing mystic foliage. May day and Halloween are the times for questions about sinister witchcraft in wild woods and suburban gardens. Saint George's Day can occasion questions about Norse, Germanic and Saxon originating religion.

If it is easy to lampoon the obsessions of the media, the tendencies of academics are no less predictable and disappointing. Paganism, it is regularly asserted, is not a religion because it is too recent and too diverse. It does not have a proper tradition, authority, text or creed. Its individualism might define is as a "spirituality" but not as a "religion". Hervieu-Léger proposes that:

> there is no religion without the explicit, semi-explicit, or entirely implicit invocation of *the authority of a tradition*, an invocation that serves as support for the act of believing. Within this perspective, one designates as "religious" all forms of believing that justify themselves, first and foremost, upon the claim of their inscription within a *heritage of belief.*
> (Hervieu-Léger 2008: 256)

Setting aside the problematic insistence that religionists must "believe" rather than experiment and verify (made three pages earlier in defining "believing" as a particular, non-scientific kind of experientialism), this seems to allow that religions begin when people invoke a heritage or tradition. Pagans often talk of the sub-divisions of their movement as "paths" rather than "denominations". That is, they are not institutions with secure labels but journeys following the steps of others. They are traditions or heritages – and this is so even before Pagans claim authoritative sources from prior to the twentieth century.

It is not difficult to find examples of deliberate and knowing invention among Pagans, and among the sources they cite. Knowing that Iolo Morganwg forged his Druidic wisdom while in prison in 1786 has not stopped Pagan Druids drawing on his work to establish "bardic chair" public performance events (Harvey 2012a). More radical forms of invention include Star Trek rituals and the very notion that those persecuted as "witches" in early modern Europe were members of a Pagan fertility cult (Harvey 2007).

Time will tell if these ideas and practices continue long enough to be recognized by our more sceptical colleagues as a "tradition". At some date, the evident fact that religions are invented by someone, somewhere, and that heritages develop when others celebrate the value of those inventions as a way of engaging with their contemporary world, ceases to be particularly interesting. Modernity might just be a good time to invent religions or potential religions but the invention of Anglican Christianity is not remarked upon every time the Archbishop of Canterbury usurps the originally Roman Catholic cathedral at Canterbury.

I propose then, that while we should pay attention to processes of origination and evolution, we need not treat "heritage" or "invention" as particularly helpful in defining religion.

ETHNIC, ELECTIVE AND ETHICAL RELIGIONS

That Pagans and those who study Paganism identify this religion as a "nature religion" has implications for comparative efforts. The (often disappointed) expectation that a "nature religion" should attract and encourage ecological activism has been a subject of considerable discussion (e.g. Letcher 2000, 2005; Harris 2008; Jamison 2011). The locative pull of "nature religion" deserves further discussion (to apply Appadurai 1996: 178–99; Knott 2005a; and Howell 2011), especially in light of the mobility of its practitioners and attractions.

However, care is required with all our categories, infected as they are by our still too early-modern and theological frameworks. It could legitimately be expected, I think, that "nature religions" might tend to become inherited rather than elective traditions. That is, people will be born into them rather than convert. Indeed, one common way in which people speak of becoming Pagan is "coming home" rather than "converting" – but there again, many religionists make similar claims. In reality, the whole notion that there are "ethnic religions" into which people are born and "elective religions" which people chose to opt into is deeply flawed. The majority of the British population continue to identify as Christians, regardless of whether academics have worked out what this means for defining "Christianity" or "religion", or for tracing the wave of secularization.

Similarly, after an indigenous elder (aged over 90 at the time) declared on Facebook that he was pleased by the numbers of his people who continue to honour their ancestral, traditional, given religion, he indicated that he was referring to Roman Catholic Christianity. If nothing else, these brief notes on religious affiliation and affection should encourage us at least to take more care with the categories we use to compare religious traditions, or more robustly to jettison the packaging together of alleged types of religion. Pagans and other religionists rarely fit the categories and our analyses are likely to be confused.

PAGAN STUDIES

In this chapter I have set out some of the ways in which research among Pagans casts light on the inadequacies of various ways in which religions are sometimes approached. In contrast with those who claim to have resisted the lure of religious approaches to religion, I suggest a more vigorous divorce from the rhetorics of elite Christianity. The notion of syncretism (sometimes pompously disguised as hybridity) continues to invigorate the imaginary "bounded religions" and "bounded religion". The declaration that religion should be separated out from the secular world, that it can be theorized apart from its mingling in with other facets of lived reality, continues the Reformation and Enlightenment projects. This cannot be objective scholarship, and crying "theology" against others masks an alternative partisanship. We are all, necessarily, partisans of one ideology or another. The task of our discipline should be to test our analyses and interpretations by one means or another. Setting up modernism as a yardstick can only result from a delusion of separatism.

More strongly, I have come to wonder why some scholars of religion think the object of our research and teaching is so utterly different from that of anthropological, sociological or philosophical colleagues. Why is it that debate in many disciplines can challenge the dominance of modernism's obsessions? Why is it that our colleagues in other academic arenas are free to find inspiration for challenging thoughts in dialogue with those they study? Is there something about "religion" that makes those who claim the status of scientific scholars of religion worried? Is theology a threat because, far from being diametrically opposed to the project of modernity, it provides much of the language and structure of objectivism? Why is it easy to accuse others (Pagans who research Paganism, Christians who research Christianity, Buddhists who research Buddhism) of being promoters of particular worldviews without recognizing that the promotion of modernism is little different? It is not, after all, as if modernity is a secure, given and natural fact. It requires hard work and has failed to convince many. What is it about "religion" that makes it so different to culture, literature, music, ideas, politics, economics or catering? If those who study such activities can enjoy and promote them (or particular aspects of them) what is it about religion that is different?

The problem, I am arguing throughout this book, is twofold. First, and most easily dealt with, "religion" has been wrongly defined as believing in transcendence. But the larger problem is that opposing religion to rationality has led modernist academics to invest considerable energy in avoiding contagion by religious postulations. If, instead, we attend to religions as everyday performances, they seem no more dangerous to study than cooking or sports. Studying a religion that evolved within modernity but often resists the allure of modernism can help liberate us to do our scholarly work better. That is, real world religion can be studied in the real world.

I am not, here or elsewhere, promoting the wholesale demolition of modernity. I do not need to. "We have never been modern" (Latour 1993). Or perhaps we have been modern in a range of creative or rebellious ways. Certainly, there is no singular form taken by modernity everywhere.

Enchantment has not been superseded by bureaucracy, intellectualism and rationalism. Such dualities are unliveable. Instead we have evolved, as always, new hybridities. Perhaps now, with colleagues in other disciplines, scholars of religion can face the fact that religious people continue to resist (implicitly at least) the wildest fantasies of modernism and mingle religion with materiality, relationality with experimentation, and their religions with other religions.

In the evolution of Paganism a wide range of influences have blended. The choices made and experiments conducted by Pagans, paralleling those of other religionists, indicate that religion has been poorly interpreted through lenses designed by Reformation and Enlightenment ideologies. Certainly, Pagan Studies can make better contributions to the debates about religions, and will do as its practitioners become more skilled in reflexivity and dialogue. It will not advance our understanding of religion, however, if colleagues continue to set up fantasies of separation (between scholars and religions, between religions and religions, or between religions and science) as if these were natural and necessary.

11. Christians do religion like other people

This relatively brief chapter demonstrates that my earlier assertion that Christianity is not a religion was faulty. Its point, like that of this whole book, is twofold. We have mis-defined Christianity as belief, and we have approached studying Christianity wrongly by seeking to understand believing. We may have inherited the first error, but we remain responsible for continuing it by pursuing the second.

What if we (scholars of religion) had taken Judaism as the starting place for our project of understanding, analysing and debating religion and had only then researched among Christians? What if we had taken studying rather than believing texts as a core practice to examine? If lived Judaism (and not Judaism as imagined by Christians) was our definitional starting point, would we have looked for ways in which stories (rooted in and generative of texts) shape daily observances and world-structuring ceremonies as Neusner (2002: 256–60) shows them to do in Judaism? Would we have researched, written and taught more about the eating and drinking habits of Christians? To some degree we have done so, noticing, for example, that Christian denominational differences are not always about doctrines and ideas but about styles of leadership, liturgy and ritualism. Sometimes, too, we have paid attention to the diversification of Christian practice and lifestyle as it relates to cultural and geographical location. However, some of us have ruined that effort by writing about syncretism and most of our textbooks tend to follow the lead of theological works, imagining that the key matters for attention should be famous names, canonical texts and correct doctrines.

More radically, perhaps, what if we had taken Maori *tapu* processes as definitive of religion? What if we look for *tapu* in the Church of England? Would it, for instance, be easier to see how Christianity is a religion like

---

other religions if we analysed the kind of data that gets the media's attention? The current ferment over the possibility of some women becoming Church of England bishops makes more sense if this Christianity is really all about what people do with or as gendered bodies than it does if we continue to think that Christianity is about beliefs to do with transcendence. The vitriol with which some British Christians respond to legislation that might compel the Church of England (as a state-funded body) to conduct marriages between gay and lesbian couples also seems to be evidence of contested taboos. It would probably serve as the perfect case study with which to update Mary Douglas's *Purity and Danger* (1992).

CONTRARY INDICATORS

Christianity is, after all, a religion like others. Like other religions, it is not and never has been fully or accurately defined by belief and believing. Like them, It is embodied, emplaced, performative and not *fully* dualistic, interiorized or individualized. Despite the undoubted power of the processes of disenchantment, individualization and interiorization, Christians have continued to perform collective, relational acts. Charles Taylor correctly identifies the continuing post-Reformation trend towards "taking religion seriously … more personally, more devotionally, inwardly, more committedly" (C. Taylor 2008: 179). He is equally correct that conjoined commitment (to sincerely, inwardly held beliefs) and confession (as much as of faith as of doubt and other faults) have empowered processes of disenchantment. Nonetheless, despite strident rhetoric and vigorous reformation of religion and society, people have not ceased either ritualizing or being social embedded in groups, cosmos or notions of goodness (well-being or proper living as much as morality).

If it is true generally that "we have never been modern" (Latour 1993), perhaps many of the Christians among us also remain only imperfectly disenchanted. Perhaps the more resistant or rebellious (against modernizing) of them either remain fully enchanted or are energetically re-enchanting. This might explain Taylor's second-thought in which he distinguishes not "bounded selves" but "buffered selves" from the "porous self of the earlier enchanted world" (C. Taylor 2008: 183). Indeed, even the most thoroughgoing secularist, atheist recluse continues to live in a participative cosmos and to interact with a communal world. They can imagine atomized individualization and devote considerable effort to hyperseparatism but have to buffer themselves against participative reality – because there are no impermeable boundaries. They live because bacteria live with, in and through them. They live because matter energetically mingles and fuses all our realities. Similarly, pietistic Protestant Christian movements may provide classic examples of disenchantment, but the very fact that they are movements in which people act together, becoming intimates even as they preach or hear imaginaries, demonstrates the continuity of degrees of enchantment.

If Christianity is a religion in which Christians continue to do what other religious people do (e.g. ritualize, commune while consuming or restraining themselves from consumption, celebrate similarity while enforcing separations, employ ritualists and other virtuosi), it can be studied in the same way as other religions. So it is important that there are significant studies that show various ways in which this can be done. Although too much writing about Christians obsessively reproduces the imagination and project of theological, text-centred elites, it is evidently possible to theorize these aspects of Christianity (i.e. belief and transcendence) not as defining "religion" but as defining particular mechanisms within a specific religion. This chapter provides some examples of the kind of analyses and theorizations that have arisen from scholarly attention to historical and/or contemporary Christianity in lived reality and/or as everyday life. One of the difficulties in doing so, is the struggle to use a language (English) redolent with interiorizing, individualizing and anthropocentricism to speak about the real world. Nonetheless, the experiment is worth pursuing and testing.

NEGOTIATING ALTERITIES

In a series of works, Thomas Csordas discusses the lives and acts of charismatic Christians and points to new directions for academic analysis and debate. His work powerfully attends both to embodiment and alterity (see Csordas 1994, 1997, 2004) and insistently demonstrates that religion (and life more generally) is necessarily intercorporeal and intersubjective (Csordas 2008). To put this another way, since materiality and difference are constitutive features of cosmic reality, they are, by necessity and sometimes by design, central to human social, political and religious lives. Csordas invites us to consider the entanglement or embraidedness (my terms which attempt to see where some things are confused and others are deliberately fused) of putatively different aspects of life. The apparent effervescence of charismatic Christian events, framed by Catholic or Pentecostalist heritages, evidences fascinating tensions between imagination and intimacy. In healing ceremonies, charismatics invoke powerful others (Jesus or the Virgin Mary), visualizing their intimate and tactile presence and healing power. They gain knowledge of themselves and empowerment to consider new possibilities.

All of this, and more, is evident in Csordas's work, but I cite it not because of its provocative and ramifying theorizations (exciting as these are), nor because he says "What I am saying has nothing to do with belief" (Csordas 2004: 183), but because of its careful attention to the performances and lived realities of Christian lives. He writes not only of dramatic ceremonies and curious ideas, but provides examples (e.g. Csordas 1994) of alterity in the everyday intimate learning of appropriate habits for prayer and in the everyday intimate avoidances of alcohol and other (taboo) matters.

SURVEILLANCE AND ABSTINENCE

Although there are certainly many differences between the medieval and modern worlds, marked by terms like "Reformation", "Wars of Religion" and "Enlightenment", there are also interesting continuities. Monasteries continue to be places where people subject themselves both to divine and self surveillance. Talal Asad writes:

> The formation/transformation of moral dispositions (Christian virtues) depended on more than the capacity to imagine, to perceive, to imitate ... It required a particular program of disciplinary practices. The rites prescribed by that program ... aimed to construct and reorganise distinctive emotions – desire (*cupiditas/caritas*), humility (*humilitas*), remorse (*contritio*) – on which the central Christian virtue of obedience to god depended.   (Asad 1993: 134)

It is important that the "rites" here include not only ceremonies in church but also manual labour in gardens, kitchens and other venues. Bodies and souls (to the degree that there is any dualism among these monks) are trained, not merely restrained or repressed. The practice of legitimized "technologies of the self" and especially of self-surveillance (Foucault 1999: 162) shaped the embodied, emplaced performance of a Christian elite. While other Christians were not intended or able to (con)form themselves to monastic rules they were certainly expected to aim to remodel their lives to become more godly in acts, imaginations, desires, knowledges and deportment. Gustavo Ludueña (2005) demonstrates how some of these practices and analyses are relevant to a Latin American monastery today. His attempt to understand a silent monastic Order by subjecting himself to the slightly more relaxed rules of a "retreat" in the guest accommodation tells us much about the shaping of *habitus* (Bourdieu 1977) by attentive exercise. Significantly, he also reflects on implications for scholarly practices restrained but attentive participation.

Taboos, tensions and transgressions around sexuality may be most evident in the performance of priesthood. In discussing ways in which priestly bodies and duties can be acted at the altar, Liz Stuart (2009) clearly sets out what is possible when sexuality and gender are "erased". Efforts to bring these imaginaries into intimate reality involve further examples of communal and personal training, surveillance and labour. Conversely, media and court reports of clerical sexual abuse evidence failures of restraint, as well as many failures by Church and other authorities to act on information from surveillance and testimony. This resonates with Douglas's (1992) insight that disputes over communal and cultural imagined boundaries are often played out in bodies and/or concerns about bodies. By bringing issues related to "restraint" into dialogue with those around "sacrifice" it also chimes with Girard's (1988, 2004) discussions of religious violence.

Asceticism is not alien to Protestant Christianities. Koerner's (2005) discussion of purpose-built Lutheran churches as gathering and sermon-focused places illustrates an early example of the retraining of Protestant embodiment to harmonize with desired or proclaimed habits. It would also be possible to trace evolving Calvinist efforts to practise restraint, such as those which attracted the attention of Max Weber (1930). More recent material and performative data are provided by Marie Griffith in her examination of *Born Again Bodies*, demonstrating. the ways in which Evangelical Christian women seek to conform to standards advertised by the diet, beauty and fitness industries and distance themselves from "the excesses associated with nonwhite culture" (Griffith 2004: 225). This is possible rather than aberrant because of a tradition (not always enunciated or fully familiar to those that maintain it) of practices that diminish gender. Sexual taboos are similarly empowered among American Evangelicals as surveillance over virginity and abstinence is extended by public declarations and material culture like the "silver ring thing" or "purity ring".

SYNERGY, MIGRATION AND RESISTANCE

Christianity, like all lived religions, evolves by dint of adjusting or adapting to, and/or accommodating or acclimatizing within surrounding influences, religious or otherwise. As religious people migrate they take their habituated observances with them but learn and retrain themselves as they relish or resist what they find elsewhere. Studies of Christianity that privilege the "founder, text, creeds and institutions" tradition generally mis-present such matters, encouraging a view that definitive Christian beliefs are poorly expressed by popular activities.

In contrast, studies of Latin American, African and other "non-western" Christian lives and communities are much richer. Studies of migrating and/ or subaltern Christians are often particularly valuable as discussions of the resistant potential of lived religion (Orsi 1997: 15). For example, Thomas Tweed's rich ethnography of Cuban migrants to Miami (Tweed 1997) provided an excellent foundation for his more recent retheorization of the fluid dynamics both of religion and of research about religion (Tweed 2005, 2006). Similarly, Charlie Thompson discusses Jacalteco Maya (from Guatemala, but migrating from and to Mexico and the USA) and the synergies emerging as and in their veneration of an indigenous Virgin and their performance of dances that remember the Spanish Conquest and resist ongoing colonialisms (Thompson 2000, 2001, 2005).

Another noteworthy example of the value of research concerned with the migration of subaltern Christians is provided when Vásquez resists the temptation of seeing locative "emplacement" as an entirely positive and harmonious experience, writing instead about "domination and resistance" (Vásquez 2011: 261–90). Here he considers all manner of ambiguous tensions and unambiguous dominations in real lives and lived religioning, not forgetting the subtle and not-so-subtle acts of resistance that often fall outside the surveillance or sacralizing of religious hierarchies. Lived Christianity is a complex and unbounded phenomena and is unlikely to be captured in one study. Concerted efforts to introduce students to this Christianity (rather than the elite imaginary version with posture of obeisance to a too-neat, too-textual lineage) might prove difficult but ought to demonstrate the great value of our discipline's ability to speak about the real world.

VERNACULAR AND VICARIOUS RELIGION

Primiano makes it crystal clear that he coined the term "vernacular religion" (Primiano 1995, 2012) to emphasize the need for and value of studying lived religion, the only kind there is. Those who use the term to distinguish the religious acts of "the laity" or of "ordinary people" from those of religious hierarchies have, despite Primiano's clarity, misunderstood. What the Pope or the Dalai Lama do, even were they to do the same thing every day, and even if they were to do precisely what their predecessors did, is lived religion. It is vernacular religioning. It is religion in today's practice. Douglas Davies and Mathew Guest's *Bishops, Wives and Children* (2007) resonates with this approach. While analysing the processes by which Christian "tradition is transmitted, modified, embraced or rejected" (in the words of the book's cover blurb), they attend to the ordinary lives of bishops within families and other relational webs. Any illusion about the embodiment, emplacement or shifting, everyday vernacular performance of Christianity is shattered by this carefully empirical study of real lives.

Real differences, however, are signalled by terms like clergy and laity, or preacher and congregation. It is not that any of the groups identified by these labels should be given priority in defining their religion. Christianity, like other religions, is what people do. However, part of what Christians, like other religionists, do is employ individuals to conduct ceremonies, teach histories and encourage observance of taboos. As elsewhere, some of these people are given the job of living unusual or distinctive lives so that others, knowing that rituals are being maintained and restrained lives being lived, can live less devoted or ritualized lives. This is part of a wider phenomenon that might be identified by using Grace Davie's term "vicarious religion", meaning "The notion of religion being performed by the active minority but on behalf of a much larger number, who (implicitly at least) not only understand, but, quite clearly, approve of what the minority is doing" (Davie 2002: 46; 2010).

Davie actually means more than a group which employs clergy. She seeks to identify the phenomena by which some people who rarely if ever attend (let alone participate in) church ceremonies are keen to maintain church institutions. Europeans who pay church taxes when they could easily opt out are good examples of this trend. Similarly, perhaps some of the 59.3 per cent of the population of England and Wales who declared themselves to be Christians by voluntarily ticking a box in the 2011 national census (Office of

National Statistics 2012) were indicating their desire to maintain Christian institutions.

Another of Davie's admirable phrases, "believing without belonging" (Davie 1990, 1994), encompasses the "vicarious religionists" within an even larger phenomenon of those who continue to answer affirmatively to questions such as "do you believe in god?", but assert that "you do not have to go to church to be Christian". Some, certainly, "cherish" the continued existence and availability of churches (buildings and congregations), wanting them "to be there, partly as a holder of ancestral memory, partly as a resource against some future need (e.g., their need for a rite of passage, especially a funeral; or as a source of comfort and orientation in the face of some collective disaster)" (C. Taylor 2008: 224).

Perhaps this is well expressed in Abby Day's phrase "believing in belonging" (Day 2009, 2011). In Davie's usage, "vicarious religion" is a new and growing trend made possible by the "secularizing" separation of religion from public life. However, there are continuities with entirely traditional religious practices of expecting the few to do ceremonies on behalf of the many. Indeed, it seems possible that the normal or majority way of being Christian has always been the kind of religion identified by Yang (1967: 20) as "diffuse" or by Jeffrey Cox (1982) and John Wolffe (1994) as "diffusive". Perhaps, too, Robert Bellah's "civil religion" (1967) – especially as elaborated by Gerald Parsons (2004, 2008) in relation to Siena, and by Paul Johnson (2005) in relation to the atrocity in New York in September 2011 – might point us towards the majority form rather than the modern exception to ways in which religion has always been performed by most people.

BELIEF-ERS

While belief and believing do not define religion, they are significant aspects of the activities of Christians. To understand believing as something done within Christianity we have to stop theorizing belief as connected to postulation, ideas, interiority, subjectivity. Rather, we have to think of believing as another kind of relational activity. Citing an interesting array of authorities to support his contention that belief is something people do, de Certeau says: "Cut off from the act that posited it, regarded as a 'mental occurrence', belief received the comprehensively negative definition of corresponding to what one does not know or see, in other words, of being the *other* of knowledge or sight" (de Certeau 1985: 198).

Believing, however, can be retrieved as an action, and especially as the kind of action that promotes further actions, when we pay attention to the ways in which people learn to be believers. That is, within the kinds of Christianity in which believing is significant, people do not only learn about the objects of belief (e.g. deity, miracles, salvation) but also, and more importantly, they learn to enact belief-ing. I use this clumsy term to aid my mental exercise of trying not to think believing happens "within" people. Belief-ing is a practice or activity which needs to be learnt and properly performed within particular Christian groups because the ways in which people do belief differ. Pentecostalists, for instance, learn words to speak publically about belief-ing and beliefs and, in speaking (or "witnessing") they become Pentecostalists (Seamone 2013). Intimacy between neophytes to the movement and existing congregations requires the learning of the protocols for witnessing. The imagined faithful community becomes a face-to-face intimate group as people act together by speaking and hearing in ways that are deemed appropriate. Entering a congregation and gaining acceptance is a process of mutual make-believing and make-believers.

While the specifics of any Christian group's belief and belief-ing should not be taken to be applicable elsewhere and, as argued in Chapter 3, while belief is not definitive of religion but only of some kinds of Christianity, similar process are observable elsewhere. Jews, Pagans, Buddhists, Maori and others learn appropriate ways to speak and act that show they are within the intimate fold of the desired community. Thus, studying religion requires attention not only to the specific content of locally meaningful discourse and performance, but also to the general processes by which people learn and improve their doing of religion with others.

CHRISTIANITY AS MATERIALITY

In Chapter 3 I noted that Caroline Walker Bynum's careful attention to late medieval Christian materiality (2011) offers something of a challenge to Lévi-Strauss's culture/nature contrast. Without doubting that indigenous Puerto Ricans tested the humanity of Europeans by seeing if their bodies rotted or that Spanish councils debated evidence as to whether "natives" could believe or not, the contrast is too strong, too fixed and too polemical. Bynum writes:

> The problem for medieval worshippers and theorists, both those who doubted and those who believed, was change – not the line between

person and thing, or the line between life and death, but the divide between what something is (its identity) and its inevitable progression towards death. (Bynum 2011: 284)

This is close to what Lévi-Strauss represents as the view of indigenous Puerto Ricans rather than Spanish Catholics. Bynum's work demonstrates in considerable detail that late medieval Christians (clergy and laity, reformist and orthodox) were often deeply concerned and strongly motivated to struggle with materiality. Indeed, she shows that this concern with materiality pervaded the era. She concludes that "the assumptions – and the anxiety – about materiality that we find in religious discourse and religious behavior can be seen in scientific thought and vernacular literature as well" (*ibid.*: 271).

Perhaps what the councils noted by Lévi-Strauss illustrate is not a sustained or systematic difference from indigenous Puerto Ricans but a moment in the transition from the late medieval to the early modern world. Nonetheless, in every period of Christian history from late antiquity until today evidence of a central and definitive interest in material proliferates. This is not to say that the interest remains static, or that the assumptions and anxieties are constant. Bynum is clear that paradox was familiar among late medieval Christians. It seems likely that reformers (both Catholic and Protestant) tried to resolve matters by emphasizing interiority, subjectivity and, above all, faith. Nonetheless, in every period, faith in an incarnate deity who promised bodily resurrection fuse Christian interests in transcendence and immanence, souls and bodies, spiritual and material benefits (e.g. salvation and healing), supernatural and sensual ways of being in the world.

There is, in the end, something utterly ridiculous in the notion that Christianity is disinterested in bodies and things. Large public matters such as the great cathedrals (massively heavy even if some give the illusion of lightness) and the arrangement of cities and city-living around them demonstrate this. Small private matters like devotional cards and annotated bibles reinforce it. The evidence of the profound corporeality of Christianity has been a key theme in recent scholarly research. A few excellent examples will suffice: Fenella Cannell's *Power and Intimacy in the Christian Philippines* (1999) and *The Anthropology of Christianity* (2006), Davies and Guest's *Bishops, Wives and Children* (2007), Simon Coleman's *The Globalisation of Charismatic Christianity* (2007), Webb Keane's *Christian Moderns: Freedom and Fetish in the Mission Encounter* (2007), and Ruth Marshall's *Political Spiritualities* (2009). In specific and different ways, all of these demonstrate that believing is a performative, emplaced, material and materializing disposition, competence, and experience. Christianity, like other religions is a discipline mediated in and by bodies and things.

VANTAGE POINTS

Chapter 3 was predicated on the notion that if Christianity is about belief it is unique. If it is unique either it is the only religion or it is not a religion at all. Therefore, either the proper subject of the study of religions is Christianity and those phenomena that have become like it (Protestant Buddhism, Protestant Paganism, etc.) or Christianity should be ignored altogether. However, this chapter has contested that view and insisted that in reality Christianity is not about belief. At least, it is not about believing as some interior, personal, individual experience of affirming some truth. Some kinds of Christianity (and similar kinds of Protestant-influenced traditions) may emphasize believing in this way. Nonetheless, even they too are not *about* believing. Even they are about performing affirmation, commitment and witnessing. In short, they are about public confession of faith. They are about relationships of trust. They are quests to become increasingly intimate with others. They are disciplined ways of behaving among others with whom one wants to belong in distinction from those people who are imagined to behave differently.

Christianity, as a way of life or even as a set of performances, looks quite different if it is approached not as beliefs derived from authoritative teachers and texts but as something more like other religions. Lived Christianity can be studied, like other religions, as an embodied, emplaced, performative, material and relational activity. Such a Christianity is a plural (if not always pluralistic) phenomenon. Just as some kinds of Judaism do not look particularly Jewish to some Jews, so some kinds of Christianity look radically strange from some Christian vantage points. The effort we need to make is to stop treating vantage points as providing objective, incontestable, universally and permanently valid perspectives. Whatever other faults have followed from accepting that Christianity is a belief-system, and that believing in transcendence is definitive of religion, it is the folly of imitating a putatively objective deity that has most damaged scholarly practices. Our engagements with particular local communities, as they increase intimacy or bar strangers, as they act (in ceremonies or speech) to disseminate or test imagined possibilities, provide valuable data for further debate, theorizing and theory-testing.

The exciting thing for the future project of religion is to see what happens when we stop using a faulty model of Christianity not only as a pattern for presenting religion or religions, but also as a pattern for scholarly practice. Too many of us are "believers in belief" (Latour 2010) but we can act differently. Studies of lived Christianity are showing how dramatic and impressive the results can be. It is not only that we might experiment with seeing Christianity through the lens of *dharma*, *din*, *halakah* or *taboo*, but that Christianity might turn out to be another "elsewhere". Its theorization of disciplined relationality in a multi-species world might cast light on neighbouring religions.

12. Religion is etiquette in the real world

Religion evolved in a relational and material world. The recent human experiment of hyperseparation may have misled interpreters of religion, but it has not entirely rerouted the trajectory of religioning. Not only within the many ways of resisting modernism, but also within the many ways of being modern, religions are perhaps most easily observed (seen, heard, smelled, tasted and touched) when people ritualize together. The bits of religion where people teach others are required because people need to be formed and reformed to relate in ways that are deemed locally appropriate. In such ways, persons are made, and so are communities. But these rituals and teaching practices should not be treated in isolation from everyday life. Just as life cannot be divided between secular and spiritual phases, religion is diffused throughout everything people do. It is integral to everyday human encounters in a multispecies material, relational world.

RESEARCHING DELUSIONS

Understanding religion has been made difficult by our entanglement in confusions about what kind of modernity we inhabit. In truth, there has never been a pure modernity, so we have never been completely modern. We have, however, been trying rather hard. Similarly, we have never really been completely disenchanted, but we have succumbed to a particular kind of rationalism. We have imagined ourselves divorced from bodies, communities and places. These things are true generally. But there are some specifically academic fantasies that are nested within those larger commitments to particular kinds of modernism. Too often, we academics have attributed objectivity to ourselves, claiming to analyse objects (subjective persons, material artefacts or inert scenery) without being reciprocally affected or relationally involved. In reality it is not possible to avoid participation or interaction. Our efforts objectify and pacify the world while simultaneously suppressing our relationality. In imagining the possibility of separation we have partially embodied and enacted it. We have conducted research and teaching while struggling to impose the imaginary modernist world on the intimate relational, participative and material world. In doing so we have only researched a fragment of the real world. This has largely been a figment of our modernist framework.

Researching a double fiction – our own delusions in a virtual reality – has not required us to escape the constraints of particular perspectives. The commonplace rhetoric by which scholars of religion(s) distinguish ourselves from theologians seems to have been easier to assert than to achieve. Belief, interiority, subjectivity, personal experience and other matters that were given strong emphasis in Reformation and early modern Europe continue to shape teaching and research regardless of where or among whom we work. This criticism is well established but continues to be forcefully reiterated because a satisfactory solution has not been reached. The closing down of departments of religious studies (by whatever name) only diminishes the number of scholars dedicated to understanding and discussing what "religion" means in the contemporary world. Regardless of the ranting of those who still have not realized that their secularism is largely a product of Christian Reformation world-remaking, various phenomena are usefully labelled religion. There is something we need to define and debate while people assert that they are religious, as well as ethnic, gendered, aged, political, and otherwise self-identified.

In the preceding chapters I have aimed to do two things. One is to seek data "elsewhere" that might inform a revised definition of religion. The second is to contribute to imagining what a real world approach to researching and teaching about religion might involve. Both of these matters are related to my doubts that religion is something so different from the other phenomena which academics study. It should not require such peculiar acrobatics to avoid contagion. Can the evident signs of phobia or animosity be anything more than a barely suppressed knowledge of the Euro-Christian shaping of academic practice and self-understanding? For all the posturing, if the best that self-declared scientific study of religions can do is replicate debates about beliefs (ideology, postulation, irrationality) and transcendence (metaphysical or non-empirical imaginaries; or culture separate from nature, or vice versa), then it has not gone far enough.

200

TURNING THE TABLES

It is liberating to discover, however, that there are many ways to be modern. Just as Yoruba moderns can deploy animist materialism, and just as Pagan moderns can ritualize against disenchantment, so scholarly moderns can act differently. There are plenty of signs of good scholarship being done in ways that promise better understanding and more exciting debates in the future. Feminist scholarly attention to the gendered realities of religious practice and rhetoric led the way, and continues to do so. Postcolonial challenges to dominant ways of being academic have enriched reflection on more just and more accurate theorizing of lived realities (e.g. Connell 2007; Tuhiwai Smith 2012). Approaches to performance and material culture have greatly advanced recent engagements with vernacular religion. Research among indigenous peoples has strengthened the project of focusing on non-supernaturalist religion as it is done by the majority of religionists. Placing such religious imaginaries as founders, texts, and dogmas within the performative, materializing, relational intimacies of religious living has begun to enable a far richer sense of what people do when they maintain and develop their religions and religioning.

As noted in Chapter 3, when Catholic Christian inquisitional commissions sought to know whether indigenous peoples in the Americas were human, one of the things they looked for was evidence of religion. To them, "true religion" was self-evidently Christianity, but something like Christianity would show that people could be converted. Later, missionaries in Australia tried to find something like Christianity within Aboriginal cultures. Failing that, some went to Aotearoa to try their luck among Maori. In these and similar cases, to have a religion would mean believing in something or someone like the Christian god, having teachings and ways of teaching them, and participating in rituals for other-than-secular purposes. In the Victorian period moralizing became increasingly more important than ritualizing as a positive indicator of religion. There was no need to define religion as anything other than "something like Christianity" because modern Christianity had replaced pre-modern Christianity as the model for "religion". Nonetheless, "modern" Christianity continued to emphasize the kinds of interiorities valorized in the early modern project of elevating the newly conceived state.

Most of the textbooks used to introduce religions to high school and university students continue to assume that Christianity is more definitively religion than is any other phenomena. This rightly provokes many scholars of religion to object strongly to the resulting "world religions paradigm". Others similarly object to the continuing evidence of theological interests

201

in such teaching programmes. Founders, texts, creeds and the imaginations of elites continue to frame the ways in which all religions are taught. Secondary emphasis on "expressions of belief" brings narratives of diversification, degeneration or revival, syncretism and popularization into the picture. In the end, students gain a Protestant view of Buddhism, Jainism, Judaism, Paganism and all other religions. These are the versions that adapt most closely to the demands made by the modernizing state ideology. Alternatively, students learn to understand the Protestant, modernity-adapted versions of these religions while remaining either ignorant of or confused about religions which are not belief-systems.

Food, Sex and Strangers is my effort to turn the tables on this learning about belief-systems. I have imagined that by seeking to bring "religion" into dialogue with *taboo*, *bimaadiziwin* or *halakah* we might gain a richer and better understanding. By putting putatively religious performances into other frames, those formed by the evolution of relational repertoires and intimacies elsewhere, I share the hope that we might understand similarities and differences more clearly. I do not propose that we hammer local facts into systems established elsewhere. It would serve only negatively polemical purposes to force matters into a mould shaped by *dharma* or *din* or any of a thousand other locally appropriate terms. However, having recognized that "belief in god" has not served us well, we must now do better than defining religion as "non-empiricism". Conversely, understanding what people mean by *taboo*, *bimaadiziwin*, *halakah*, *dharma*, *din* and so on might enable us to think and research about lived religion more interestingly and effectively. We might also notice some matters and activities to which we have not yet paid sufficient attention.

Therefore, the effort to turn the tables is not limited to challenging the dominance of Christian theological topics in defining the objects we might study. The more difficult task is to reflect on the impact of Christianity and its modernism on the perspectives, approaches and methods which we have become accustomed to thinking of as critical. The fact that "secular" is an aspect of a post-Reformation project to establish modernist ways of living and behaving ought to have warned us against too strongly separating religion off from other activities. Instead we have gone further and imagined ourselves in the image of the allegedly omniscient Christian deity. We have thought ourselves able to become utterly objective and all-knowing if only we could just do one more experiment without subjective entanglements. Thus, while some of us criticize others for being too theological, we have almost all celebrated a modern Christian idea of scholarly rectitude and surveillance.

In attempting to do the "god-trick" (Haraway 1991: 189), we have sought to understand people's interiority (soul, mind, emotion, intention, desire, believing) while imagining both them and ourselves as hyperseparated individuals in a dualistic world. This is partly related to the fact that we have an unsustainable notion of ourselves as minds observing discrete facts. More powerfully, it is also due to our having not yet fully considered the potential of approaching people as relational beings in a relational cosmos. We have failed to follow Darwin into a vibrantly relational world. It is time to move on. If our world is relational rather than Cartesian, all sorts of things flow. Here are four of them:

- This world is inhabited only by social beings.
- Our first need (as humans) is to negotiate with other persons (most of whom are not human).
- Negotiation most passionately seeks either respectful or resistant outcomes.
- The most significant outcome of negotiation is openness to further acts of relating.

These four assertions will receive some elaboration at the finale of this conclusion.

In demonstrating that ritual drives ways of being "deeply into the bone", Ronald Grimes argues that "ordinary acts, when extraordinarily practiced, break open, transforming human conventions and revealing what is most deeply desirable, most cosmically orientating, and most fully human" (Grimes 2000: 346). But even the regular repetition of ordinary acts in ordinary ways mould habits which form *habitus* (Bourdieu 1977, 1984), entraining people together in locally appropriate ways of being or becoming persons. A definition of religion that enables us to research and teach about the real world will need to embrace its relationality, performativity, materiality, fluidity and locality. This is, most certainly, not to require religious people to understand or treat the world in any particular way (other than those they define for themselves and their intimates). Rather, it is an assertion about academic practice and tools. Useful approaches to researching and teaching about religion as it is done by real people will require further effort to dwell within a relational, performative and mattered cosmos and to attend to the ways in which religions work in the real world. The two together (defining and approaching) will entail both table-turning and being elsewhere.

REAL WORLD ACADEMIA

In a previous chapter I wondered what it is about "religion" that makes it seem so different – so impure, infectious, suspicious, dangerous, corrupting – that some academics insist it is an improper subject for study. I am still wondering. They do not say that politics, gender, sexuality, war or catering should not be studied. Do they imagine that because religion is the twin of their own alleged secularity to research or teach about it would undermine their unstable rationalist objectivity? Is religion really more threatening than other things that such people might define themselves by? Is religion just too queer? Does studying it have the potential to unmask the posture of separation from religion and, terrifyingly, thereby show that all manner of other separatisms are fictional? Do our colleagues think that destabilizing the religion/secular division might involve a dangerous rebellion against the state? These seem possible but unhelpful fantasies which limit scholarly ability to engage with reality. While others keep shouting "we are not theologians!" to drown out the possibility that in reality "we have never really, fully achieved being modern", others of us have taken another look at the world. Or at least, in case my enthusiasm has led me to read people in ways they did not intend, let me say only that I think academic work is already being done differently.

Music studies departments are not full of composers, performance studies departments are not full of dancers or actors, and literature studies departments are not full of creative writers. However, colleagues in such places do seem to recognize the positive value of some kind of participation – whether by themselves, other colleagues or their students. Some anthropologists and some physicists, meanwhile, have recognized that fuller modes of participation are not only helpful, not only necessary, but utterly inescapable. Greatly inspired by finding that colleagues like Manuel Vásquez are thinking carefully and hard about the participative universe, I want to reinforce my previously tentative efforts to understand what doing academia in the real world might mean.

Karen Barad states that:

Theories are not sets of free-floating ideas but rather specific material practices in the ongoing intra-active engagement of the world with itself, and as such they are empirically open and responsive. That is, they are always already part of what the world does in its ongoing openness and responsiveness to itself. Why would we want it to be otherwise? Why would we want theories to be shielded from the world?
(Barad 2011: 4–5)

Why? Because we have imagined ourselves and the world differently. We have thought of science differently. Ignoring all our mediating devices, we have imagined science as a quest for unmediated knowledge (Latour 2010). Barad, however, insists that research is something we do as "a way of understanding the world from within and as part of it" (Barad 2007: 88). If the world and cosmos are, as Barad argues, thoroughly relational, then the separations we have forced to intervene between relationships are barriers to engagement and, therefore, to understanding. Barad's proposal is that we need "agential realism": acknowledging that material reality exists in its own right as a participant in the myriad relational inter-activities that constitute the cosmos. That which we encounter "kicks back", i.e. there is no "innocent, symmetrical form of interaction between the knower and the known" (*ibid.*: 2). There is only relational matter, active stuff. Our research, then, must entail participation and presence. Recognizing this can only enhance our ability to understand and analyse. Barad, then, notes of the "more familiar approaches" (i.e. a naive empiricism that elides important social factors or a social constructivist approach that excludes natural factors or agencies) that they:

> take the nature/culture dichotomy for granted, whereas agential realism understands the objective referent for empirical claims to be material-discursive phenomena (with the notions of objectivity and referent appropriately redefined). I noted that we could all agree that one experiment never makes or breaks any theory, and with this proviso, agential realism offers a possibility for thinking "the social" and "the natural" together in a way that is responsive and responsible to the world
> (Barad 2011: 5)

Barad concludes: "Our meta/physics, like all good scientific theories, should be alive, responsible, and responsive to the world. How else will our theories matter?" (*ibid.*: 9). I can think of no good reason why the study of religion should be excluded from this rethinking of scholarly performance.

BRACKETING ASIDE

One benefit of material and performative approaches to religion as material and performative phenomena is that we may be released from the effort of "bracketing out". Phenomenology has continued to emphasize subjectivity as the main object for research, taking it to be the main locus of experience, sometimes transcending nature and culture. As Vásquez writes:

> In religious studies, the pure subjectivity of the believer – whether
> expressed in the raw power of his/her inner states, or through his/her
> "ultimate concerns," or in the search for meaning – provides the ulti-
> mate, authentic, and irreducible foundation to avoid getting lost amid
> the diverse and ever-changing world of discourses, practices, and
> institutions. The result of this "jargon of authenticity" (McCutcheon
> 2003: 173) has been consistently the same: the denigration of "exter-
> nal" religious phenomena, often tied to the body, as mere manifesta-
> tions of a deep inner and supra-historical reality.
>
> (Vásquez 2011: 64)

Once we are fully liberated from the obsession with belief, subjectivity, affective and cognitive experience, and other forms of interiority (except as aspects
of the performances that interest us), we will concentrate more fully on what
people do.

To be clear, belief is at the heart of the way that some Christians do their
religion. It is at the heart of the religioning of other people who do their
religions like Christians do theirs. Respect is at the heart of many indigenous religions. Purity is a core concern of Jews and Shintoists, among others.
Belief, respect and purity are, however, not interior attitudes but expressive
acts. They are not expressions of soul, mind, spirit or some other postulated
interiority. They are actions or performances. They are deeds that contribute
to living life. Religion is something people do. When scholars study what
people do they are not studying the expression of attitudes, ideas, postulations. They are not bracketing out the allegedly interior or transcendent
spiritual, soulful essentials of religion. They are studying religion. They can
study religion as fully relational and participative persons because religion is
not an alien subjectivity but a(nother) relational activity.

LOOKING AGAIN AT LIVED RELIGION

I propose that we take believing to be a corporeal and corporate performance of some religionists, but not in all religions. It is not an activity that
motivates the majority of religious people, except where they have been significantly influenced by Reformation Christianity and the Protestant-rooted
Enlightenment. Therefore, believing (communally confessing commitment)
is not definitive of religion. How, then, should we define the object of our
disciplined scholarly activities? I have argued that to understand religion we
need to understand the real world.

Instead of theorizing religion as if Luther correctly identified the constitution of our world as a place where (divine) reality is "in, with and under" ordinary reality and therefore requires faith and preaching, we should start again elsewhere. Instead of theorizing religion as if Descartes correctly advanced objectivity by separating mind from matter, we should start again in the real world. Instead of theorizing religion as if the framers of the Peace of Westphalia correctly entombed religion in a private realm where it could not legitimately affect the power of the state, we must start again. We must be more radical than we have been.

This is a world in which humans have co-evolved alongside and among myriad related species as embodied, emplaced, and interactive co-creative persons. It is a world without hyperseparations, in which nothing is unique about humans except the specific mix that constitutes us in each emergent and interconnected temporal-and-located interaction. Religion, in this world, is unlikely to be a uniquely human activity. It is unlikely to be separated out (except heuristically) from other activities. Speaking of something diffused throughout life might be difficult because it is, by definition, not distinct from other objects or acts. But the truth is that no such hyperseparated objects or acts exist in reality. We have to find ways to study matters and acts as they flow and blend and reform and re-emerge.

Vásquez notes:

> As Russell McCutcheon puts it in his helpful review of this manuscript, today there is a new generation of scholars who critique past scholarship "because it did not allow them to find religion in enough places." While appearing radical, this critique, in fact, gives religious studies a new lease on life, since it opens the possibility of seeing religion everywhere, in everyday life. (Vásquez 2011: 325)

As Primiano (1995, 2012) persuasively demonstrates, there is no other kind of religion than the everyday, vernacular kind. As McGuire (2008) reveals, lived religion is far more interesting that the imaginary religion defined by texts or creeds. We ought only to have to say "religion" to be understood to mean everyday, lived, performative, material, vernacular religion. To that end, I have engaged with some of the "elsewheres" where religion is done in the real world. These are not premodern or primitive cultures. They are not claimed to be authentically traditional and untouched by global mostmodernity. They are "elsewhere" for varied reasons which include that they remain resolutely communal, relational, material, performative and entangled with other everyday activities. These elsewheres help us to see that wherever religion is done it is not fixed but fluid – although practitioners sometimes erect barriers against change. It is performed with intimates and either invites or excludes strangers (who might become intimates or enemies).

The project of generating new theories of religion utilizing materialist and performative approaches has been enormously empowered by Vásquez as he builds on other recent work. It is clearly not enough to propose definitions of religion as if religion alone required redefinition. In particular, our definitions arise from and bring with them definitions of the *study* of religions. A researcher who finds a lofty position from which to survey religious facts is likely to miss entirely the diffusion and fluidity of religious performance. More participative, dialogical and reflexive practices are required. Latour suggests this is possible in science:

> Truth is not to be found … in correspondence … between the original and the copy (in the case of religion) – but in taking up again the task of *continuing* the flow, of elongating the cascade of mediations one step further. … God did not tell us not to make images … but not to freeze-frame, that is not to isolate an image out of the flows that only provide them with their real – their constantly re-realized, re-represented – meaning. (Latour 2010: 122–3)

We (religion researchers) ought, then, to be able to theorize religion not so as to nail down a true representation of static complexes (e.g. something called "Jainism" discrete from any fusions or admixtures) but so as to enrich engagement with living, dynamic, ongoing relationships.

EMERGENT MATERIALS FOR A DEFINITION

What does all this amount to? What are the building blocks of a redefinition of religion that picks up these themes? If the sacrificing of goats could define particular religions or be integral to ritual complexes in those religions, should we seek their analogues elsewhere as we once did with belief? I think that by now (years into the work of studying religions) some facts ought to be uncontentious.

Religion is a performance, an activity, something people do. Religion is not distinct from other activities, except heuristically. Like gender, age and ethnicity, "religion" is diffuse either as something that informs everything people do, or available as a resource for when difference or similarity, intimacy or strangeness, seem to require emphasis. Just as "everything is political" and "everything is personal", so (to religious people at least) "everything is religious". Just as feminist women enact both feminism and woman-ness when doing both private and public, personal and political, reflexive and activist things, so religionists do religion in a similar range of contexts. All facets of their performed, relational, emplaced and embodied identities are at least affected by religion. If they wash their dishes, fire their guns, marry their spouses, cook their lentils, name their children, oppose their neighbours, dislike other people's religiously-inspired noises, distrust other's publications, then they do these things religiously. These are not additions or marginal activities. They are not expressive of the definitive core of religion (i.e. believing). They are religion.

There are lots of things (networks of actors and acts) that are often identified as religions or religious. Earlier generations of scholars, under the strong influence of European Reforming Christianity, emphasized belief (interiority, confessionalism, transcendence and sometimes salvation) as definitive of religion. It might be that a different starting point – for example, among Tawhai's ([1988] 2002) guest-making Ngati Uepohatu or Neusner's (2002) Torah-observing Jews – would result in a different way of structuring data gathered about these and other religions. Since all of them evolve precisely because of encounters with others (however imaginary or intimate, however welcome or opposed) it is to be expected that there will be similarities as well as differences. They all entail flows and fusions, permeable boundaries and imagined cores, invented pasts and conflicted performances. We may, then, have to work hard to determine which performances are definitive of particular religions and which might be definitive of a larger phenomenon called religion. We can, however, identify networks that ought to be worth visiting and considering.

Stepping back from trying to survey what named complexes (Judaism, Maori religion, Paganism, Zoroastrianism and so on) might offer data towards a definition of religion, there are also some facts that ought now to be uncontentious about the world in which we live. The world is integrated by intra-actions between always co-evolving species. Matter and action are shared. Participation and encounter are commonplace and unavoidable. What looks like an "environment" to those accepting of modernity's constitution is a society in which beings are integral members and of which they are constituent parts. There are no separations when we approach the world ecologically. All acts are acts of relating. Religion in this world must be some kind of activity in which matter (bodies and places) is affective and affected. Religion in this world must be some kind of act of relating. But if everything matters and everything relates, which bit shall we call religion?

FOOD, SEX AND STRANGERS: AN EXPERIMENT

In a pervasively relational world, what kind of relationships are involved in religion? Given that all acts are acts of relating, what kind of acts are religious performances? We have words for the performance of intimate inter-personal relationships: sexuality, family, gender and so on. Intra- and inter-generational relationships are "kinship". Larger nests of relationships are "community" or "society". Inter-community relationships are "politics", "diplomacy" or "war". Inter-producer relationships are "economics" or "gift". Synergies of politics and economics can be identified as "capitalism" or "socialism". These are all imagined to be labels for definable groups of actions that can be observed and/or theorized. Groups of people can be clustered together because of their predilection for doing particular batches of these actions in particular ways. Alternatively, they can be victimized for being imagined to perform acts in allegedly improper ways. So we can, provisionally, divide the world into intimates and strangers, and further think of strangers as potential intimates or potential enemies.

There are other actions which, similarly, seem to describe networks of activities: catering, sport, business, science and the rest of the terms taken up and prefaced with "study of", suffixed with "-ology", or in other ways made the subject/object of an academic discipline. "Religion" is unlikely to be either entirely synonymous with or entirely different from those words. Academics rightly focus on some phenomena selected out of the range of activities which are in reality intimately embraided with other actions to constitute the world. This disciplined focus allows clarity about the parts. It cannot be "religion" alone that should be rejected as a fiction of early modern construction. (If there was any candidate for excision on such grounds, surely it is the state.) None of our other scholarly "-ologies" approaches something untouched and uninteresting to other disciplines. If we are to research and teach about religion at least as well as others research and teach about catering, gender, economics or politics we need to say something about the particular flows and fusions that interest us.

As an experiment, I propose that we could treat religion as beginning with interspecies relationality. The primary activity we could look for is the performance of respect, appropriate etiquette, across species boundaries. We should understand etiquette as entrained habits and learnt behaviours (not merely as rule codes). This would enable us to show how people not only treat other-than-human persons but also how their intimate familial and local relationships are constrained or constructed by systems of control or celebration. Religion would be about the disciplining and enlivening of lives and would include the ways in which people teach others to act respectfully and deal with those who act disrespectfully. It need not be nice.

We have Tawhai's argument that "the purpose of religious activity here is to seek to enter the domain of the superbeing and do violence with impunity" ([1988] 2002: 244) to provoke us. In case we felt misled by the word "superbeing" into engaging once more with metaphysics, we should be reminded that Hallowell's (1960) term "other-than-human persons" refers not to alleged "spiritual" beings but to rocks and eagles. We might also listen to what Aua, an Iglulik Inuit shaman, told Rasmussen, a Danish explorer and ethnographer, in the 1920s:

> The greatest peril of life lies in the fact that human food consists entirely of souls. All the creatures that we have to kill to eat, all those that we have to strike down and destroy to make clothes for ourselves, have souls, like we have, souls that do not perish with the body and which must therefore be propitiated lest they should avenge themselves on us for taking away their bodies.   (Rasmussen 1929: 55–6)

Whether or not "the creatures that we have to kill" have imperishable "souls", they are our relations, many with flesh, bones, families and activities that look quite like our own. This much we could have learnt from Darwin too (e.g. Crist 2002). Our relationships with other animals are fraught both because of their similarities with and differences from us and also because we (and probably they) do not entirely approve of violence and life-taking. Nonetheless, killing is necessary. It is a crucial element of everyday life in the real world, even for those of us who employ others to kill for us. We cannot, even if we wished, escape the cycle of violence by ending our own lives because as symbionts our skin and guts are home to myriad lively bacteria. It seems likely that Maori and Inuit are far from alone in seeking ways to commit necessary, life-sustaining violence with impunity.

Many religions, certainly, have rules not only about killing but also about eating respectfully. Rituals connected with hunting, gardening, catering, feasting and fasting are among the most common acts that might deserve identification as "religious" or even as emblematically "religion". The giving of thanks before or after meals, and efforts to eat or not eat according to dietary rules, can be simple everyday matters or can occur in dramatic, public ceremonial occasions. They may even structure time (thanksgiving and world renewal ceremonies) and space (farms, gardens, kitchens and dining rooms). We have also noted that obtaining and consuming food play central roles among the activities enmeshed in the dynamic, socializing rules called *tapu* among Maori and *kashrut* among Jews. From them, we might gather that a useful definition of religion ought to take into account the ways in which people restrain themselves from consuming all that might be available. They build social networks out of these inherited and inculcated choices.

Similarly, religions often have rules about sexuality. Once again, these can invoke borders and restraints. They are frequently transgressed. In particular religions such rules are placed within the sub-category of human morals or ethics but they may also have explicit implications for human dwelling among and encounters with other-than-human persons. Sexual codes are about how humans are constituted as persons among other persons, bodies among other bodies, and as beings of whom defined behaviours are expected. Deities or prey animals, for example, may dislike any suspicion or even talk about sex. They might expect proper marital or other domestic relations, such as the avoidance of sex during menstruation. Like food, sex is a domain that makes it obvious who is an intimate and who is a stranger. Strangers might be potential intimates, but sexual engagement with them can be an intensely dangerous possibility. In the physical and relational world, such everyday, embodied matters are core elements of the performance of religion.

Systems of rules do not stand alone but generate texts, oratory and other educative performances. Again, everyday lives and elaborate ceremonies can arise from these efforts to abide by such rules. Ways of structuring activities further illustrate the impossibility of separating "religion" out from other social acts. Importantly, this "social" must refer to the activities and interests of a larger-than-human community. In Chapter 7, recognizing that some relations are closer than others, especially when people think of who it is appropriate either to eat or to eat with, I considered the Anishinaabe originated term "totem". Humans and other animals, and plants too, are kin both in traditional Algonkian and in recent Darwinian understandings of the world. Consideration of degrees of intimacy reinforces issues about consumption and sexuality. They contribute to our effort to understand "religion" by indicating the possibility (insisted on in many religions but also by some ethologists) that humans are far from alone in performing rituals. I tried to encapsulate that thought by telling a story about the flight of an eagle during a powwow honour song at Conne River Mi'kmaq reserve in Newfoundland. In a participative world, the likelihood must be that our other-than-human kin not only perform their own rituals but also recognize and participate in our ceremonies. Similarly, if one group of chimpanzees avoids eating plants that others do eat, perhaps they too have food taboos as well as sexual and gendered hierarchies. We should be open, at least, to such possibilities unless we have good evidence that humans are unique in this single way.

To sum up my thought experiment so far: religion may be, at its core, a way of dealing with the eating of relational and related beings. Its ceremonies allow people (human and other-than-human) to continue relating despite the necessity of predation or consumption. It does so by inculcating and energizing restrictions and celebrations of all manner of activities that might otherwise be uncontentious, unmarked or ordinary. Taboos are recommended and/or required so as to reinforce the performative, embodied knowledge that total consumption or indulgence is disallowed. No individual or single species has the right to take or consume without limits. There are boundaries that define appropriate relations. Giving up and giving back (taboos and sacrifices) are ways in which people dramatize the limits their community encourages. Religion is about disciplined living.

To this we must add that religion is not only about eating others, it is also about eating or not eating *with* others. Sharing food is among the most intimate acts imaginable. Boundaries between those who are like us and those who are different from us are constructed, maintained, policed and/or transgressed in meals and other ways of consuming. It is no accident that many Christians have adopted the term "communion" for a central communal ritual. It is not only the drinking of wine and the eating of bread (whether these are symbolic, representational or something significantly different) but the drinking of tea or the smoking of tobacco that indicate that this rite involves more than souls and their deity. Similarly, the Church of England's frequent presentation in the news media as being energetically divided about gay marriages and women bishops says much about contemporary constructions of relational persons. Religion is not a misunderstood representation, manifestation or mystification of something called society. It is a social act between persons, not all of whom are human, but all of whom are participants in imagining ways of being in the world and seeking to bring imagination into intimate reality. In this way, we can find a place for teaching, texts, leaders, institutions and future hopes in our studies of religion. They are among the boundary making and community building acts of persons in a complex multi-species world.

Religion, as the etiquette of relating within a multi-species world, is diffused throughout the lives of embodied, located and performative persons. It entails negotiations between the need to consume others and the need to maintain both diversity and (larger-than-human) community. It entails negotiations between intimates and strangers – both often defined when rules are made explicit about who can legitimately have sex with whom. Religion is not always and definitively "nice" but commonly excludes and opposes those who perform their personhood and world-making differently. It has imagined elements as people set up role models, hopes and ambitions. These sometimes become codified in texts but it is the use of texts and other archiving and teaching media that is significant for defining the doing of religion. We should not mistake imaginaries for the intimate activities of religious people. Static texts (religious or academic ones) do not define religion. This is achieved in the ongoing fluid fusions that emerge when people seek to bring imagination into intimate reality. While religions can stagnate, the call of the real world invites people to enhance society, welcoming intimates and resisting others.

Test 1: origins

Sitting on the strand outside Lásságámmi, the house of the late Sámi multimedia artist and performer Nils-Aslak Valkeapää, I wondered if religious art and performance may have begun when our remote ancestors memorialized the places of significant interspecies encounters. They may have raised a small cairn of stones at a place where the bones of respectfully consumed animals were returned to the land. They may have shown their children how to return fish bones to the sea. They may have taught others songs or chants that seemed acceptable to the mountains or the ravens. The evolution of religion as an etiquette of cross-species communication may, in these or similar ways, have been shaped for the encouragement of others to engage in similar acts.

This is, of course, a flight of fantasy. The purpose of sharing it here is to suggest an implication of an embodied, performative understanding of religion. The recognition that the world really is full of interspecies communication and pervaded by intentionality challenges approaches to religion and culture that define them as cognitive errors, albeit with evolutionary value. A more straightforward account of religion's origins may have to seek evidence elsewhere than in the chemistry or hard-wiring of human brains. If religion is not principally about interiority but relationality, etiquette in a larger-than-human world, diffusely affecting the whole of human lives, we might seek evidence for its origins or early dissemination in such ritual acts as cairn building or chant singing. Noting that chimpanzees, crows and other animals use tools (Shumaker *et al.* 2011), that earthworms decorate their burrows (Crist 2002), and that many mammals and birds have been observed mourning their dead (Bekoff 2012), perhaps more careful attention to a world without hyperseparations would help us see religion happening more widely than in human beliefs and cognition.

Test 2: Buddhism and football

The question of whether Buddhism and football are religions seems perennial. Buddhists are said not to "believe in god" and football is said to provide an arena for the construction of communities who share powerful experiences and who ritualize their responses to heroes and sporting "idols". Although there are plenty of Buddhists who acknowledge the existence (and request the aid of) deities, it remains true that some kinds of Buddhism cannot be defined as "belief in deity". One way round this, for those who wish to include this Buddhism under the label "religion", has been to replace "deity" with "ultimate reality" or "the sacred" or some such mystification. Another tradition popular among students and teachers is to deny football a place among religions because it does not teach traditions of transcendence. It is, at best, quasi-religious, producing a froth of emotional experiences and only temporary *communitas*. However, if religion is not defined by Protestant Christianity or rationalist mysticism, it is futile to make Buddhism or football fit such patterns.

Identifying religion with the etiquette of interspecies relationality may serve us better in both cases. Even if all appearances are ultimately illusory, Buddhist practice and living do implicate other-than-human persons. All beings are expected to achieve enlightenment and, in more popular forms, desiring the well-being of others is not limited to human communities. Football, on the other hand, seems almost entirely about humans. Only if we allow, as we probably ought, that our objects or made-things are members of our relational communities might we find a place for football as a kind of religion. The usual data (of rituals and ecstatic experiences) can be drawn

215

into a consideration of encounters between humans and balls. Whether this would succeed remains for others to test. I have a different thought to pursue about Buddhism, football and religion.

One key element of this book's work is to enquire not only about defining religion but also about defining academic practices. One fault in many debates about whether Buddhism or football are religions is that they seem to seek something boxed or separated out from other activities. Religion, however, cannot be treated as a discrete object. But neither can football. Academics interested in the game do not all work in sports studies departments. They bring expertise about entertainment, economics, politics, gender, health, business and much more to bear in their research and teaching. Some may focus on the players during matches but, like religion, football interests can be diffused throughout many aspects of life (individual and communal). Buddhism, too, is in reality rarely treated as a belief-system or faith. Research concerned with what Buddhists do is far richer than that. In short, considering Buddhism and football may reinforce the need to deploy a range of understandings and approaches that deal better with diffuse phenomenon.

Test 3: non-religion

Colin Campbell once asserted that "The study of irreligious phenomena appears to offer a unique and untried vantage-point from which to gain a fresh grip on the slippery tangle of assumptions, hypotheses and predictions which constitute the sociology of religion" (Campbell 1971: 14). Since then, increasing amounts of "irreligion", "non-religion" and/or secularity have generated considerable attention to such matters. For some these remain fresh vantage-points, for others they seem like exhausted pastures or scarred battlefields. Among the most exciting contribution to debate here is a special issue of the *Journal of Contemporary Religion* devoted to "Non-religion and Secularity" (Bullivant & Lee 2012). Its articles analyse data from varied international contexts about the social and cultural trends that result in census and survey data about shifting (but generally declining) patterns of religious "believing" and "belonging". They pay attention to economics, gender and generational change as well as other factors. Among other "puzzles", David Voas and Siobhan McAndrew (2012) focus on the ways in which British people evidence having or not having a religion, believing or not believing in god, and attending or not attending services at least monthly. To oversimplify a rich argument, it seems that people can identify ownership of or belonging to a religion for quite different reasons to those of belief or attendance, that they can express belief and doubt at the same time, and can make use of regular services without feeling the need to believe or belong. While there are people who strongly do or do not own, believe or attend, many of them are in Voas's "fuzzy fidelity" category – that is, doing one or more, but not all three, of those things (also see Voas 2009). Religion and non-religion are complex beasts.

Given this complexity, I doubt that William Bainbridge's dictum that "Any wide-ranging theory of religion needs to be tested with evidence not only about religion itself, but also about its absence" (Bainbridge 2005: 22) is workable. Bainbridge seems to undermine his own argument by following this up with an assertion that "learning more about the lack of faith" will help us "understand better the role of faith in modern society". He probably does aid understanding of theism and atheism (the subject of his article) but these are specific forms of religion and non-religion rather than definitive of them. I am far from convinced that religion must be a bounded phenomenon contrastable with a clear something that is other than religion. If feminists are right (as I think they are) that the personal is political, then studies of politics need assert no "non-politics" in order to discuss its chosen focus. Anthropologists have, by and large, found it unhelpful to continue contrasting culture and nature but manage quite well to discuss cultures without recourse to theorizing something definitively "non-culture". Belief, belonging and attendance are religious phenomena (and/or political, economic, social and cultural phenomena) but they are not the entirety of the everyday, embodied, emplaced, material, performative activities that interests the study of religion. If there is nothing that gender studies or ethnic studies cannot study, there is nothing that religious studies cannot study. Thus, once again, the vantage point that we need for doing the job of studying (researching and teaching) is not a safe and stable "outside" place but somewhere within the fuzzy fluid messiness of relational reality.

Test 4: Vodou and art

Vodou seems to upset people. Its offence appears to be that it is a hybridity: it is neither Christianity nor an African traditional religion, it is neither traditional nor entirely new. Or, rather, it is all these things in varying, shifting ways. This is suggested, at least, by the regularity with which Vodou is identified as a "syncretistic" and "popular" or "folk" religion. Or, worse, it is

217

defined as "magic" (a mystification that probably just means "not my religion"). In truth, Vodou's offence might be its role in the successful republican revolution of slaves that established Haiti as an independent nation (albeit one economically indebted to France and the USA – and, more than once, militarily endangered by them). Vodou carries the scars of slavery and revolution openly as flags parading consolation and resistance. It does not always play the "religion is nice" card but, even in its secrecy, contests ease and comfort. When ex-slaves and still-indebted popular masses invite possession by tricky and ambiguous deities (among others), they cannot be naïve about the perils of ownership. There is much more that could be said about Vodou in relation to the effort to define religion as an everyday activity in a relational world. In particular, attention to Vodou and Haitian everyday life could make an understanding of unpleasant, hierarchical, aggressive, colonial and not-yet-postcolonial relationality quite edgy. It could test an attempt to define religion not as supernaturalist but as this-worldly. It could do much more. Here, however, I use it to initiate brief reflections on the intersection between religion (as a material and materializing activity) and art.

The display of religious materiality (paintings, banners, chalices, costumes, buildings) is far from rare. Museums and galleries are full of religious art. Religious buildings are among the most frequently photographed destinations of many tourists. The academic discipline of art history devotes considerable attention to European Christian objects. In these and many other contexts it is not rare for people to ponder whether words like "art" and "object" are correct, and whether it is appropriate to display particular things or types of things. When an object of devotion is put on display to those who are not devoted is the result understanding or misunderstanding? These and other issues are the subject of significant works within museum studies (e.g. Crispin Paine's edited *Godly Things*; Paine 2000).

Exhibitions of Haitian art dramatically illustrate or emphasize such questions about the definition of religion and art. I note only two here. The University of California's Fowler Museum of Cultural History opened "The Sacred Arts of Haitian Vodou" in 1995. Events during the exhibition and within the galleries included dramatic personal engagements between devotees and *lwa* (deities), possibly including possession. While controversial, it seems these acts of devotion were positively anticipated and even built into the "mounting" of the exhibition (Cosentino 2000). In 2012–13 Nottingham Contemporary presented a somewhat more traditional gallery experience in which Haitian paintings, sculptures and flags were displayed. No receptacles were evident for making offerings. No ritual-like performances were advertised. Nonetheless, the exhibition catalogue contains many evocations of the power of Vodou and the displays (Farquharson & Gordon 2012). The origins of many of these works in popular ("peasant" or "naïve") craft or in "found" objects or assemblages seems to encourage a view that they can be more accessible, more engaging or more likely to elicit a powerful response than the "elite" art of the high renaissance.

It seems commonplace now for "religious art" to be labelled and treated differently from other art. The latter, for example, might be appraised for its aesthetic qualities while the former is often noted for some additional value such as its "spirituality" or its transformative effectiveness. Vodou altars on display may be expected to work on people, demanding responses not expected of other similarly crafted material. Agency may be attributed to them in ways that suggest a more-than-inert physicality is present. If offered for sale, there may be a concern that religious "artworks" (not only "Vodou art") might possess those who possess them or might make owners religious. In all these possibilities and potentialities, themes generative in and of early modernity are complicit. Immediate experience, subjectivity and commitment, for instance, are at least implicit. This is not to say that people might not be relationally engaged and transformed corporately by coming into the presence of a deity in "art" form. It is only to notice the entanglement of quandaries about displaying and defining "religious art" with the kind of questions that run throughout this book. While art seems self-evidently performative and material, something of transcendence and interiority make it more complex to define. Vodou's fluidity, non-neatness and contingency make the issues of defining religion and art, and "religious art" more stark than some other material culture traditions. If this is so in relation to a religion that is so thoroughly about bodies, matter and places, it deserves further consideration in the project of defining and studying religions.

It seems to me, however, that everyday religion in the real world is likely to include many things that do not require acrobatic worrying about faith and experience. Vodou exhibitions ought to demonstrate that our kinship with matter invites us to consider viewing and visiting in the framework of etiquettes. The question is not "do you have to believe to understand this picture?" but "what is the appropriate way to act in its presence?" There are, as ever, more questions to discuss.

DOING RELIGION, DOING ACADEMIA

It is likely that I have exaggerated the way that religious people live religion in *every* facet of their lives. There are people for whom religious activities are quite separate from their other activities (e.g. politics, sport, employment). Nonetheless, even if people can identify some activities as separate from others, religion is like gender, age, income, education and class in affecting all activities. For example, ritual experts may be employed to perform religious ceremonies on behalf of others. Then the majority of people can get on with politics, sport and other employments. Nonetheless, knowing that such ritualists are working and that such ceremonies are happening is part of the enabling of everyday life. It reinforces the key point: that religion is an everyday matter of people living lives among others in a multi-species, relational and participative world.

Religion in this world is an aspect of relationality. It is performative and material (embodied, emplaced, generative). Even if the effort to be modern has involved trying to ignore human kinship with all other beings (and with constitutive matter), we remain involved participants in complex webs of predation, consumption and recycling. In these webs religion usefully labels negotiations over appropriate taking and giving. Religion is seen in the locally specific disciplines of giving up and giving back. It is an acknowledgement that humans are not the only important beings and therefore cannot consume freely without penalty. Finding the society of others important, people maintain community (among and beyond humanity) by disciplined living. Others are given room and room is expected in return. Openness to proliferating acts of relating is bounded only by resistance to the sociable sharing of life's necessities. Rules about food and sex are leitmotivs in religions because such intimacies most dramatically identify "us" and "them". Rules are so frequently transgressed because the kinship of all species means that there are no impenetrable boundaries in reality. Religion is a negotiation between persons who dwell together in this relational, material, participative world.

Bibliography

Abram, D. 1997. *The Spell of the Sensuous*. New York: Vintage.

Abram, D. 2010. *Becoming Animal: An Earthly Cosmology*. New York: Pantheon.

Abram, D. 2013. "The Invisibles: Towards a Phenomenology of the Spirits". See Harvey (2013), 124–32.

Adogame, A. 2009. "Practitioners of Indigenous Religions of African and the African Diaspora". See Harvey (2009a), 75–100.

Albanese, C. L. 2002. *Reconsidering Nature Religion*. Harrisburg, PA: Trinity Press International.

Altieri, P. 2000. "Knowledge, Negotiation and NAGPRA: Reconceptualizing Repatriation Discourse(s)". In *Law and Religion in Contemporary Society: Communities, Individualism and the State*, P. Edge & G. Harvey (eds), 129–49. Aldershot: Ashgate.

Amato, J. A. 2004. *On Foot: A History of Walking*. New York: New York University Press.

Anttonen, V. 1996. "Rethinking the Sacred: The Notions of 'Human Body' and 'Territory' in Conceptualizing Religion". In *The Sacred and Its Scholars: Comparative Methodologies for the Study of Primary Religious Data*, T. A. Idinopulos & E. A. Yonan (eds), 36–64. Leiden: Brill.

Anttonen, V. 2000. "Sacred". In *Guide to the Study of Religion*, W. Braun & R. T. McCutcheon (eds), 271–82. London: Cassell.

Anttonen, V. 2005. "Space, Body, and the Notion of Boundary: A Category-Theoretical Approach to Religion". *Temenos* 41 (2): 185–201.

Appadurai, A. 1996. *Modernity at Large: Cultural Dimensions in Globalization*. Minneapolis, MN: University of Minnesota Press.

Apter, E. & W. Pietz. 1993. *Fetishism as Cultural Discourse*. Ithaca, NY: Cornell University Press.

Asad, T. 1993. *Genealogies of Religion*. Baltimore, MD: Johns Hopkins University Press.

Ashgate 2011. Catalogue copy for Pace 2011, available at www.ashgate.com/default. aspx?page=637&calcTitle=1&title_id=11270&edition_id=14746 (accessed 11 November 2011).

Axtell, J. 1988. *After Columbus: Essays in the Ethnohistory of Colonial America*. New York: Oxford University Press.

Bainbridge, W. S. 2005. "Atheism". *Interdisciplinary Journal of Research on Religion* 1: 1–24.

Barad, K. 2007. *Meeting the Universe Half Way: Quantum Physics and the Entanglement of Matter and Meaning*. Durham, NC: Duke University Press.

Barad, K. 2011. "Erasers and Erasures: Pinch's Unfortunate 'Uncertainty Principle'". *Social Studies of Science*, http://humweb.ucsc.edu/feministstudies/faculty/barad/barad-social-studies.pdf (accessed 19 February 2012).

Barth, K. 1956. *Church Dogmatics*, vol. I, pt. 2. Edinburgh: T. & T. Clark.

Bartley, J. K. 2002. "Liaisons of Life, from Hornworts to Hippos, How the Unassuming Microbe Has Driven Evolution". *Palaios* **17**(4): 414–15.

Baudrillard, J. 1988. "Simulacra and Simulations". In his *Selected Writings*, Mark Poster (ed.), 166–84. Palo Alto, CA: Stanford University Press.

Bauman, Z. 2000. *Liquid Modernity*. Malden, MA: Blackwell Publishing.

Beaudoin, T. 2012. "Everyday Faith in and Beyond Scandalized Religion". In *Religion, Media and Culture: A Reader*, G. Lynch & J. Mitchell with A. Strhan (eds), 236–43. London: Routledge.

Bekoff, M. (ed.). 2004. *Encyclopedia of Animal Behavior*; 3 vols. Westport, CT: Greenwood Press.

Bekoff, M. 2008a. *The Emotional Lives of Animals: A Leading Scientist Explores Animal Joy, Sorrow, and Empathy – and Why They Matter*. Novato, CA: New World Library.

Bekoff, M. 2008b. *Animals at Play: Rules of the Game*. Philadelphia, PA: Temple University Press.

Bekoff, M. 2010. *The Animal Manifesto: Six Reasons for Expanding Our Compassion Footprint*. Novato, CA: New World Library.

Bekoff, M. 2011. "Dead Cow Walking: The Case against Born-Again Carnivorism". *Animal Emotions – Do Animals Think and Feel?* Blog, online at www.psychologytoday.com/blog/animal-emotions/201112/dead-cow-walking-the-case-against-born-again-carnivorism (accessed 2 January 2013).

Bekoff, M. 2012. "Birds Tweet about the Dead but Do They Know What They're Doing?" www.psychologytoday.com/blog/animal-emotions/201209/birds-tweet-about-the-dead-do-they-know-what-theyre-doing (accessed 2 January 2013).

Bekoff, M. & J. Pierce 2009. *Wild Justice: The Moral Lives of Animals*. Chicago, IL: University of Chicago Press.

Bellah, R. N. 1967. "Civil Religion in America". *Daedalus* **96**(1): 1–21.

Benavides, G. 1998 "Modernity". See M. C. Taylor (1998), 186–204.

Benjamin, W. [1936] 1968. "The Work of Art in the Age of Mechanical Reproduction". In his *Illuminations*, H. Arendt (ed.), 217–51. New York: Schocken.

Bird-David, N. 1999. "'Animism' Revisited: Personhood, Environment, and Relational Epistemology". *Current Anthropology* **40**: S67–91. Reprinted in Harvey (2002), 73–105.

Bird-David, N & D. Naveh. 2008. "Relational Epistemology, Immediacy, and Conservation: Or, What Do the Nayaka Try to Conserve?" *Journal for the Study of Religion, Nature and Culture* **2**(1): 55–73.

Black, M. B. 1977. "Ojibwa Power Belief System". In *The Anthropology of Power*, R. D. Fogelson & R. N. Adams (eds), 141–51. New York: Academic.

Blackburn, T. C. (ed.). 1975. *December's Child: A Book of Chumash Oral Narratives*. Berkeley, CA: University of California Press.

Bloch, M. 1992. *Prey into Hunter*. Cambridge: Cambridge University Press.

Bocking, B. 2006. "Mysticism: No Experience Necessary?". *Diskus* **7**, www.basr.ac.uk/diskus/diskus7/bocking.htm (accessed 23 October 2011).

Bourdieu, P. 1977. *Outline of a Theory of Practice*. Cambridge: Cambridge University Press.

Bourdieu, P. 1984. *Distinction: a Social Critique of the Judgement of Taste*. Cambridge, MA: Harvard University Press.

Bruce, S. 2011. *Secularization: In Defence of an Unfashionable Theory*. Oxford: Oxford University Press.

Bruce, S. & D. Voas 2010. "Vicarious Religion: An Examination and Critique". *Journal of Contemporary Religion* **25**(2): 243–59.

Bullivant, S. & L. Lee (eds) 2012. *Journal of Contemporary Religion* **27**(1). Special Issue: Non-religion and Secularity.

Bunson, M. E. Undated. "Twenty-Six Crosses on a Hill". *Catholic Answers*, www.catholic.com/magazine/articles/twenty-six-crosses-on-a-hill (accessed 9 November 2011).

Burchett, P. & D. Vaca. 2009. "Belief Matters: Reconceptualizing Belief and Its Use". Call for papers, conference at Columbia University, www.columbia.edu/cu/religion-gsa/2009conference/index.html (accessed 11 November 2011).

Bynum, C. W. 1987. *Holy Feast and Holy Fast: The Religious Significance of Food to Medieval Women*. Berkeley, CA: University of California Press.

Bynum, C. W. 2011. *Christian Materiality: An Essay of Religion in Late Medieval Europe*. New York: Zone Books.

Campbell, C. 1971. *Toward a Sociology of Religion*. London: Macmillan.

Cannell, F. 1999. *Power and Intimacy in the Christian Philippines*. Cambridge: Cambridge University Press.

Cannell, F. 2006. *The Anthropology of Christianity*. Durham, NC: Duke University Press.

Carrette, J. & R. King 2005. *$elling Spirituality: The Silent Takeover of Religion*. London: Routledge.

Cavanaugh, W. T. 1995. "A Fire Strong Enough to Consume the House: 'The Wars of Religion' and the Rise of the State". *Modern Theology* **11**(4): 397–420.

Chabad-Lubavitch Media Center 2012. "Meron", www.chabad.org/special/israel/points_of_interest_cdo/aid/588227/jewish/Meron.htm (accessed 12 April 2012).

Chabal, P. 1996. "The African Crisis: Context and Interpretation". In *Postcolonial Identities in Africa*, R. Werbner & T. Ranger (eds), 29–54. London: Zed.

Clark, A. 1997. *Being There: Putting Brain, Body, and World Together Again*. Cambridge, MA: MIT Press.

Clarke, K. M. 2004. *Mapping Yoruba Networks: Power and Agency in the Making of Transnational Communities*. Durham, NC: Duke University Press.

Clarke, P. B. & P. Beyer (eds) 2009. *The World's Religions: Continuities and Transformations*. London: Routledge.

Clifford, J. 1990. "Notes on (Field)notes". In *Fieldnotes: The Making of Anthropology*, R. Sanjek (ed.), 47–70. Ithaca, NY: Cornell University Press.

Clifton, C. S. 2006. *Her Hidden Children: The Rise of Wicca and Paganism in America*. Lanham. MD: Altamira Press.

Coleman, S. 2007. *The Globalisation of Charismatic Christianity*. Cambridge: Cambridge University Press.

Connell, R. 2007. *Southern Theory: The Global Dynamics of Knowledge in Social Science*. Cambridge: Polity.

Cook, J. [1777] 1967. *A Journal of a Voyage Round the World in HMS Endeavour 1768–1771*. New York: Da Capo Press.

Cosentino, D. 2000. "Mounting Controversy: the Sacred Arts of Haitian Vodou". In *Godly Things: Museums, Objects and Religion*, C. Paine (ed.), 97–106. London: Leicester University Press.

Cox, J. 1982. *The English Churches in a Secular Society: Lambeth 1870–1930*. Oxford: Oxford University Press.

Cox, J. L. 2007. *From Primitive to Indigenous: The Academic Study of Indigenous Religions*. Aldershot: Ashgate.

Crist, E. 2002. "The Inner Life of Earthworms: Darwin's Argument and Its Implications". In *The Cognitive Animal: Empirical and Theoretical Perspectives on Animal Cognition*, M. Bekoff, C. Allen & G. M. Burghardt (eds), 3–8. Cambridge, MA: MIT Press.

Csordas, T. J. 1994. *The Sacred Self: A Cultural Phenomenology of Charismatic Healing*. Berkeley, CA: University of California Press.

Csordas, T. J. 1997. *Language, Charisma, and Creativity: The Ritual Life of a Religious Movement*. Berkeley, CA: University of California Press.

Csordas, T. J. 2004. "Asymptote of the Ineffable: Embodiment, Alterity, and the Theory of Religion". *Current Anthropology* **45**(2): 163–85.

Csordas, T. J. 2008. "Intersubjectivity and Intercorporeality". *Subjectivity* **22**: 110–21.

Curry, P. 2010. *Divination: Perspectives for a New Millennium*. Farnham: Ashgate.

Curry, P. 2011. "What It's About", www.patrickcurry.co.uk (accessed 16 July 2012).

Damasio, A. 1994. *Descartes' Error: Emotion, Reason, and the Human Brain*. New York: HarperCollins.

Dav 2011. "New Topic for 2012–14: Belief and Unbelief". Shelby Cullom Davis Center for Historical Studies, Princeton University, www.princeton.edu/dav/program/new_topic/index.xml (accessed 10 November 2011).

Davenport, F. G. 1917. *European Treaties Bearing on the History of the United States and its Dependencies to 1648*, vol. 1. Washington, DC: Carnegie Institution of Washington.

Davie, G. 1990. "Believing without Belonging: Is This the Future of Religion in Britain?" *Social Compass* **37**: 455–69.

Davie, G. 1994. *Religion in Britain Since 1945: Believing without Belonging*. Oxford: Blackwell.

Davie, G. 2002. *Europe: The Exceptional Case*. London: Longman & Todd.

Davie, G. 2007. "Vicarious Religion: A Methodological Challenge". In *Everyday Religion: Observing Modern Religious Lives*, N. T. Ammerman (ed.), 21–35. Oxford: Oxford University Press.

Davie, G. 2010. "Vicarious Religion: A Response". *Journal of Contemporary Religion* **25**(2): 261–6.

Davies, D. J. 1997. *Death, Ritual and Belief: The Rhetoric of Funerary Rites*. London: Cassell.

Davies, D. J. 2011. *Emotion, Identity and Religion: Hope, Reciprocity, and Otherness*. Oxford: Oxford University Press.

Davies, D. J. & M. Guest 2007. *Bishops, Wives and Children: Spiritual Capital Across the Generations*. Aldershot: Ashgate.

Day, A. 2009. "Researching Belief without Asking Religious Questions". *Fieldwork in Religion* **4**(1): 86–104.

Day, A. 2011. *Believing in Belonging: Belief and Social Identity in the Modern World*. Oxford: Oxford University Press.

de Aquino, P. 2005. "An Assembly of Humans, Shells and Gods". See Latour & Weibel (2005), 454–7.

de Brosses, C. 1970. *Du culte des dieux fétiches, ou Parallèle de l'ancienne Religion de l'Egypte avec la Religion actuelle de Nigritie*. Farnborough: Gregg.

de Certeau, M. 1985. "What Do We Do When We Believe?". In *On Signs*, M. Blonksy (ed.), 192–202. Baltimore, MD: Johns Hopkins University Press.

Dennett, D. C. 2006. *Breaking the Spell: Religion as a Natural Phenomenon*. London: Allen Lane.

Detwiler, F. 1992. "'All My Relatives': Persons in Oglala Religion". *Religion* **22**: 235–46.

de Vries, H. (ed.) 2008. *Religion: Beyond a Concept*. New York: Fordham University Press.

Douglas, M. 1992. *Purity and Danger: An Analysis of Concepts of Pollution and Taboo*. London: Routledge.

Dowden, K. 2000. *European Paganism: The Realities of Cult from Antiquity to the Middle Ages*. London: Routledge.

Dueck, B. 2007. "Public and Intimate Sociability in First Nations and Métis Fiddling". *Ethnomusicology* **51**(1): 30–63.

Dueck, B. 2013. *Musical Intimacies and Indigenous Imaginaries: First Nations and Métis Dance in Public Performance*. New York: Oxford University Press.

Durkheim, É. 1915. *The Elementary Forms of the Religious Life*. London: George Allen & Unwin.

Ehrenreich, B. 2003. "Maid to Order". In *Global Woman*, B. Ehrenreich & A. R. Hochschild (eds), 85–103. London: Granta.

Eilberg-Schwartz, H. 1994. *God's Phallus and Other Problems for Men and Monotheism*. Boston, MA: Beacon.

Eliade, M. 1959. *The Sacred and the Profane: The Nature of Religion*. New York: Harcourt Brace Jovanovich.

Evans-Pritchard, E. E. 1937. *Witchcraft, Oracles and Magic among the Azande*. Oxford: Clarendon.

Farquharson, A. & L. Gordon 2012. *Kafou: Haiti and Art*. Nottingham: Nottingham Contemporary.

Fernández Olmos, M. & L. Paravisini-Gebert 2003. *Creole Religions of the Caribbean: An Introduction from Vodou and Santeria to Obeah and Espiritismo*. New York: New York University Press.

Fitzgerald, T. 2000. *The Ideology of Religious Studies*. Oxford: Oxford University Press.

Fitzgerald, T.2007. *Discourse on Civility and Barbarity: A Critical History of Religion and Related Categories*. New York: Oxford University Press.

Flood, G. 1999. *Beyond Phenomenology: Rethinking the Study of Religion*. London: Cassell.

Foucault, M. 1973. *The Order of Things: An Archaeology of the Human Sciences*. New York: Vintage.

Foucault, M. 1999. *Religion and Culture by Michel Foucault*, J. Carrette (ed.). New York: Routledge.

Frazer, J. G. 1910. *Totemism and Exogamy*; 4 vols. London: Macmillan.

FSM Consortium 2010. *The Loose Canon*, http://tinyurl.com/dyt2a5j (accessed 20 April 2013).

Fulbright, J. 1992. "Hopi and Zuni Prayer-Sticks: Magic, Symbolic Texts, Barter or Self-Sacrifice?". *Religion* **22**: 221–34.

Fuller, R. C. 2004. *Spiritual, but Not Religious: Understanding Unchurched America*. New York: Oxford University Press.

Garuba, H. 2003. "Explorations in Animist Materialism: Notes on Reading/Writing African Literature, Culture, and Soceity". *Public Culture* **15**(2): 261–85.

Geertz, A. 1999. "Definition as Analytical Strategy in the Study of Religion". *Historical Reflections/Reflexions Historiques* **25**(3): 445–75.

Geertz, C. 1973. *Interpretation of Cultures*. New York: Harper & Row.

Geertz, C. 1983. *Local Knowledge: Further Essays in Interpretative Anthropology*. New York: Basic Books.

Gendlin, E. 1981. *Focusing*. New York: Bantam.

Gerth, H. H. & C. W. Mills (eds) 1948. *From Max Weber: Essays in Sociology*. London: Routledge.

Girard, R. 1986. *The Scapegoat*. Baltimore, MD: Johns Hopkins University Press.

Girard, R. 1988. *Violence and the Sacred*. London: Athlone Press

Girard, R. 2004. "Violence and Religion: Cause and Effect?" *Hedgehog Review* **6**(1): 8–20.

Goldschmidt, H. 2009. "Religion, Reductionism, and the Godly Soul: Lubavitch Hasidic Jewishness and the Limits of Classificatory Thought". *Journal of the American Academy of Religion* **77**(3): 547–72.

Gombrich, R. F. 1971. *Precept and Practice*. Oxford: Clarendon.

Graeber, D. 2005. "Fetishism as Social Creativity: or, Fetishes are Gods in the Process of Construction". *Anthropological Theory* **5**(4): 407–38.

Griffith, R. M. 2004. *Born Again Bodies: Flesh and Spirit in American Christianity*. Berkeley, CA: University of California Press.

Grimes, R. 2000. *Deeply into the Bone: Re-inventing Rites of Passage*. Berkeley, CA: University of California Press.

Grimes, R. 2002. "Performance Is Currency in the Deep World's Gift Economy: An Incantatory Riff for a Global Medicine Show". *Interdisciplinary Studies in Literature and Environment* **9**(1): 149–64.

Grimes, R. 2003. "Ritual Theory and the Environment". *Sociological Review* **51**: 31–45.

Gross, L. 1996. "Making the World Sacred, Quietly, Carefully: Silence, Concentration and the Sacred in Soto Zen and Ojibwa Indian Experience". Address to Harvard Buddhist Studies Forum, 1 April 1996, Harvard University, Cambridge, MA.

Hallowell, A. I. 1955. *Culture and Experience*. Philadelphia, PA: University of Pennsylvania Press.

Hallowell, A. I. 1960. "Ojibwa Ontology, Behavior, and World View". In *Culture in History: Essays in Honor of Paul Radin*, S. Diamond (ed.), 19–52. New York: Columbia University Press. Reprinted in Harvey (2002), 18–49.

Hallowell, A. I. 1992. *The Ojibwe of Berens River, Manitoba: Ethnography into History*, J. S. H. Brown (ed.). Fort Worth, TX: Harcourt Brace Jovanovich.

Halman, L. & V. Draulans 2004. "Religious Beliefs and Practices in Contemporary Europe". In *European Values Studies*, vol 7, W. A. Arts & L. Halman (eds), 283–316. Leiden: Brill.

Hamayon, R. 2013. "Shamanism and the Hunters of the Siberian Forest: Soul, Life Force, Spirit". See Harvey (2013), 284–93.

Hanegraaff, W. 1996. *New Age Religion and Western Culture: Esotericism in the Mirror of Secular Thought*. Leiden: Brill.

Haraway, D. 1991. *Simians, Cyborgs and Women: The Reinvention of Nature*. New York: Routledge.

Harris, A. 2008. "The Wisdom of the Body: Embodied Knowing in Eco-Paganism". PhD thesis, University of Winchester.

Harris, A. 2013. "Focusing in Nature". *Bodymind Place* (4 April), www.adrianharris.org/blog (accessed 11 April 2013).

Harvey, G. (ed.) 2000. *Indigenous Religions: A Companion*. London: Cassell.

Harvey, G. (ed.) 2002. *Readings in Indigenous Religions*. London: Continuum.

Harvey, G. 2003a. "Guesthood as Ethical Decolonising Research Method". *Numen* **50**(2): 125–46.

Harvey, G. (ed.) 2003b. *Shamanism: A Reader*. London: Routledge.

Harvey, G. 2005a. *Animism: Respecting the Living World*. London: Hurst & Co.

Harvey, G. 2005b. "Performing and Constructing Research as Guesthood". In *Anthropologists in the Field*, L. Hume & J. Mulcock (eds), 168–82. New York: Columbia University Press.

Harvey, G. (ed.) 2005c. *Ritual and Religious Belief: A Reader*. London: Equinox.

Harvey, G. 2006. *Listening People, Speaking Earth: Contemporary Paganism*, 2nd edn. London: Hurst & Co.

Harvey, G. 2007. "Inventing Paganisms". In *The Invention of Sacred Traditions*, J. Lewis & O. Hammer (eds), 277–90. Cambridge: Cambridge University Press.

Harvey, G. (ed.). 2009a. *Religions in Focus: New Approaches to Tradition and Contemporary Practices*. London: Equinox.

Harvey, G. 2009b. "Animism Rather than Shamanism: New Approaches to what Shamans do (for other animists)". In *New Interpretations of Spirit Possession*, B. Schmidt & L. Huskinson (eds), 14–34. London: Continuum.

Harvey, G. 2011a. "Field Research: Participant Observation". In *The Routledge Handbook of Research Methods in the Study of Religion*, M. Stausberg & S. Engler (eds), 217–44. London: Routledge.

Harvey, G. 2011b. "Paganism: Negotiating between Esotericism and Animism under the Influence of Kabbalah". See Huss (2011), 267–84.

Harvey, G. 2012a., "Bardic Chairs and the Emergent Performance Practice of Pagans". In *Handbook of New Religions and Cultural Production*, C. Cusack & A. Norman (eds), 399–416. Leiden: Brill.

Harvey, G. 2012b. "Ritual is Etiquette in the Larger than Human World: The Two Wildernesses of Contemporary Eco-Paganism". In *Wilderness and Religion: Approaching Religious Spatialities, Cosmologies and Ideas of Wild Nature*, L. Feldt (ed.), 265–91. Boston, MA: de Gruyter.

Harvey, G. 2013. *Handbook of Contemporary Animism*. Sheffield: Equinox.

Harvey, G. & K. R. MacLeod (eds). 2001. *Indigenous Religious Musics*. Aldershot: Ashgate.

Harvey, G. & R. Wallis 2010. *The A to Z of Shamanism*. Lanham, MD: Scarecrow Press.

Henare, A., M. Holbraad & S. Wastell (eds) 2007. *Thinking Through Things: Theorising Artefacts Ethnographically*. London: Routledge.

Henderson, B. 2005. "Open Letter To Kansas School Board", www.venganza.org/about/open-letter (accessed 3 January 2012).

Hervieu-Léger, D. 2000. *Religion as a Chain of Memory*. Cambridge: Polity.

Hervieu-Léger, D. 2008. "Religion as Memory: Reference to Tradition and the Constitution of a Heritage of Belief in Modern Societies". See de Vries (2008), 245–58.

Holbraad, M. 2007. "The Power of Powder: Multiplicity and Motion in the Divinatory Cosmology of Cuban Ifá (or *Mana* Again)". In *Thinking Through Things: Theorising Artefacts Ethnographically*, A. Henare, M. Holbraad & S. Wastell (eds), 189–225. London: Routledge.

Holbraad, M. 2008. "Definitive Evidence, from Cuban Gods". *Journal of the Royal Anthropological Institute* **14**: S93–109.

Holbraad, M. 2010. "Afterword: Of Ises and Oughts: An Endnote on Divinatory Obligations". In *Divination: Perspectives for a New Millennium*, P. Curry (ed.), 265–74. Farnham: Ashgate.

Holler, L. 2002. *Erotic Morality: The Role of Touch in Moral Agency*. New Brunswick, NJ: Rutgers University Press.

Hornborg, A. 1992. "Machine Fetishism, Value, and the Image of Unlimited Good: Towards a Thermodynamics of Imperialism." *Man* **27**(new series): 1–18.

Hornborg, A. 2013. "Animism, Fetishism, and the Cultural Foundations of Capitalism". See Harvey (2013), 244–59.

Howell, F. 2011. "Sense of Place and Festival in Northern Italy: Perspectives on Place, Time and Community". PhD thesis, Open University.

Hultkrantz, Å. 1983. "The Concept of the Supernatural in Primal Religion". *History of Religion* **22**: 231–53.

Humphrey, C. with U. Onon. 1996. *Shamans and Elders: Experience, Knowledge, and Power among the Daur Mongols*. Oxford: Oxford University Press.

Huss, B. 2011. *Kabbalah and Contemporary Spiritual Revival*. Be'er Sheva: Ben Gurion University of the Negev Press.

Hutton, R. 1991. *The Pagan Religions of the Ancient British Isles*. London: Blackwell.

Hutton, R. 1994. *The Rise and Fall of Merry England: The Ritual Year 1400–1700*. Oxford: Oxford University Press.

Hutton, R. 1996. "The Roots of Modern Paganism". In *Paganism Today*, G. Harvey & C. Hardman (eds), 3–15. London: Thorsons.

Hutton, R. 1999. *The Triumph of the Moon: A History of Modern Pagan Witchcraft*. Oxford: Oxford University Press.

Hutton, R. 2003. *Witches, Druids and King Arthur*. London: Hambledon.

Hutton, R. 2007. *The Druids: A History*. London: Hambledon.

Hutton, R. 2009. *Blood and Mistletoe*. New Haven, CT: Yale University Press.

Ingold, T. 2000. *The Perception of the Environment*. London: Routledge.

Ingold, T. 2011. *Being Alive: Essays on Movement, Knowledge and Description*. London: Routledge.

Ingold, T. & J. L. Vergunst (eds). 2008. *Ways of Walking: Ethnography and Practice on Foot*. Aldershot: Ashgate.

Irwin, L. 1992. "Contesting World Views: Dreams among the Huron and Jesuits". *Religion* **22**: 259–69.

James, W. [1902] 1997. *The Varieties of Religious Experience: A Study in Human Nature*. New York: Simon & Schuster.

Jamison, I. 2011. "Embodied Ethics and Contemporary Paganism". PhD thesis, Open University.

Johnson, P. C. 2000. "The Fetish and McGwire's Balls". *Journal of the American Academy of Religion* **68**(2): 243–64.

Johnson, P. C. 2002a. *Secrets, Gossip and Gods: The Transformation of Brazilian Candomblé*. Oxford: Oxford University Press.

Johnson, P. C. 2002b. "Migrating Bodies, Circulating Signs: Brazilian Candomble, the Garifuna of the Caribbean, and the Category of Indigenous Religions". *History of Religions* **41**(4): 301–27.

Johnson, P. C. 2005. "Savage Civil Religion". *Numen* **52**: 289–324.

Johnson, P. C. 2013. "Whence 'Spirit Possession'?". See Harvey (2013), 325–40.

Joy, M. 2010. *Why we Love Dogs, Eat Pigs and Wear Cows: An Introduction to Carnism, the Belief System that Enables us to Eat Some Animals and Not Others*. San Francisco, CA: Conari Press.

Keane, W. 2007. *Christian Moderns: Freedom and Fetish in the Mission Encounter*. Berkeley, CA: University of California Press.

Kent, S. A. 2009. "Post-World War II New Religious Movements in the West". See Clarke
& Beyer (2009), 492–510.

Kim, C. 2003. *Korean Shamanism: The Cultural Paradox*. Aldershot: Ashgate.

King, R. 2007. "The Association of 'Religion' with Violence: Reflections on a Modern
Trope". In *Religion and Violence in South Asia: Theory and Practice*, J. R. Hinnells &
R. King (eds), 226–57. London: Routledge.

Knight, C. 1996. "Totemism". In *Encyclopedia of Social and Cultural Anthropology*,
A. Barnard & J. Spencer (eds), 550–51. London: Routledge.

Knott, K. 2005a. *The Location of Religion: A Spatial Analysis*. London: Equinox.

Knott, K. 2005b. "Spatial Theory and Method for the Study of Religion". *Temenos* **41**(2):
154–84.

Knott, K. 2009. "Geography, Space and the Sacred". In *The Routledge Companion to the
Study of Religion*, J. Hinnells (ed.), 476–91. London: Routledge.

Koerner, J. L. 2005. "Reforming the Assembly". See Latour & Weibel (2005), 404–33.

LaFleur, W. R. 1998. "Body". See M. C. Taylor (1998), 36–54.

Lakoff, G. & M. Johnson 1980. *Metaphors We Live By*. Chicago, IL: University of Chicago
Press.

Lakoff, G. & M. Johnson 1999. *Philosophy in the Flesh: The Embodied Mind and Its
Challenge to Western Thought*. San Francisco, CA: HarperCollins.

Landes, R. 1968. *Ojibwa Religion and the Midewiwin*. Madison, WI: University of
Wisconsin Press.

Latour, B. 1993. *We Have Never Been Modern*. New York: Harvester Wheatsheaf.

Latour, B. 2002. *War of the Worlds: What about Peace?* Chicago, IL: Prickly Paradigm
Press.

Latour, B. 2005. *Reassembling the Social: An Introduction to Actor–Network Theory*.
Oxford: Oxford University Press.

Latour, B. 2010. *On the Modern Cult of the Factish Gods*. Durham, NC: Duke University
Press.

Latour, B. & P. Weibel (eds) 2005. *Making Things Public: Atmospheres of Democracy*.
Karlsruhe: ZKM.

Lear, L. 2007. *Beatrix Potter: A Life in Nature*. New York: St Martin's Press.

Lefebvre, H. 1991. *The Production of Space*. Oxford: Blackwell.

Letcher, A. 2000. "'Virtual Paganism' or Direct Action? The Implications of Road
Protesting for Modern Paganism". *Diskus* **6**, www.basr.ac.uk/diskus/diskus1-6/
letcher6.txt (accessed 16 May 2011).

Letcher, A. 2001. "The Scouring of the Shires: Fairies, Trolls and Pixies in Eco-Protest
Culture". *Folklore* **112**: 147– 61.

Letcher, A. 2005. "Eco-paganism". In *Encyclopedia of Religion, Culture and Nature*,
B. Taylor (ed.), 556–7. London: Continuum.

Levenson, J. D. 1993. *The Death and Resurrection of the Beloved Son*. New Haven, CT:
Yale University Press.

Lévi-Strauss, C. [1952] 1973. *Anthropologie structurale deux*. Paris: Plon.

Lévi-Strauss, C. [1955] 1961. *Tristes tropiques*. London: Hutchinson.

Lévi-Strauss, C. 1969. *Totemism*. Harmondsworth: Penguin.

Lopez, D. S. 1998. "Belief". See M. C. Taylor (1998), 21–35.

Ludueña, G. A. 2005. "Asceticism, Fieldwork and Technologies of the Self in Latin
American Catholic Monasticism". *Fieldwork in Religion* **1**(2): 145–64.

Malinowski, B. 1948. *Magic, Science and Religion and Other Essays*. Glencoe, IL: Free Press.

Malotki, E. & M. Lomatuway'ma 1984. *Hopi Coyote Tales/Istutuwutsi*. Lincoln, NE: University of Nebraska Press.

Mark, Z. 2011. "The Contemporary Renaissance of Braslav Hasidism: Ritual, Tiqqun and Messianism". See Huss (2011), 101–16.

Marshall, R. 2009. *Political Spiritualities: The Pentecostal Revolution in Nigeria*. Chicago, IL: University of Chicago Press.

Masuzawa, T. 2000. "Troubles with Materiality: The Ghost of Fetishism in the Nineteenth Century". *Comparative Studies in Society and History* **42**(2): 242–67.

Masuzawa, T. 2005. *The Invention of World Religions Or, How European Universalism Was Preserved in the Language of Pluralism*. Chicago, IL: University of Chicago Press.

Mataira, P. 2000. "Mana and Tapu: Sacred Knowledge, Sacred Boundaries". See Harvey (2000), 99–112.

Mauss, M. [1923–4] 1954. *The Gift: Forms and Functions of Exchange in Archaic Societies*. London: Cohen & West.

McCutcheon, R. 1997. *Manufacturing Religion: The Discourse on Sui Generis Religion and the Politics of Nostalgia*. New York: Oxford University Press.

McCutcheon, R. 2001. *Critics Not Caretakers: Redescribing the Public Study of Religion*. Albany, NY: SUNY Press.

McCutcheon, R. 2003. *The Discipline of Religion: Structure, Meaning, Rhetoric*. London: Routledge.

McGuire, M. B. 2008. *Lived Religion: Faith and Practice in Everyday Life*. New York: Oxford University Press.

McNally, M. 2009. *Honoring Elders: Aging, Authority and Ojibwe Religion*. New York: Columbia University Press.

Midgley, M. 2004. *The Myths We Live By*. London: Routledge.

Mills, C. W. 1951. *White Collar: The American Middle Classes*. New York: Oxford University Press.

Morrison, K. M. 1992a. "Beyond the Supernatural: Language and Religious Action". *Religion* **22**: 201–5.

Morrison, K. M. 1992b. "Sharing the Flower: A Non-Supernaturalistic Theory of Grace". *Religion* **22**: 207–19. Reprinted in Harvey (2002), 106–20.

Morrison, K. M. 2000. "The Cosmos as Intersubjective: Native American Other-than-Human Persons". See Harvey (2000), 23–36.

Morrison, K. M. 2002. *The Solidarity of Kin: Ethnohistory, Religious Studies, and the Algonkian-French Religious Encounter*. Albany, NY: SUNY Press.

Morrison, K. M. 2013. "Animism and a Proposal for a Post-Cartesian Anthropology". See Harvey (2013), 38–52.

Morrison, T. 1987. *Beloved: A Novel*. New York: Knopf.

Mutiga, M. 2011. "Push for Pope's Trial in Clergy Child Abuse Cases". *Daily Nation* (2 October), http://allafrica.com/stories/201110031256.html (accessed 21 October 2011).

Narayanan, V. 2000. "Diglossic Hinduisms: Liberation and Lentils". *Journal of the American Academy of Religion* **68**(4): 761–79.

Naveh, D. & N. Bird-David. 2013. "Animism, Conservation and Immediacy". See Harvey (2013), 27–37.

Nelson, R. 1983. *Make Prayers to the Raven: A Koyukon View of the Northern Forest*. Chicago, IL: University of Chicago Press.

Neusner, J. 1981. *Judaism: Evidence of the Mishnah*. Chicago, IL: University of Chicago Press.

Neusner, J. 2002. *Judaism: An Introduction*. New York: Penguin.

Newcomb, S. T. 1992. "Five Hundred Years of Injustice". *Shaman's Drum* (fall): 18–20, http://ili.nativeweb.org/sdrm_art.html (accessed 15 January 2012).

Newcomb, S. T. 2008. *Pagans in the Promised Land: Decoding the Doctrine of Christian Discovery*. Golden, CO: Fulcrum.

Nichols, J. D. & E. Nyholm. 1995. *A Concise Dictionary of Minnesota Ojibwe*. Minneapolis, MN: University of Minnesota Press.

Nussbaum, M. C. 2004. *Hiding from Humanity: Disgust, Shame, and the Law*. Princeton, NJ: Princeton University Press.

Nussbaum, M. C. 2010. *From Disgust to Humanity: Sexual Orientation and Constitutional Law*. Oxford: Oxford University Press.

Nye, M. 2004. *Religion: The Basics*. London: Routledge.

Office of National Statistics 2012. "Religion in England and Wales 2011", www.ons.gov.uk/ons/dcp171776_290510.pdf.

Olcott, H. S. [1881] 1947. *The Buddhist Catechism*, 44th edn. Adyar: Theosophical Publishing House.

Olsson, T. 2013. "Animate Objects: Ritual Perception and Practice among the Bambara in Mali". See Harvey (2013), 226–43.

Orsi, R. 1997. "Everyday Miracles: The Study of Lived Religion". In *Lived Religion in America: Toward a History of Practice*, D. Hall (ed.), 3–21. Princeton, NJ: Princeton University Press.

Otto, R. 1958. *The Idea of the Holy*. Oxford: Oxford University Press.

Pace, E. 2011. *Religion as Communication: God's Talk*. Aldershot: Ashgate.

Paine, C. (ed.) 2000. *Godly Things: Museums, Objects and Religion*. London: Leicester University Press.

Parsons, G. 2004. *Siena, Civil Religion and the Sienese*. Aldershot: Ashgate.

Parsons, G. 2008. *The Cult of Saint Catherine of Siena: A Study in Civil Religion*. Aldershot: Ashgate.

Pels, P. 1998. "The Spirit of Matter: On Fetish, Rarity, Fact, and Fancy". In *Border Fetishisms: Material Objects in Unstable Spaces*, P. Spyer (ed.), 91–121. New York: Routledge.

Pels, P. 2008. "The Modern Fear of Matter: Reflections on the Protestantism of Victorian Science". *Material Religion* 4(3): 264–83.

Pentikäinen, J. 2009. "Central Asian and Northern European Shamanism". See Clarke & Beyer (2009), 99–108.

Pflug, M. A. 1992. "Breaking Bread: Metaphor and Ritual in Odawa Religious Practice". *Religion* 22: 247–58.

Pickering W. S. F. 1994. *Locating the Sacred: Durkheim, Otto and Some Contemporary Ideas*, BASR Occasional Papers 12. Leeds: British Association for the Study of Religions.

Pietz, W. 1985. "The Problem of the Fetish I". *Res* 9: 5–17.

Pietz, W. 1987. "The Problem of the Fetish II". *Res* 13: 23–45.

Pietz, W. 1988. "The Problem of the Fetish III". *Res* 16: 105–23.

Platvoet, J. 2001. "Chasing Off God: Spirit Possession in a Sharing Society". See Harvey & MacLeod (2001), 122–35.

Plumwood, V. 1993. *Feminism and the Mastery of Nature*. London: Routledge.

Plumwood, V. 2000. "Being Prey". *Utne Reader* (1 July), www.utne.com/2000-07-01/being-prey.aspx (accessed 9 February 2012).

231

Plumwood, V. 2002. *Environmental Culture: The Ecological Crisis of Reason*. London: Routledge.

Plumwood, V. 2008. "Shadow Places and the Politics of Dwelling" *Australian Humanities Review* **44**: 139–50, http://epress.anu.edu.au/wp-content/uploads/2011/04/eco02.pdf (accessed 12 February 2012).

Plumwood, V. 2009. "Nature in the Active Voice". *Australian Humanities Review* **46**: 113–29, www.australianhumanitiesreview.org/archive/Issue-May-2009/plumwood. html (accessed 9 February 2012). Reprinted in Harvey 2013.

Primiano, L. N. 1995. "Vernacular Religion and the Search for Method in Religious Folklife". *Western Folklore* **54**(1): 37–56.

Primiano, L. N. 2012. "Afterword. Manifestations of the Religious Vernacular: Ambiguity, Power, and Creativity". In *Vernacular Religion in Everyday Life: Expressions of Belief*, Ü. Valk & M. Bowman (eds), 382–94. London: Equinox.

Pye, M. 1993. "Pilgrimage". In *Macmillan Dictionary of Religion*, M. Pye (ed.), 203–4. Basingstoke: Macmillan.

Pye, M. 2010. "The Way is the Goal: Buddhist Circulatory Pilgrimage in Japan with Special Reference to Selected Artefacts". In *Pilgrims and Travellers in Search of the Holy*, R. Gothóni (ed.), 163–82. New York: Peter Lang.

Raphael, M. 1994. "Feminism, Constructivism and Numinous Experience". *Religious Studies* **30**: 511–26.

Rappaport, R. A. 1999. *Ritual and Religion in the Making of Humanity*. Cambridge: Cambridge University Press.

Rasmussen, K. 1929. *Intellectual Culture of the Iglulik Eskimos*, Report of the Fifth Thule Expedition. Copenhagen: Gyldendalske Boghandel, Nordisk Forlag.

Reader, I. 1995. "Cleaning Floors and Sweeping the Mind". In *Ceremony and Ritual in Japan*, J. van Bremen & D. P. Martinez (eds), 227–45. London: Routledge. Reprinted in Harvey (2005c), 88–104.

Reader, I. 2004a. "Ideology, Academic Inventions and Mystical Anthropology". *Electronic Journal of Contemporary Japanese Studies*, discussion paper 1, www.japanesestudies. org.uk/discussionpapers/Reader.html (accessed 3 July 2012).

Reader, I. 2004b. "Dichotomies, Contested Terms and Contemporary Issues in the Study of Religion". *Electronic Journal of Contemporary Japanese Studies*, discussion paper 3, www.japanesestudies.org.uk/discussionpapers/Reader2.html (accessed 3 July 2012).

Ricoeur, P. 1979. "The Model of the Text: Meaningful Action Considered as a Text". In *Interpretive Social Science: A Reader*, P. Rabinow & W. Sullivan (eds), 73–102. Berkeley, CA: University of California Press.

Rorty, R. 1979. *Philosophy and the Mirror of Nature*. Princeton, NJ: Princeton University Press.

Rose, D. B. 1992. *Dingo Makes Us Human: Life and Land in an Australian Aboriginal Culture*. Cambridge: Cambridge University Press.

Rose, D. B. 1997. "Common Property Regimes in Aboriginal Australia: Totemism Revisited". In *The Governance of Common Property in the Pacific Region*, P. Larmour (ed.), 127–43. Canberra: NCDS.

Rose, D. B. 1998. "Totemism, Regions, and Co-management in Aboriginal Australia". Paper presented at Crossing Boundaries, International Association for the Study of Common Property 7th Annual Conference, Vancouver, June 10–14, http://dlc. dlib.indiana.edu/dlc/bitstream/handle/10535/1187/rose.pdf (accessed 19 February 2012).

Rose, D. B. 2004. *Reports from a Wild Country: Ethics for Decolonisation.* Sydney: University of New South Wales Press.

Ross, D. 2011. "Introduction". In *Image and Pilgrimage in Christian Culture*, V. Turner & E. Turner, xxix–lvii. New York: Columbia University Press.

Rubenstein, S. L. 2012. "On the Importance of Visions among the Amazonian Shuar". *Current Anthropology* **53**(1): 39–79.

Ruel, M. 1997. "Christians and Believers". In his *Belief, Ritual and the Securing of Life: Reflexive Essays on a Bantu Religion*, 36–59. Leiden: Brill. Reprinted in Harvey (2005c), 243–64.

Saler, B. 1977. "Supernatural as a Western Category". *Ethnos* **5**: 31–53.

Saler, B. 1993. *Conceptualising Religion: Immanent Anthropologists, Transcendent Natives, and Unbounded Categories.* Leiden: Brill.

Saler, B. 2000. "Conceptualising Religion Responses". In *Perspectives on Method and Theory in the Study of Religion*, A. W. Geertz & R. R. McCutcheon (eds), 323–38. Leiden: Brill.

Sangharakshita u. 1998. *What is the Dharma? The Essential Teachings of the Buddha.* Birmingham: Windhorse Publications.

Schmidt, B. & L. Huskinson (eds) 2010. *Spirit Possession and Trance: New Interdisciplinary Perspectives.* London: Continuum.

Schwartz, Y. 1999. "The *Hillula* of Rabbi Shimon bar Yohai at Meron". In *To The Tombs of the Righteous: Pilgrimage in Contemporary Israel*, R. Gonen (ed.), 46–59. Jerusalem: Israel Museum.

Seamone, D. 2013. *This is My Story, This is My Song: A Pentecostal Woman's Life Story and Ritual Performance.* Berkeley, CA: University of California Press.

Sedaris, D. 2001. *Me Talk Pretty One Day.* London: Abacus.

Shields, J. M. 2000. "Sexuality, Blasphemy, and Iconoclasm in the Media Age: The Strange Case of the Buddha Bikini". In *God in the Details: American Religion in Popular Culture*, M. Mazur & K. McCarthy (eds), 80–101. New York: Routledge.

Shumaker, R. W., K. R. Walkup & B. B. Beck 2011. *Animal Tool Behavior: The Use and Manufacture of Tools by Animals.* Baltimore, MD: Johns Hopkins University Press.

Singer, S. 1962. *Authorised Daily Prayer Book of the United Hebrew Congregations of the British Commonwealth of Nations.* London: Eyre & Spottiswoode.

Smith, J. Z. 1978. *Map is Not Territory: Studies in the History of Religions.* Chicago, IL: Chicago University Press.

Smith, J. Z. 1987. *To Take Place: Toward a Theory of Ritual.* Chicago, IL: Chicago University Press.

Smith, W. C. [1962] 1978. *The Meaning and End of Religion.* London: SPCK.

Southwold, M. 1979. "Religious Belief". *Man* **14**(4): 628–44.

Soyinka, W. 1970. *The Interpreters.* London: Heinemann.

Soyinka, W. 1976. *Myth, Literature and the African World.* Cambridge: Cambridge University Press.

Spelman, E. 1988. *Inessential Woman: Problems of Exclusion in Feminist Thought.* Boston, MA: Beacon.

Spretnak, C. 1999. *The Resurgence of the Real: Body, Nature, and Place in a Hypermodern World.* New York: Routledge.

Spretnak, C. 2011. *Relational Reality: New Discoveries of Interrelatedness that Are Transforming the Modern World.* Topsham: Green Horizon Books.

Steinberg, M. 2005. *The Fiction of a Thinkable World: Body, Meaning, and the Culture of Capitalism.* New York: Monthly Review Press.

233

Stover, D. 2001. "Postcolonial Sun Dancing at Wakpamni Lake". *Journal of American Academy of Religion* **69**(4): 817–36. Reprinted in Harvey (2002), 173–93.

Strenski, I. 2006. *Thinking About Religion: An Historical Introduction to Theories of Religion*. Oxford: Blackwell.

Stuart, E. 2009. "The Priest at the Altar: The Eucharistic Erasure of Sex". In *Trans/formations*, L. Isherwood & M. Althaus-Reid (eds), 127–38. London: SCM.

Sullivan, W. F. 2008. "Neutralizing Religion; or, What is the Opposite of 'Faith-based'?". See de Vries (2008), 563–79.

Tarlo, E. 2010. *Visibly Muslim: Fashion, Politics and Faith*. Oxford: Berg.

Taussig, M. 1998. "Transgression". See M. C. Taylor (1998), 349–64.

Tawhai, T. P. [1988] 2002. "Maori Religion". See Harvey (2002), 238–49. Originally published in *The Study of Religion: Traditional and New Religion*, S. Sutherland & P. Clarke (eds), 96–105 (London: Routledge, 1988).

Taylor, B. 2010. *Dark Green Religion*. Berkeley, CA: University of California Press.

Taylor, C. 2008. "The Future of the Religious Past". See de Vries (2008), 178–244.

Taylor, M. C. (ed.) 1998. *Critical Terms for Religious Studies*. Chicago, IL: University of Chicago Press.

Thistlethwaite, S. B. 2011. "It's Not 'Class Warfare', it's Christianity". *Washington Post* (19 September), www.washingtonpost.com/blogs/on-faith/post/its-not-class-warfare-its-christianity/2011/09/19/gIQAkoMxfK_blog.htm (accessed 2 October 2011).

Thomas, T. 1994. *"The Sacred" as a Viable Concept in the Contemporary Study of Religions*, BASR Occasional Papers 13. Leeds: British Association for the Study of Religions. Reprinted in *Religion: Empirical Studies*, S. J. Sutcliffe (ed.), 47–66 (Aldershot: Ashgate, 2004).

Thompson, C. D. 2000. "The Unwieldy Promise of Ceremonies: The Case of the Jakalteko Maya's Dance of the Conquest". See Harvey (2000), 190–203.

Thompson, C. D. 2001. *Maya Identities and the Violence of Place: Borders Bleed*. Aldershot: Ashgate.

Thompson, C. D. 2005. "Natives of Bleeding Land: The Case of the Jacalteco Maya". In *Indigenous Diasporas and Dislocation*, G. Harvey & C. Thompson, 57–77. Aldershot: Ashgate.

Tuhiwai Smith, L. 2012. *Decolonising Methodologies: Research and Indigenous Peoples*, 2nd edn. London: Zed.

Turner, D. H. 1999. *Genesis Regained: Aboriginal Forms of Renunciation in Judeo-Christian Scriptures and Other Major Traditions*. New York: Peter Lang.

Turner, E. 1993. "Bar Yohai, Mystic: The Creative Persona and his Pilgrimage". In *Creativity/Anthropology*, S. Lavie, K. Nayran & R. Renaldo (eds), 225–51. Ithaca, NY: Cornell University Press.

Turner, V. 1973. "The Center out There: Pilgrim's Goal". *History of Religions* **12**(3): 191–230.

Tweed, T. 1997. *Our Lady of the Exile: Diasporic Religion at a Cuban Catholic Shrine in Miami*. New York: Oxford University Press.

Tweed, T. 2005. "Marking Religion's Boundaries: Constitutive Terms, Orienting Tropes, and Exegetical Fussiness". *History of Religions* **44**(3): 252–76.

Tweed, T. 2006. *Crossing and Dwelling: A Theory of Religion*. Cambridge, MA: Harvard University Press.

Tweed, T. 2009. "Crabs, Crustaceans, Crabiness, and Outrage: A Response". *Journal of the American Academy of Religion* **77**(2): 445–59.

Tylor, E. [1871] 1913. *Primitive Culture*; 2 vols. London: John Murray.

Uberoi, J. P. S. 1978. *Science and Culture*. Delhi: Oxford University Press.

Valk, Ü. & M. Bowman (eds). 2012. *Vernacular Religion in Everyday Life: Expressions of Belief*. London: Equinox.

Varela, F. J., E. Thompson & E. Rosch. 1991. *The Embodied Mind: Cognitive Science and Human Experience*. Cambridge, MA: MIT Press.

Vásquez, M. A. 2011. *More than Belief: A Materialist Theory of Religion*. Oxford: Oxford University Press.

Veisson, M. 2011. "Widowhood Rites in North-eastern Ghana". Paper presented at British Association for the Study of Religions Conference, 5–7 September, Durham University, Durham, UK.

Victoria and Albert Museum 2012a. "Beatrix Potter and Randolph Caldecott", www.vam.ac.uk/content/articles/b/beatrix-potter-randolph-caldecott (accessed 17 February 2012).

Victoria and Albert Museum 2012b. "Beatrix Potter: Nature's Lessons", www.vam.ac.uk/content/articles/b/beatrix-potter-natures-lessons (accessed 17 February 2012).

Vincett, G. 2008. "The Fusers: New Forms of Spiritualized Christianity". In *Women and Religion in the West: Challenging Secularization*, K. Aune, S. Sharma & G. Vincett (eds), 133–46. Aldershot: Ashgate.

Vincett, G. 2009. "Quagans: Fusing Quakerism with Contemporary Paganism". *Quaker Studies* 13(2): 220–37.

Viveiros de Castro, E. 1998. "Cosmological Deixis and Amerindian Perspectivism". *Journal of the Royal Anthropological Institute* 4(3): 469–88, www.jstor.org/pss/3034157 (accessed 19 February 2012).

Viveiros de Castro, E. 2004. "Exchanging Perspectives". *Common Knowledge* 10(3): 463–85.

Vizenor, G. 1998. *Fugitive Poses: Native American Indian Scenes of Absence and Presence*. Lincoln, NE: University of Nebraska Press.

Voas, D. 2009. "The Rise and Fall of Fuzzy Fidelity in Europe". *European Sociological Review* 25: 155–68.

Voas, D. & S. McAndrew 2012. "Three Puzzles of Non-religion in Britain". *Journal of Contemporary Religion* 27(1): 29–48.

von Stuckrad, K. 2002. "Reenchanting Nature: Modern Western Shamanism and Nineteenth-Century Thought". *Journal of the American Academy of Religion* 70(4): 771–99.

Wade, N. 2008. "Bacteria Thrive in Inner Elbow; No Harm Done". *New York Times* (23 May), www.nytimes.com/2008/05/23/science/23gene.html (accessed 17 February 2012).

Wakeford, T. 2001. *Liaisons of Life, from Hornworts to Hippos: How the Unassuming Microbe has Driven Evolution*. New York: John Wiley.

Weber, M. 1930. *The Protestant Ethic and the Spirit of Capitalism*. Boston, MA: Unwin Hyman.

Welch, C. 2007. "Complicating Spiritual Appropriation: North American Indian Agency in Western Alternative Spiritual Practice". *Journal of New Age and Alternative Spiritualities* 3: 97–117.

Werlang, G. 2001. "Emerging Amazonian Peoples: Myth-Chants". See Harvey & MacLeod (2001), 165–82.

Whitehead, A. 2012. "Religious Objects and Performance: Testing the Role of Materiality". PhD thesis, Open University.

Whitehead, A. 2013. "The New Fetishism: Western Statue Devotion and a Matter of Power". See Harvey (2013), 260–70.

Whitehead, N. L. & R. Wright 2004. *In Darkness and Secrecy: The Anthropology of Assault Sorcery and Witchcraft in Amazonia*. Durham, NC: Duke University Press.

Whitehouse, H. 2004. *Modes of Religiosity*. New York: Altamira.

Wiebe, D. 1999. *The Politics of Religious Studies: The Continuing Conflict with Theology in the Academy*. New York: St Martin's Press.

Wiebe, D. & L. H. Martin 2012. "Religious Studies as a Scientific Discipline: The Persistence of a Delusion". *Journal of the American Academy of Religion* **80**(3): 587–97.

Willerslev, R. 2007. *Soul Hunters: Hunting, Animism, and Personhood among the Siberian Yukaghirs*. Berkeley, CA: University of California Press.

Wittgenstein, L. [1953] 2001. *Philosophical Investigations*. Oxford: Blackwell.

Wolffe, J. 1994. *God and Greater Britain: Religion and National Life in Britain and Ireland, 1843–1945*. London: Routledge.

Yang, C. K. 1967. *Religion in Chinese Society*. Berkeley, CA: University of California Press.

Yarwood, A. T. 1967. "Marsden, Samuel (1765–1838)". In *Australian Dictionary of Biography*, National Centre of Biography, Australian National University, http://adb.anu. edu.au/biography/marsden-samuel-2433/text3237 (accessed 31 January 2012).

Yasin, S. 2010. "An Interview with Emma Tarlo, Author of *Visibly Muslim*". *Muslimah Media Watch* (24 February), http://muslimahmediawatch.org/2010/02/an-interview-with-emma-tarlo-author-of-visibly-muslim (accessed 21 October 2011).

Index